This Book Belongs to

Christmas
Book 3

Content and Artwork by **Gooseberry Patch Company**

LEISURE ARTS
Vice President and Editor-at-Large: Anne Van Wagner Childs
Vice President and Editor-in-Chief: Sandra Graham Case
Director of Designer Relations: Debra Nettles
Publications Director: Kristine Anderson Mertes
Design Director: Cyndi Hansen
Editorial Director: Susan Frantz Wiles
Creative Art Director: Gloria Bearden
Photography Director: Karen Hall
Art Operations Director: Jeff Curtis
Licensed Product Coordinator: Lisa Truxton Curton

EDITORIAL STAFF

EDITORIAL
Managing Editors: Suzie Puckett and Linda L. Trimble
Senior Associate Editor: Jennifer L. Riley
Associate Editor: Susan McManus Johnson

TECHNICAL
Managing Editor: Theresa Hicks Young
Technical Writers: Sherry Solida Ford and Leslie Schick Gorrell
Knitting Editors: Lois J. Long and Linda Luder
Technical Associate: K.J. Smith

FOODS
Foods Editor: Jane Kenner Prather

OXMOOR HOUSE
Senior Editor: Susan Carlisle Payne
Editor: Kelly Hooper Troiano
Senior Photographer: Jim Bathie
Senior Photography Stylist: Kay E. Clarke
Test Kitchen Director: Elizabeth Tyler Luckett
Test Kitchen Assistant Director: Julie Christopher
Recipe Editor: Gayle Hays Sadler
Contributing Test Kitchen Staff: Jennifer A. Cofield; Gretchen Feldtman, R.D.; David Gallent; Ana Price Kelly and Jan A. Smith

DESIGN
Designers: Polly Tullis Browning, Diana Sanders Cates, Cherece Athy Cooper, Peggy Elliott Cunningham, Anne Pulliam Stocks, Linda Diehl Tiano and Becky Werle
Executive Assistant: Debra Smith
Technical Assistant: Karla Edgar

ART
Art Director: Mark Hawkins
Senior Production Artist and Color Technician: Mark Potter
Production Artist: Elaine Barry
Staff Photographer: Russell Ganser
Photography Stylists: Tiffany Huffman and Janna Laughlin
Publishing Systems Administrator: Becky Riddle
Publishing Systems Assistants: Myra S. Means and Chris Wertenberger

PROMOTIONS
Associate Editor: Steven M. Cooper
Designer: Dale Rowett
Graphic Artist: Deborah Kelly

BUSINESS STAFF
Publisher: Rick Barton
Vice President, Finance: Tom Siebenmorgen
Director of Corporate Planning and Development: Laticia Mull Cornett
Vice President, Retail Marketing: Bob Humphrey
Retail Marketing Director: Margaret Sweetin
Vice President, Sales: Ray Shelgosh
Vice President, National Accounts: Pam Stebbins
Vice President, Operations: Jim Dittrich
Comptroller, Operations: Rob Thieme
Retail Customer Service Manager: Wanda Price
Print Production Manager: Fred F. Pruss

Copyright© 2001 by Gooseberry Patch, 149 Johnson Drive, Delaware, Ohio 43015, **www.gooseberrypatch.com** (illustrations, recipes and crafts). Copyright© 2001 by Leisure Arts, Inc., 5701 Ranch Drive, Little Rock, Arkansas 72223-9633, **www.leisurearts.com** (layout, photography, crafts and recipes). All rights reserved. No part of this book may be reproduced in any form or by any means without the prior written permission of the publishers, except for brief quotations in reviews appearing in magazines or newspapers. We have made every effort to ensure that these recipes and instructions are accurate and complete. We cannot, however, be responsible for human error, typographical mistakes or variations in individual work. Made in the United States of America.

Library of Congress Catalog Number 99-71586
Hardcover ISBN 1-57486-217-0
Softcover ISBN 1-57486-218-9

10 9 8 7 6 5 4 3 2 1

Christmas

Book 3

A LEISURE ARTS PUBLICATION

Christmas

Gooseberry Patch

For all our Gooseberry friends…
you make every day delightful!

How Did Gooseberry Patch Get Started?

You may know the story of Gooseberry Patch...the tale of two country friends who decided one day over the backyard fence to try their hands at the mail order business. Started in JoAnn's kitchen back in 1984, Vickie & JoAnn's dream of a "Country Store in Your Mailbox" has grown and grown to a 96-page catalog with over 400 products, including cookie cutters, Santas, snowmen, gift baskets, angels and our very own line of cookbooks! What an adventure for two country friends!

Through our catalogs and books, Gooseberry Patch has met country friends from all over the world. While sharing letters and phone calls, we found that our friends love to cook, decorate, garden and craft. We've created Kate, Holly & Mary Elizabeth to represent these devoted friends who live and love the country lifestyle the way we do. They're just like you & me... they're our "Country Friends®!"

Your friends at Gooseberry Patch

Holly   Mary Elizabeth   Kate   Spotty

Just For You

Contents

Homespun Christmas Memories

Homespun Christmas Memories

There's no place like home for the holidays…and there's no better time to bring out Christmas keepsakes, the family photo albums and those greeting cards that are just too pretty to discard! You can make this year's celebration extra special by enjoying favorite family traditions, and creating exciting new ones. Get set for the most memorable holiday ever!

These holiday ornaments are the perfect way to display cherished family photographs. You can easily make your own using photo transfers of snapshots. Instructions begin on page 120.

Have a "Make-It-&-Take-It" craft night. Every month, meet at a different friend's house and learn to make a craft for Christmas. By the time December rolls around, you'll have enough neat new gifts and decorations to go around! Keep the craft simple enough to complete in one night, then take home and hide for the holidays.

Be prepared for the first snow day of the year: Keep a small box filled with items needed to make a snowman…hats, mittens, woolly scarves, twigs and small lumps of coal or rocks for eyes and buttons.

Pick one room in which to do all your Christmas wrapping and crafting. Don't worry about keeping it tidy. Wrap the door to look like a package with a sign that reads "Do not open until Christmas," or "Santa's Workshop," or "Do Not Enter… Authorized Elves Only!"

Tie a big red bow on the antenna of your car. This makes it easier to find in those crowded parking lots.

Here's a great project for the kids. Save the shiny metal lids from frozen juice cans. During the year, set aside their best little photos, such as those taken at school or on their birthdays. (Double prints are great!) Take out the photos and cut the images to fit inside the lids. Help the children glue some rickrack, ribbon or lace around the edge and glue a loop of pretty fabric ribbon to the back…you'll have a Christmas ornament for Grandma & Grandpa. Or buy some disk magnets in the craft section and glue them onto the backs of the lids. Then the relatives can look at their little angels all year 'round!

A bit of German folklore…if you keep herring or cabbage in the house on New Year's Eve, you'll have money all year. If you eat a piece of herring as the clock strikes midnight, you'll be lucky all year.

An old Yugoslavian custom is to bake bread on Christmas Eve for family and friends. What is so special about this bread? After it's baked, a large gold coin is inserted inside, and when it's served, it's anyone's guess who will receive that special piece. Children especially enjoy this old-fashioned tradition for the holidays!

You'll want to choose an extra-special photo to adorn this piecework hanging pillow! Instructions are on page 120.

Animals have Christmas traditions all their own. So the legend goes, for one hour on Christmas Eve, all animals can speak.

Early American folklore says that on New Year's Day the lady of the house would open first the front door and then the back door, letting the cold air flow through the house. After a moment she would say, "letting out the old and letting in the new!"

Early settlers of Massachusetts lit their Christmas candles from the stub of a candle remaining from the previous year's Christmas.

In Victorian times, it was customary to hang a glass pickle ornament somewhere on the tree. On Christmas morning, the first child to find the pickle received a special little gift. Why not try it at your house!

According to Irish folklore, if you find a bird's nest in your Christmas tree, it is a sign of life and good fortune for the coming year.

Make these quick & easy keepsake ornaments to give to family & friends at your holiday festivities. Use paint pens to draw simple designs and handletter names, dates and seasonal messages on colorful glass balls.

'Tis the season to show off your favorite treasures. If you don't already have a collection, start one…try Santas (like ours), snowmen or Christmas cottages.

A collection of Santas looks wonderful on the shelves of a pie safe…add lots of tiny votives to cast a soft glow. Fold a red & white quilt over an open pie safe door or hang stockings from a length of jute.

Display all of your holiday books in a basket by a cozy chair. Set aside a night to gather the family around and read your favorites together.

Start a collection of Christmas books to hand down over the years. Books with Christmas themes, illustrations, stories, poems, recipes…old and new…will be treasured always. You can search new and used bookstores, garage sales and tag sales. The older books are becoming scarce, but occasionally you can find delightful old Christmas stories. Bring the books out every December to enjoy and share with family.

Dress your favorite Teddy bears in mufflers and stocking caps to form a holiday "greeting committee."

a happy memory never wears out.
—LIBBIE FUDIM—

Looking for a great way to display this year's Christmas cards? Salvage old window shutters, paint them bright red and accent with homespun and buttons. Complete instructions are on page 120.

Organizing is what you do before you do something, so that when you do it, it's not all mixed UP. ~A.A. MILNE

Use pictures cut from last year's Christmas cards for this year's gift tags!

Purchase an old glass milk bottle at a flea market. Perfect for setting out once a year...for Santa's milk and cookies, of course!

A holiday keepsake: Use a permanent marker to trace your children's hands on a solid color tablecloth. Have them write their names and ages with a pencil, then embroider over the pencil lines. Gently wash to remove all pencil markings.

Help a young couple start their own Christmas collection...special ornaments, Santas and snowmen.

Don't forget to check the batteries in your camera! Stock up on extra batteries for toys, film, light bulbs and hooks for your ornaments.

When you have family members visiting for the holidays (especially those who live far away), get out the old picture albums, slides and family films! What a joy to reminisce together, laugh and share special memories of childhood and Christmases past!

A charming Bavarian custom: On Saint Barbara's Day (December 4), cut several branches from a flowering fruit tree, such as apple, pear or cherry, and place them in water inside the house. If the branches blossom by Christmas, legend has it, the family will be blessed in the new year.

A favorite tradition that we have passed on to our daughter and her family involves cutting down the Christmas tree each year. We pack either a breakfast or a picnic lunch to have in the woods after we get our tree. How nice it is to have a winter picnic, complete with fire to cook bacon or hot dogs. Yum-yum!

— Carrol Begley

Craft whimsical memory album pages to complement special holiday memories, like a trip to the tree farm. Or showcase a family picture on a rustic tray with a homespun fabric mat…just the thing to give to Grandma! Instructions for both projects begin on page 120.

CHRISTMAS MAGIC

Just ask Kate, Holly & Mary Elizabeth...Christmas is the most magical time of the year! Kate likes to keep her decorations natural: popcorn and cranberries are among her favorite trims. Mary Elizabeth creates a wonderland of sweets, and Holly is crazy about Santas of all shapes and sizes. Turn the page to find lots of great holiday trims.

Ticking peppermint candy canes and felt redbirds look so nostalgic with a popcorn-and-cranberry garland. Instructions begin on page 121.

16

Sweet Christmas Greetings

Sugarcoat your home for the holidays with decorations featuring candy cane stripes. The nostalgic red & white ticking fabric is ideal for ornaments and other refreshing trims.

"WELCOME HOME" DOOR PILLOW

- muslin
- fusible interfacing
- striped and plaid fabrics
- tissue paper
- gold and red embroidery floss
- fabric glue
- four buttons
- polyester fiberfill
- jute

Refer to Embroidery Stitches, page 133, before beginning project. Use 3 strands of floss for all embroidery.

1. Cut a 4¹/₂"x7" piece from muslin; pull threads to fringe edges ¹/₄-inch. Cut a 3"x6" piece from interfacing. Cut two 7"x9¹/₂" pieces from striped fabric for pillow front and back. Tear one ¹/₂"x6" strip from plaid fabric for hanger; tear two ¹/₂"x3¹/₂" and two ¹/₂"x6¹/₂" strips from plaid fabric for trim.

2. Trace Welcome Home pattern, page 142, onto tissue paper. Center and pin pattern on muslin. Using red floss, work *Back Stitches* over words. Use gold floss to work *Running Stitches*, *Straight Stitches* and *French Knots* over star and sprinkles; carefully tear away paper.

3. Center and fuse interfacing on wrong side of stitched piece. Overlapping ends, glue strips around stitched area.

4. Center muslin on right side of one pillow piece. Use floss to sew one button at each corner of strips to attach stitched piece to pillow front.

5. Leaving an opening for turning, matching right sides and catching ends of hanger in seam at top of pillow, use a ¹/₂-inch seam allowance to sew pillow pieces together. Turn pillow right side out. Lightly stuff pillow with fiberfill and sew opening closed.

6. Tie a length of jute into a bow…tack bow at top center of pillow.

Welcome one & all to your holiday home with the smiling faces of your family! Just trim a grapevine door basket with greenery and snapshots framed with paper-doily snowflakes. See page 121 for instructions.

Snowy day delights

Remember how much fun you had making those paper fold-and-snip snowflakes? You'll love them just as much today. Hang them in a window to celebrate the first snowfall… or choose especially pretty ones to frame. You'll find the instructions on page 122.

Kids will enjoy Christmas snow cones! Gather a pail of freshly fallen snow and top with their favorite flavor fruit juice. Make an old-fashioned treat by drizzling warm maple syrup over a bowl of fresh snow.

Dear Santa

The jolly old elf we love so much always brings warm feelings to the Christmas season. Add to the nostalgia with our collection of handmade ornaments and homespun decorations.

STENCILED SANTAS

For each shelf sitter, use the patterns on page 138, and follow *Making Patterns*, page 134, to make an entire Santa pattern and an oval pattern. Follow *Stenciling*, page 134, to make stencils, then stencil Santa on muslin. Lightly paint red cheeks, black eyes, a black line for nose, pink ears on lamb, and berries on hat; allow to dry.

Cut out Santa ³/₄-inch outside painted lines. Using painted piece as a pattern, cut out another piece from muslin for the back. Matching right sides and raw edges and leaving bottom edge open, sew pieces together using a ¹/₄-inch seam allowance; clip curves and turn right side out. Press bottom edge ¹/₄-inch to the wrong side. Stuff Santa with fiberfill to one inch from bottom. For base, draw around oval pattern on muslin, then cut out ¹/₂-inch outside drawn line; clip curves and press edge ¹/₂-inch to the wrong side.

Leaving an opening for filling, stitch base to bottom of Santa. Fill Santa with plastic filler beads and sew opening closed. Thread a bell onto 5 inches of ribbon, tie into a bow and sew to tip of hat.

For each ornament, stencil top of Santa onto muslin; cut out ³/₄-inch outside painted lines. Draw around the piece on batting, poster board and muslin; cut out pieces ³/₄-inch inside drawn lines. Center batting, then poster board on the wrong side of the painted piece; clip curves and glue the edges to the back. Glue the remaining muslin piece over the back. Making a loop at top for a hanger, hot glue jute along the edges of the ornament. Thread a bell onto 5 inches of ribbon, tie into a bow and sew to tip of hat.

Each of these jolly gentlemen has a one-of-a-kind look because you shape them by hand using paper maché.

WOODSY SANTAS

- bobby pins
- aluminum foil
- toothpick
- paintbrushes
- white gesso
- soft cloth
- assorted colors of acrylic paint
- brown water base stain
- instant paper maché
- matte clear acrylic spray
- craft glue (optional)
- glitter (optional)

Allow gesso, paint, stain and sealer to dry after each application.

1. For each ornament, slightly separate the prongs of a bobby pin.

2. Leaving top ¹/₂-inch of the pin exposed for a hanger, wrap and crush a 12-inch square of aluminum foil firmly around pin prongs. Wrap additional aluminum foil around shape as needed to form a 3 to 4-inch long head.

3. Follow manufacturer's instructions to mix paper maché. Apply an ¹/₈-inch thick layer of paper maché over aluminum foil, smoothing with finger. Use additional paper maché to sculpt nose, hat and hat trim as desired.

4. Use a toothpick to carve details into beard and hat; hang ornament to dry.

5. After ornament is thoroughly dry, apply a coat of gesso to ornament. Paint ornament as desired.

6. Apply stain to ornament and immediately wipe off excess with a soft cloth. If glitter is desired, spread a thin coat of glue over area to be covered; apply glitter to glue-covered area, then gently shake excess glitter from ornament and allow to dry. Apply 2 to 3 coats of sealer to ornament.

I collect Santas and my prize one was bought in 1938, the year I married. He followed us everywhere the Navy sent us…the first on our tree, the last off. My husband and I had 57 years together, and our Santa is still around; somewhat tarnished, but so loved.

— Mae Blevins
Oak Harbor, WA

When I was a child, I loved candy-coated milk chocolate candies, so Santa filled my whole stocking with just those! Children may have favorites that they would like delivered that way as well.

— Martha Terrell

There is no remedy for love ♡ but to love more. —THOREAU—

25

BUTTON ORNAMENT

- 4-inch diameter paper maché ornament with hanger
- green acrylic paint
- paintbrushes
- Santa face motif
- craft glue
- assorted red buttons
- hot glue gun
- homespun fabric strip

1. Paint ornament green and allow to dry.

2. Mix one part glue with one part water. Use glue mixture to glue Santa motif to ornament. Smooth motif in place and apply one coat of glue mixture over motif; allow to dry.

3. Layering buttons as desired and framing Santa motif, hot glue buttons to ornament.

4. Tie fabric strip into a bow around ornament hanger.

Ornaments can be stored inside a locking plastic bag. Leave a little air in the bag when you seal it, and you will provide a cushion for the ornament. Don't blow into the bag however; this creates moisture which may damage the ornament.

JOLLY BUTTON FRAME

Santa's little cherry nose is cute as a button...and so is this festive frame! Extra easy to make, it goes together in no time. Simply spray paint a wooden picture frame green and hot glue lots of red buttons over the frame...make sure you layer some buttons on top of others. This is a great quick & easy craft to do with the kids...just make sure you use a low temperature glue gun to protect little fingers.

Here's a neat way to show off your collection of antique buttons: Thread narrow satin ribbon through the button holes and tie onto the branches of a tabletop tree.

Spotty strings jute across his windows & mantel and hangs up his Christmas cards with painted clip clothespins.

SANTA TREE FENCE

A whimsical picket fence around your tree says "No peeking!" Make this jolly row of Santas with some wired picket fencing painted red, then add a band of paint to each picket for the face. The fluffy beards are torn triangles of cotton batting hot glued around the pickets...use the cotton batting to make the hat bands, too. For each mustache, knot a length of thread around the center of about eight pieces of 6-inch long yarn...glue the mustache to the fence and trim it as desired. Add painted eyes (a new eraser on a pencil works great for this) and your Santa security is ready for patrol.

WARM THOUGHTS JAR

'Twas a month before Christmas and all through the land, sweet and warm thoughts were close at hand. The Warm Thoughts Jar, such a holiday treat…to top it all off, you get something to eat!

Photocopy the warm thoughts label, page 139, onto card stock. Use a red marker to color the checkerboard border, then glue it to the front of a jar with a lid. Draw around the lid on the wrong side of a piece of homespun. Cut out the circle 1¹/₂-inches outside the drawn line. Hot glue a ball of fiberfill to the top of the lid. Cover the lid with the fabric circle and glue the edges to the sides of the lid; trim the fabric even with the lid. Place the lid on the jar and glue a length of homespun trim around the edge of the lid. Use raffia to attach a Woodsy Santa from page 24 to the jar.

Use decorative-edge craft scissors to cut out twenty-four 1"x1¹/₂" pieces of paper. Fold each piece in half and punch a ¹/₈-inch diameter hole through one corner of the folded edge. Write your warm Christmas thoughts on the papers and tie them to tissue-wrapped candies. Fill the jar with the warm thoughts.

Beginning on December 1ˢᵗ, read one wish a day to remind you of the warmth of the season and to count down to Santa's arrival.

Peppermint Dreams

It just wouldn't be Christmas without peppermints and gumdrops! Why not use these colorful candies to trim a tiny tree or glue them to foam balls to create sweet kissing balls.

GUMDROP KISSING BALL

Use a ¼-inch diameter dowel rod to push a hole all the way through a 4-inch diameter plastic foam ball. For the hanger, knot the ends of a 24-inch length of ⅝-inch wide ribbon together to form a loop; use dowel to push the loop through the hole in the ball. Hot glue the knot of the hanger to the bottom of the ball. Using hot glue, add gumdrops to the ball until it's completely covered. Tie a length of ribbon into a bow around the hanger at the top of the ball.

How stripes get on the peppermints

CANDY ORNAMENTS

The kids will love to help make these quick & easy sweet ornaments! Simply hot glue gumdrops, red hots or broken pieces of peppermint sticks over a 2-inch diameter plastic foam ball. Use ¼-inch wide grosgrain ribbon to make a hanging loop; overlap the ends and thread them onto a large head straight pin that matches the ribbon color. Use the same ribbon to make a bow with lots of loops. Thread the center of the bow onto the pin. Apply a little hot glue to the pin and stick it onto the ornament.

Re-create the joy of going to an old-fashioned candy store. Gather together several old-time canning jars and fill them with all sorts of wonderful holiday treats! Nestle among some greenery…a tempting display!

— Stacey Spaseff
Lakewood, CA

A quick & easy craft…hot glue two candy canes together; add a bow and a jingle bell and hang on the tree.

Peppermints & Jelly Beans & yummy Gumdrops in between!

CANDY TREE

A real "kid can do" project…glue tips from gumdrops to round peppermint candies, then glue candies to ribbon bows. Attach your ornaments to a miniature tree using hot glue. Thread colorful jelly beans on string for a garland, then finish with a pinked ticking tree skirt…so sweet!

String an assortment of ribbon candy onto a holiday wreath. Your family will love to snip off a treat!

To bring up a child in the way he should go, travel that way yourself once in a while.
—JOSH BILLINGS—

For colorful fun with Christmas treats, layer different candies in a glass jar, paint the lid red and top it off with a peppermint bow.

PEPPERMINT TOPIARY

Fill a 3-inch tall can with plaster of paris...insert a $1/2$-inch diameter, 10-inch long dowel in center and allow plaster to harden. Slide a 4-inch diameter plastic foam ball $21/2$ inches onto top of dowel. Wrap the dowel with ribbon and glue ends to secure. Glue candy sticks around the outside of the can; glue round candies on top of the can. Glue edges of round candies in rows on foam ball until ball is completely covered. Finish off your topiary with a festive red bow tied around the dowel.

Nothing you do for children is ever wasted.
—GARRISON KEILLOR

By the Chimney with Care

If you're like Kate, you can't wait to see what Santa stuffs in your stocking! Hang your roomiest sock on the mantel, but also place little stocking ornaments on your tree and occasionally slip tiny surprises into them. Your family will enjoy peeking inside all season long! Instructions begin on page 122.

OH BOY!

"The stockings were hung by the chimney with care, in hopes that Saint Nicholas soon would be there..."

— Clement Clarke Moore

A friendly snowman and Santa fill these country stockings with holiday cheer. Knitting instructions begin on page 122.

Dreaming of a White Christmas

Seems like there's nothing better for making special memories than the excitement a Christmas snow brings. Use pearly buttons and homespun fabrics to fill your home with snowy decorations like our button candle, nostalgic ticking tree and lace-trimmed stocking. These and other simple projects are sure to turn your home into a winter wonderland the whole family will enjoy!

An assortment of pearl buttons and a cheery bow make this simple-to-create holiday wreath a wintry welcome. Instructions begin on page 124.

DREAMY WHITE CANDLE COLLECTION

Mix a few slightly weathered wooden candlesticks with lots of assorted crystal candleholders. Topped with white candles and tucked between sprigs of greenery, they're perfect for a mantel or table centerpiece! You can create your own "weathered" candlesticks using wooden spindles or pillars. Sand the wooden pieces until smooth and clean, then paint brown. Apply a thin coat of paste floor wax and a topcoat of white paint; let paint dry between coats. Lightly sand each candleholder for a beautiful aged look.

QUICK and EASY CANDLES

BUTTON CANDLE

This candle is so easy to make that Kate used dozens to decorate her house! Start with a plain pillar candle and an assortment of white buttons, then begin gluing…hot glue works best. Be creative! Use the buttons to make designs or you could even layer buttons, too.

Line the steps of an open staircase with layers of fresh cedar sprigs and scented candles in votive holders. You can also stencil on white lunch-size paper sacks, then fill the sacks partially with sand and set a votive inside each one.

"Peace, like charity, begins at home."

— *Franklin Roosevelt*

 *Give a tabletop tree country charm using star ornaments, handmade of ticking.
Why not make a matching tree topper and skirt, too? Instructions begin on page 41.*

Paper-white narcissus bulbs are easy to plant and fast-growing, too! Plant about 4 to 6 weeks before Christmas and you'll have an explosion of tiny white, fragrant flowers for your holiday table.

Create a lacy border for the mantel…use white shelf paper and cut a decorative border along one edge, then add lots of fresh pine and white candles.

TICKING TREE

Tree Topper Star

- tracing paper
- tan ticking
- buttons
- embroidery floss
- polyester fiberfill
- pinking shears

1. Trace large star pattern, page 142, onto tracing paper. Use pattern to cut 2 stars from ticking.

2. Sew a cluster of buttons at center on right side of one star shape.

3. Matching wrong sides and leaving an opening for stuffing, use 3 strands of floss to work *Running Stitches*, page 133, along the edges of the star to sew pieces together.

4. Lightly stuff star with fiberfill, then sew opening closed. Use pinking shears to trim edges of star.

(Star Ornaments & Tree Skirt continued on page 124)

A vintage ornament box lets you share a collection of sweet memories, while still keeping them safe. Making arrangements of your favorite ornaments is a sentimental reminder of precious holiday memories.

Antique lace and buttons dress up a stocking made from cotton ticking. Instructions begin on page 125.

EMBOSSED CARDS

Embossing adds a charming personal touch to blank cards. Place the card wrong side up on a metal stencil. Use a stylus to rub over the design...don't be afraid to use a little pressure so you'll get a good imprint. Use the cards yourself, or give a set as a gift!

COUNTRY GIFT WRAP

Perfect for your special hand-delivered gifts! Adorn your surprises in simple ticking or sponge-painted gift wrap. Using acrylic paint and a 1 1/2-inch square sponge piece, follow the easy *Sponge Painting* instructions, page 134, to decorate white paper. Wrap your gift in fabric or painted paper, tie it closed with raffia and hot glue a pretty button to the raffia knot. For a gift tag, write your message on card stock, glue it to a larger piece of ticking-covered card stock, then add buttons.

Simple Stitches

CROSS-STITCHED ORNAMENTS

- embroidery floss
  (see color key for desired
  design, page 145)
- 3¼"x4" piece of 18-ct Aida
- green felt

- pinking shears
- flannel fabric
- buttons
- black craft wire

Refer to Cross Stitch, page 132, and Embroidery Stitches, page 133, before beginning project.

1. Using 2 strands of floss for *Cross Stitches* and one strand of floss for *Backstitches* and *French Knots*, center and stitch desired design from pages 144-145 on Aida.

2. Cut two 4¾"x5¼" pieces from felt. Use pinking shears to cut a 4"x4¾" piece from flannel. Center and pin the flannel, then the stitched piece on one felt piece. Use 6 strands of red floss to work Blanket

Trim a country tree with charming cross-stitched ornaments on flannel patches. Our friendly reindeer, snow woman, gingerbread boy, angel, snowman and Santa are eager to spread holiday cheer! Finished with curly wire hangers, they'll be enjoyed for years to come!

Stitches along the edges of the stitched piece to sew the pieces together. Add buttons, bells and floss bows as desired.

3. Layer the felt pieces together. Use 6 strands of red floss to work *Blanket Stitches* along edges of the felt pieces to sew the pieces together.

4. Curl the center of a 10-inch length of wire. Thread a button onto each end of the wire. Poke the ends of the wire through the top corners of the ornament, then coil the ends to secure.

Fresh Traditions

This Christmas, decorate your tables with beautiful centerpieces featuring colorful fruit and fragrant evergreens arranged in vintage bowls or pretty glass serving pieces. Include candles to provide a warm holiday glow.

FRUIT CENTERPIECE

Create a healthy centerpiece brimming with all the best of an old-fashioned Christmas...arrange seasonal fruits and greenery on a clear glass cake stand (you may need to use a piece of floral foam and floral picks to secure the fruit). Hollow out some of the fruit for clever votive holders.

NESTLED FRUIT BOWLS

Choose a large and a small yellowware bowl from Grandma's cupboard. Fill the bowls with your favorite fresh fruits, and stack the small bowl on top of the large one. Tuck greenery between the fruit to fill any empty spaces.

FRUITFUL WREATH

To welcome visitors with an inviting door wreath, hot glue fresh greenery and berries to an 18-inch diameter grapevine wreath and use floral picks to attach colorful fresh fruit. Follow the instructions on page 132 to top off the look with a cheery red bow. Our bow used nine 8-inch loops, a center loop and four 7-inch streamers. Wire the bow in place on the wreath.

TOPIARIES

FRESH FRUIT TOPIARIES

Paint 6-inch diameter clay pots as desired with acrylic paint, let dry and spray with clear sealer. Fill pots with floral foam. Insert and glue a $\frac{1}{2}$-inch diameter, 15-inch long twig in the center of the foam. Fill the pots with greenery and fruit; use greenery pins and floral picks to secure in place, if necessary. For apple topper, glue a 4-inch diameter plastic foam ball onto top 3 inches of the twig. Use floral picks to attach apples to ball; fill between apples with greenery. For wreath topper, slide and glue the bottom of a 6-inch diameter grapevine wreath onto the top of the twig...hot glue greenery to the wreath.

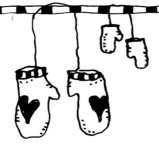

HANGING JAR LUMINARIES

Create a warm welcome for guests with glass jar luminaries. Using 2 lengths of heavy-duty wire, wrap one around each side of a jar. Twist the ends together on each side to tighten the wires under the lip of the opening…bend the ends to form hooks. Loop ends of another length of heavy-duty wire through the hooks to form a handle. Wrap black craft wire around the handle for decoration…bend the ends to form spirals, squiggles and curly-q's! Add a homespun bow, greenery and miniature pine cones at one side of the handle, then fill jar with rose hips and a votive candle.

Make it an herbal Christmas…garlands, topiaries, fragrant trees and wreaths, spicy pomanders, bundles of herbs, berries, dried apples, oranges, red roses and potpourris all bring wonderful scents to your holiday home.

LANTERN NIGHTLIGHT

Re-create the glow of an old, oil-burning lantern from yesteryear. Remove the wick hardware from a clean lantern and replace it with a candelabra-size, clip-on lamp kit with a flickering bulb. Cut a piece of candelabra base cover to fit in the space between the base of the lantern and the bottom of the lamp kit socket. Fill the base with sand to weight it down, glue sprigs of artificial greenery to the top and then tie on a homespun bow.

An antique lantern and a chicken feeder filled with candles become nostalgic holiday decorations when surrounded with fresh greenery, colorful fruit and cheery homespun bows. Instructions for the feeder begin on page 125.

Pinecone Firestarters

* PARAFFIN
* RED OR GREEN WAX DYE
  USED IN CANDLE·MAKING
* SCENTED OIL ~ CINNAMON,
  BAYBERRY OR CITRUS SPICE

* DRIED PINECONES
* CANDLEWICK

1. Melt paraffin in coffee can placed in an electric skillet filled with water. Add colored wax dye & drops of oil to melted paraffin.

2. Wrap or tie a length of candlewick through top of the pinecone. Dip dried pinecones into melted paraffin. You may need to dip several times; allow to harden between dips.

3. Package in a basket or decorated bag ~ add a tag that reads, "PLACE SEVERAL PINECONES UNDER LOGS and LIGHT THEM."

Scented pine cone firestarters create a warm and friendly atmosphere. To make a festive gift tag, photocopy the label on page 157 and glue it to fabric-covered cardboard with fringed edges.

WREATH ORNAMENTS

Craft one of our mini wreath ornaments in a jiffy! Glue artificial leaves and berries, miniature pine cones or grapevine stars and buttons onto a 4-inch diameter grapevine wreath...add a homespun hanger and a jute bow to each ornament and they are ready to hang!

A wooden bowl filled with pomegranates, lady apples and juniper makes a welcoming country centerpiece.

Add greenery sprigs to lunch-size brown paper sacks, tuck in berries and display on your mantel.

For a magical show of colorful flames in the fireplace, soak your pine cones in the following solution before making them into firestarters: Mix 1/2 lb. soda, borax or salt with 1/2 gallon water. Soak cones overnight, remove from solution and hang in a mesh bag to dry thoroughly. In your fireplace, the pine cones will burn different colors.

— Joan Schaeffer

Create simple, old-fashioned holiday greetings...fill a pitcher with greenery, berries and twigs, pile pine cones in a bowl or tie decorated mini grapevine wreaths with homespun.

Hand made from the Heart

Sharing handmade gifts with special people is the best part of Christmas! Give whimsical kitchen accessories to a favorite cook, or surprise snow pals with cozy appliquéd sweatshirts. We've also included delightful packaging ideas and homemade cards, and the kids can get into the spirit with fun activities and presents they make for their friends. And don't forget the family pets!

Homespun fabrics peek through country cut-outs on these clever cards! Mail them to friends or make a set to give as a gift. Instructions for our gift tags and cards begin on page 125.

tmas comes but
a year . . . .

Aunt
Mary

to
from

tmas comes but
ce a year . . . .

to
from

M a t t

from

Package gifts in country style using boxes trimmed with rusted metal cut-outs or embossed copper. Instructions for the embossed-copper boxes are on page 126.

STACKED CANISTERS

For a holiday gift that can "bee" around all year, make our "busy" set of canisters for a special friend. Paint paper maché boxes and lids with desired colors of acrylic paint…let dry. Glue torn strips of homespun around each canister. Use a pair of decorative-edge scissors to cut a label from card stock to fit each box. Glue the labels to the boxes over the ends of the fabric strips, then glue a rusted tin cut-out to each label. Draw "stitches" along the edges and add accents on the labels with a black permanent marker.

HEY—
NO SHAKING
OR
PEEKING
ALLOWED

GOODIE ♥ BOXES

Just Give Me 1 Teensy Hint!

Little boxes are PERFECT for little gifts! Fill 'em with potpourri, jewelry, candy... surprise a country friend with a personalized box for paper clips & rubber bands... hide a secret message inside!

Nothing is more appreciated than a thoughtful gift. Think of the recipient's interests, loves and hobbies. Dream up a gift, big or small, to reflect those likes and loves. Reflect on something out-of-the-ordinary. Use your imagination.

Vintage Kitchen

Delight a country cook with handcrafted accessories. Our sweet angel can watch over the kitchen, and the decoupaged tray is perfect for serving goodies.

A wooden spoon is at the heart of this charming angel. Instructions begin on page 126.

Scope out your neighborhood antique shops for a beautiful teapot and hide bags of flavored tea inside.

Put together a family cookbook with fun photos on each page...Uncle Floyd in the kitchen or Grandpa asleep in the recliner after lunch. Include funny stories or quotes from relatives. Photocopy a family quilt or a familiar fabric (Grandma's kitchen curtains?) for the background paper.

Buy a plain canvas apron at the hobby store and personalize it with fabric paint. Tuck a spoon, spatula and jar of Chunky Chocolate Cookie Mix (page 80) in the pockets...fold neatly and tie with a ribbon. A fun gift for the cookie snacker or for a child just learning to bake! (Add a little bag of extra chocolate chunks for snackin'!)

Tuck a cornbread mix and hot pad inside a cast-iron skillet...a quick gift!

SERVING TRAY

- spray primer
- metal serving tray
- ivory spray paint
- ivory, red and brown acrylic paint
- paintbrushes
- crackle medium
- black paint pen
- desired Santa motifs from cards or wrapping paper
- decoupage glue
- wood-tone spray
- clear acrylic matte spray sealer

Allow primer, paint, glue and sealer to dry after each application.

1. Apply primer to tray. Spray paint sides and rim of tray ivory. Using brown for basecoat and ivory acrylic paint for topcoat, follow manufacturer's instructions to crackle the bottom of the tray.

2. Use the paint pen to draw the outer edges of the checkerboard border around the rim of the tray. Paint every other square red, then go over the edges of the squares with the paint pen. Write your favorite words of the season along the sides of the tray.

3. Trim motifs as desired, then glue in place on tray. Apply 2 coats of glue over motifs.

4. Lightly spray tray with wood-tone spray. Apply 2 coats of sealer to the tray.

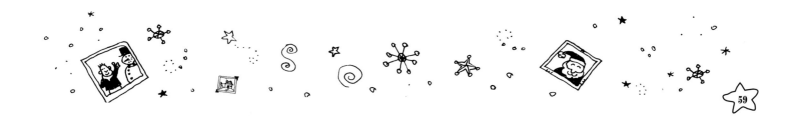

GIFTS for the Kitchen

Plaid chickens bring pocketfuls of fun to a whimsical apron set with matching oven mitt. Easy-to-fuse appliqués also perk up our trio of kitchen towels.

OVEN MITT AND APRON

Don't be chicken to try your hand at these easy kitchen accessories! Start with a purchased apron and oven mitt and add appliqués and buttons.

For the oven mitt, cut a strip of homespun to fit along the cuff of the mitt; press the edges of the strip 1/4-inch to the wrong side. Use nylon thread to sew the strip to the mitt…add a few buttons and this "handy" gift is done in no time.

For the apron, follow the mitt instructions to attach a strip of fabric across the bib. Cut two 1¹/2"x10" and two 8¹/2"x10" pieces from fabrics. Using a ¹/2-inch seam allowance, sew the pieces together to form two 9"x10" pockets…press each edge ¹/4-inch to the wrong side. Top stitch along the top edge of each pocket. Using the patterns, page 150, follow *Making Appliqués*, page 134, to make two (one in reverse) complete chicken appliqués from fabrics. Fuse one set of appliqués to each pocket…follow *Machine Appliqué*, page 134, to sew along the edges of the appliqués.

Pin the pockets on the apron and *Machine Appliqué* the sides and bottom edges. Referring to *Embroidery Stitches*, page 133, use green floss to work *Running Stitches* along the side and bottom edges of the pockets and gold floss to work *French Knots* for the eyes on the chickens. Sew buttons on the pockets and bib as desired.

APPLIQUÉ TEA TOWELS

For each towel, use a ½" seam allowance to sew three 4"x5" pieces of fabric together to form a 5"x10" rectangle. Using the patterns on pages 150-151, follow *Making Appliqués*, page 134, to make desired appliqués from fabrics. Fuse appliqués on rectangle, then follow *Machine Appliqué*, page 134, to sew along the edges of the appliqués. Fuse a 5"x10" piece of paper-backed fusible web to the back of the rectangle. Center and fuse the rectangle on one end of an 18"x28" kitchen towel. *Machine Appliqué* along the edges of the rectangle. Referring to *Embroidery Stitches*, page 133, use 3 strands of green floss to work *Running Stitches* along the edges of the rectangle and gold floss to work *French Knots* and *Straight Stitches* as indicated on the patterns. Sew a button to each corner of the rectangle.

"Live your life while you have it. Life is a splendid gift — there is nothing small about it."
— Florence Nightengale

Winter Warmers

Even when the weather outside is frightful, these merry shirts are so delightful! Raid the button box to find colorful "ornaments" for the embroidered tree and whimsical "snowflakes" for the sweatshirts, or string buttons for a fun-to-wear necklace. Instructions for the clothing begin on page 126.

BUTTON NECKLACE

Fold a 6-foot length of waxed linen thread in half. Knot the folded end to form a small loop. Measure 4 inches from the knot and knot again. Hook the loop on something, like your friend's finger (we hooked ours in the ring of a binder). Place a needle on each end of the thread. Working from opposite sides, thread the needles through the same hole on a button (Fig. 1). Now, thread the needles through the opposite hole of the same button (Fig. 2). Pull the threads to slide the button to the knot. Repeat to add as many buttons as you like, then knot the threads together close to the last button. For the clasp, choose a button that will fit through your loop. Insert the thread ends up, then back down through opposite hole in the button; knot the ends around the thread to secure.

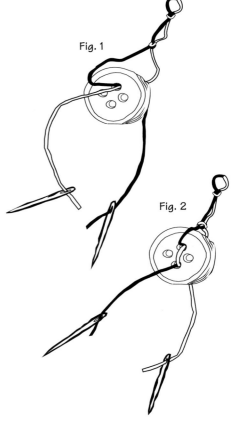

Fig. 1

Fig. 2

63

Cozy Comforts

When the cold wind blows, warm a friend's heart with these homespun pillows. Accent the friendly country cushions with buttons, appliqués and simple embroidery stitches.

Tuck holiday wishes in the pillow pocket for Santa's elves to find. Instructions for the Star Pillow are on page 127.

THROW PILLOWS

- fabric for pillow fronts, backs and welting
- paper-backed fusible web
- embroidery floss
- burlap scraps
- polyester fiberfill
- red buttons
- 1/4-inch dia. cord
- red, green & brown felt

Use a 1/2-inch seam allowance for all sewing.

Tree Pillow

1. For pillow top, cut four 7"x9" pieces from fabrics.

2. For each strip, matching right sides and short edges, sew two pieces together; repeat for remaining pieces. Matching right sides and long edges, sew strips together. Cut a piece from fabric the same size as pillow top for pillow back.

(continued on page 127)

Here's a neat gift for a college student: Buy a big canvas stocking and paint it in school colors...fill with ornaments, garlands and lights for the dorm room. Include a Christmas CD and a batch of homemade cookies, too!

Sort through your family's closets and donate "gently worn" and outgrown coats, clothes and extra blankets to a nearby shelter. They'll be much appreciated!

Lots of FUN for the Little Ones

Let the kids get in on the fun of Christmas crafting…including handmade gifts for their friends. With a little help from you, youngsters can put together a "make-it-yourself" Christmas card kit or a colorful play dough set to inspire the imagination. Instructions begin on page 128.

> "It's not the gift, but the thought, that counts."
>
> — Anonymous

> "Christmas Eve, after I had hung my stocking, I lay awake a long time, pretending to be asleep and keeping alert to see what Santa Claus would do when he came."
>
> — Helen Keller

Magic Reindeer Dust

Secret Ingredients!

* OATS (FOR ANIMALS)
* GLITTER
* PINT-SIZE CANNING JAR WITH LID

Secret How-To Instructions:

1. Fill jars with oats, sprinkling a little glitter throughout.
2. Top jars with lids and tie on a copy of "Secret Instructions for Magic Reindeer Dust" (below). You might glue it on jar, if preferred.

*Make a copy of this for each jar ↓

Magic Reindeer Dust

Come December 24th, as Santa flies here from the North,
Here's what you do, it isn't hard —
Just sprinkle this stuff in your yard...

The sparkles draw old Santa near
and oats attract his 8 reindeer...

Then just you wait — they're on their way

P.S. Happy Holiday!

KIDS' NUTTY Snowmen

...Make a whole bowl-full to hang on the tree!

You will need:

* Unsalted peanuts-in-the-shell
* Acrylic paint - white
* Small paint brush
* Fine-tip black permanent marker
* Fine-tip red permanent marker
* Red yarn
* Safety scissors

1. Pour peanuts out on a newspaper and let the kids paint 'em white. Let peanuts dry and eat a hand-full while you wait!

2. Use your markers to draw on eyes, nose & mouth — add buttons on the front of the snow peanuts, too!

3. Cut a 5" piece of yarn and tie it 'round your snowman's neck. All done!

*P.S. Thread a thin ribbon or fishing line through the back of the yarn to make a hanger.

EASY RECIPES

Mary Elizabeth's Super-Duper Play Dough

Great-smelling dough ~ perfect birthday party favors!

2-½ c. flour
½ c. salt
1 T. powdered alum
2 pkg. unsweetened fruit-flavored drink mix
2 T. vegetable oil
2 c. boiling water

Mix together flour, salt, alum & drink mix in large mixing bowl. Add oil. Pour boiling water over flour mixture ~ stir until well-combined. Knead dough until smooth. Store in airtight plastic bag or covered container.

Nutty Cocoa

All our favorite ingredients are in my Nutty Cocoa ~ peanut butter, chocolate and marshmallows!

• 4 c. MILK
• ½ c. CHOCOLATE-FLAVORED DRINK MIX
• ¼ c. CREAMY PEANUT BUTTER
• ½ t. VANILLA
• MINIATURE MARSHMALLOWS

IN A SAUCEPAN, COMBINE CHOCOLATE MIX WITH 1½ c. MILK UNTIL WELL-BLENDED. MIX IN PEANUT BUTTER, AND ADD REMAINING MILK. HEAT COCOA 'TIL ALMOST BOILING. POUR INTO MUGS AND TOP WITH MARSHMALLOWS.

Old-fashioned CANDLE SALAD

~ a fun fruit salad for kids to make for a holiday dinner!

• BIBB LETTUCE LEAVES
• CANNED PINEAPPLE RINGS
• BANANAS
• WHIPPED TOPPING
• MARASCHINO CHERRIES

PLACE ONE LETTUCE LEAF ON EACH PLATE. LAY A PINEAPPLE SLICE ON TOP OF LETTUCE. CUT BANANA IN HALF AND STAND IN HOLE OF EACH PINEAPPLE RING. TOP EACH BANANA WITH A DAB OF WHIPPED TOPPING ~ PUT CHERRY ON TOP OF WHIPPED TOPPING. Beautiful!

Make fun containers for your play dough using baby food jars and our label design on page 143. Color the photocopied artwork with permanent markers and acrylic paint.

SANTA SHAKES

MAKE UP A BATCH OF THIS COOL YOGURT SHAKE TO REFRESH THE KIDS AFTER THEY FINISH MAKING NUTTY SNOWMEN!

- 2 CUPS CHOCOLATE MILK
- 2 CUPS CHOCOLATE FROZEN YOGURT, SOFTENED
- 2 CUPS CRUSHED ICE
- ½ CUP CHOCOLATE SYRUP
- PEPPERMINTS, CRUSHED
- PEPPERMINT STICKS OR CANDY CANES

Combine all ingredients in a blender. Process until well-blended. Sprinkle with crushed peppermint and serve in tall glasses with a candy cane.

KATE'S TORTILLA TREATS

A PERFECT SNACK FOR YOUR HUNGRY YOUNG BUILDERS!

INGREDIENTS:

- FLOUR TORTILLAS
- PEANUT BUTTER
- MINI CHOCOLATE CHIPS

HOW TO:

SIMPLY SPREAD THE PEANUT BUTTER ON THE OPEN TORTILLA.

SPRINKLE CHOCOLATE CHIPS ON THE PEANUT BUTTER, THEN ROLL UP THE TORTILLA.

SCRUMPTIOUS!

Kate's Best-ever Chocolate Finger Paint

FOR THE BUDDING ARTIST IN ALL OF US ~ THE TASTIEST FINGER PAINT OF ALL! TRY VANILLA OR BUTTERSCOTCH, TOO....

4-OZ. PKG. instant chocolate pudding mix

2 c. milk
white paper

Prepare pudding mix according to package directions. Let the pudding set 'til thick. Paint on white paper with pudding. Let masterpieces dry for several hours.

RAINBOW Toast

IS IT MORE FUN TO MAKE IT OR EAT IT?

- BREAD
- FOOD COLORING
- CLEAN PAINTBRUSHES OR COTTON SWABS

PLACE 4 DROPS OF FOOD COLORING IN EACH SECTION OF A MUFFIN TIN. ADD 1 TO 2 T. WATER TO DILUTE COLORS. DIP PAINTBRUSH INTO FOOD COLORING AND PAINT DESIGNS ON BREAD. PLACE IN TOASTER AND TOAST. BUTTER & EAT IT UP!

PIZZA COBBLER

KIDS LOVE TO FIX

~ an easy and delicious snack!

- PIZZA SAUCE
- 1 CAN REFRIGERATOR BISCUITS
- 1-⅓ c. MOZZARELLA CHEESE, SHREDDED

GREASE AN 8-INCH SQUARE PAN WITH VEGETABLE OIL SPRAY. PLACE ABOUT ¼ OF THE PIZZA SAUCE IN BOTTOM OF THE PAN. CUT EACH BISCUIT IN 4 PIECES. ROLL BISCUIT PIECES INTO BALLS AND PLACE IN PAN ON TOP OF SAUCE. POUR REMAINING SAUCE OVER BISCUITS. SPRINKLE WITH MOZZARELLA CHEESE. BAKE IN 400° OVEN FOR 15 TO 20 MINUTES. ENJOY!

Pampered Pets

Pets are family too! Include them in your holiday celebration with tasty treats and other fun gifts.

HEALTHY DOG TREATS

Visiting in a dog lover's home? Bring along some homemade, easy to bake dog biscuits.

2 c. whole-wheat flour
1/2 c. all-purpose flour
1/4 c. cornmeal
1/4 c. sunflower kernels, finely
    chopped
1 t. salt
1/4 c. molasses
2 eggs, beaten
1/4 c. milk
2 T. oil

Mix all ingredients, adding more milk if needed to make dough firm. Roll out onto a floured surface to a 1/2-inch thickness. Use any shape cookie cutter to cut out biscuits, but bone shapes are fun! Bake on ungreased baking sheets at 350 degrees for 30 minutes or until lightly toasted. To make biscuits harder, leave in oven with the heat turned off for an hour or more.

Jacqueline Lash-Idler
Rockaway, NJ

For a doggone cute tree ornament, use paint pens and ribbon to decorate a dog bone…then hang it out of your pet's reach.

Any dog will love this soft, cozy bed on a cold winter's night! Instructions are on page 128.

KITTY KOOKIES

Remember that your four-legged friends love treats too.

1 c. whole-wheat flour
6-oz. can tuna in oil, undrained
1 T. oil
1 egg

Mix all ingredients in a mixing bowl, adding a little water if dough is too stiff. On a lightly floured surface, roll dough to ¼-inch thickness. Cut into shapes with your favorite cookie cutter. Place on ungreased baking sheet. Bake at 350 degrees for 20 minutes or until firm. Store in an airtight container.

Give an animal the best gift of all...go to the local animal shelter and adopt a pet!

Surprise Fluffy with catnip-filled toys; instructions begin on page 129.

Use paint pens to create a festive ceramic dish for your favorite feline.

BRAIDED BIRD WREATH

Make a picnic for the birds...they'll flock to this treat, and you'll enjoy watching them.

1 lb. frozen bread dough, thawed
peanut butter
wild birdseed

Roll out dough into a 30-inch rope. Using a sharp knife, cut the dough into thirds lengthwise and braid. Place braided dough on a greased baking sheet, forming a circle. Seal the edges of dough by pinching them together. Cover with a clean dish towel and let rise one hour or until double in size. Bake at 375 degrees for 20 to 30 minutes or until golden brown. Remove from baking sheet and let cool. Spread peanut butter on top of wreath and sprinkle with birdseed. Hang outside for the birds to enjoy!

Goodies for GIVING

Hand-packaged, homemade goodies show friends & family just how special they are to you. Take time to remember how each person has brightened your life as you share a loaf of bread, a batch of creamy fudge, or some moist, chewy cookies made just for them! Or open up your pantry and gather the ingredients to make one of the Country Friends® winning recipe mixes for friends to enjoy after the holidays are over. Whatever you choose to make, dress it up in a pretty gift basket or bag...and they will know it was made with love!

Nothing says, "You're special to me" like yummy homemade Christmas treats in a country bag or basket. Recipes begin on page 76; bag and basket instructions begin on page 130.

To: Karen

To: Pam
From: Vickie

non
ch
s

To: Betsy
From: JoAnn

ONE CUP OF EVERYTHING COOKIES

Add any of your favorite cookie ingredients!

1 c. butter, softened
1 c. sugar
1 c. brown sugar, packed
1 egg
3 c. all-purpose flour
1 c. quick-cooking oatmeal, uncooked
1 c. crispy rice cereal
1 c. semi-sweet chocolate chips
1 t. baking soda
1 t. cream of tartar
1 t. vanilla extract

Cream butter, sugars and egg together. Add remaining ingredients and stir until dough is formed. Press into one-inch balls and place on an ungreased baking sheet. Flatten balls with bottom of a greased glass. Bake at 350 degrees for 10 minutes or until bottoms are lightly browned. Makes about 6½ dozen cookies.

Claddagh Inn
Hendersonville, NC

STIR YOUR HOT TEA WITH A PEPPERMINT STICK FOR A CHRISTMAS-TIME TREAT.

CREAMY FUDGE

A delicious, creamy fudge.

12-oz. pkg. semi-sweet chocolate chips
13-oz. jar marshmallow creme
2 t. vanilla extract
2 c. chopped walnuts
5 c. sugar
1 c. butter
12-oz. can evaporated milk

Place chocolate chips, marshmallow creme, vanilla and walnuts in a mixing bowl. Heat sugar, butter and milk in a large saucepan. Bring mixture to a boil and boil for 15 minutes, stirring often. Continue to boil until mixture reaches 234 degrees or soft-ball stage on a candy thermometer. Place mixture into mixing bowl containing chips and beat on high speed until creamy. Pour into buttered 8"x8" pan. Will set in about 3 to 4 hours.

Gail Wightman

NO-COOK MINTS

Pretty holiday mints!

4¾ c. powdered sugar, sifted
⅓ c. corn syrup
¼ c. butter, softened
1 t. peppermint extract
½ t. salt
red and green liquid food coloring

Combine powdered sugar, corn syrup, butter, peppermint extract and salt; mix with spoon and hands until smooth. Divide into thirds; knead one drop of red food coloring into one third and one drop of green food coloring into another third. Leave remaining third white. Shape into small balls; flatten with fork on wax paper-lined baking sheets. Let dry several hours. Yields 72 patties.

Joan Schaeffer
Whitefish Bay, WI

CINNAMON CRUNCH BARS

Keep on hand for the grandchildren.

12 cinnamon graham crackers, 2½"x4¾" each
2 c. chopped walnuts or pecans
1 c. butter
1 c. brown sugar, packed
½ t. cinnamon

In the bottom of a greased 15"x10" jelly roll pan, arrange graham crackers in a single layer with sides touching. Sprinkle nuts evenly over crackers. In a small heavy saucepan, combine butter, brown sugar and cinnamon. Stirring constantly, cook over medium heat until sugar dissolves and mixture begins to boil. Continue to boil syrup for 3 minutes longer without stirring; pour over crackers. Bake at 400 degrees for 8 to 10 minutes or until bubbly and slightly darker around the edges. Cool completely in pan; break into pieces. Store in an airtight container. Yields about 1½ pounds of candy.

Gen Hellums
Freer, TX

HONEY-GLAZED SNACK MIX

Make several batches and give in colorful tins.

4 c. oat square cereal
1½ c. pretzel twists
1 c. chopped pecans
⅓ c. margarine
¼ c. honey

In a bowl, combine cereal, pretzels and pecans. Over low heat, melt margarine with honey until margarine is melted. Pour over mix; toss to coat. Spread on baking sheet. Bake at 350 degrees for 15 minutes. Cool and spread on wax paper.

Kathy Bolyea
Naples, FL

Slip warm holiday wishes and a loaf of hearty Cranberry Bread into a festive fabric bag. Instructions for the sawtooth-edge bag are on page 130.

CRANBERRY BREAD

Serve fresh cranberry bread with your turkey dinner.

2 c. all-purpose flour
1 c. sugar
1½ t. baking powder
½ t. baking soda
1 t. salt
juice and zest of one orange
2 T. shortening
boiling water
1 egg, beaten
1 c. chopped walnuts
1 c. fresh cranberries, chopped

Sift dry ingredients together. In a separate bowl, combine juice, zest and shortening with enough boiling water to yield a total of 3/4 cup. Cool slightly and add egg. Blend liquid ingredients in with the dry ingredients, stirring only until flour mixture is dampened. Blend in walnuts and cranberries. Pour into one 9"x5" loaf pan coated with non-stick vegetable spray. Bake at 350 degrees for 50 minutes to one hour or until center tests done.

Judy Borecky
Escondido, CA

HOLLY'S WHITE CHOCOLATE THRILLS

These set our little ♥s to pitter-pattering!

❦

1¼ lb. almond bark
1½ c. miniature marshmallows
1½ c. peanut butter cereal
1½ c. crisp rice cereal
1½ c. mixed nuts
½ c. mini chocolate chips

. . .

In a casserole dish, melt almond bark in 200° oven for 25 minutes; stir occasionally. Place marshmallows, cereal, nuts & chocolate chips in bowl. Pour melted bark over mixture, stirring to coat. Drop by spoonfuls onto waxed paper ~ allow to set.

77

Take the rush out of Christmas morning for a busy family by delivering a Sour Cream Breakfast Coffee Cake ahead of time. Instructions for decorating the box are on page 131.

SOUR CREAM BREAKFAST COFFEE CAKE

My mom was busy, but she always had time for family, friends and neighbors. This is one of her best recipes.

1 c. sugar
1 c. shortening
3 eggs, beaten
1 t. vanilla extract
2¼ c. all-purpose flour
1 t. baking soda
3 t. baking powder
1 c. sour cream
²/₃ c. brown sugar, packed
½ c. chopped nuts
1½ t. cinnamon

Cream sugar and shortening together. Add eggs and vanilla. Mix in flour, baking soda, baking powder and sour cream. Spread batter into a greased and floured tube pan. Mix together brown sugar, nuts and cinnamon. Spread on top of batter in pan. Bake at 375 degrees for 40 to 45 minutes or until a toothpick inserted in center comes out clean.

Mary Dungan
Gardenville, PA

A wrapped loaf of homemade bread tied to a wooden cutting board makes a heartwarming gift!

Simple Scottish Shortbread

A favorite cookie from Scotland that will melt-in-your-mouth!

1 c. butter, softened
1½ c. powdered sugar
½ t. vanilla
2¼ c. flour

Beat together butter, sugar & vanilla 'til well blended. Add flour, 1 cup at a time to butter mixture. On a floured surface, roll out dough to ¼ - ½" thick. With a sharp knife, cut dough into 2" squares or cut into rounds with a cookie cutter. Place on ungreased baking sheet and prick top of cookies with fork. Bake for 25-30 minutes at 325° until bottoms are golden brown and top is light in color. Cool on wire racks. Store in airtight containers.

➡ Delicious with Tea!

CRANBERRY-ORANGE CHUTNEY

An excellent relish for ham sandwiches!

4 seedless oranges
1/2 c. orange juice
1 lb. cranberries
2 c. sugar
1/4 c. crystallized ginger, diced
1/2 t. hot pepper sauce
1 cinnamon stick
1 clove garlic, peeled
3/4 t. curry powder
3/4 c. golden raisins

Peel the oranges and reserve the zest from two of them. Slice the reserved zest very thinly. Cut oranges into 1/4-inch thick slices and quarter. Combine orange zest with all remaining ingredients and simmer in a saucepan over medium heat, stirring until sugar dissolves and cranberries pop. Remove from heat and discard cinnamon and garlic clove. Add oranges and toss lightly. Serve hot or cold with ham. Makes 6 cups.

Make charming labels for canned jellies and jams using decorative-edge craft scissors, pretty papers, and markers. Dress up jar lids with colorful paper inserts.

RED PEPPER JAM

A nice hostess gift at Christmas time. I make it during the summer months and have it on hand for holiday gift-giving.

12 red peppers, seeded
2 to 4 onions, sliced
1 T. salt
2 c. vinegar
3 c. sugar

Place peppers and onions through food grinder into a saucepan. Sprinkle with salt and let stand 3 hours. Drain very well. Add vinegar and sugar and cook slowly, approximately 1 1/2 to 2 hours or until thickened. Pour mixture into clean, hot half-pint jars and process for 10 to 15 minutes in boiling water canner. Makes six half-pint jars.

Janet Myers

SUSAN'S PUMPKIN BUTTER

This recipe is very much like apple butter and has a better flavor if made with fresh pumpkin. Serve with warm, fresh bread or biscuits.

3 1/2 c. cooked or canned pumpkin
1 T. pumpkin pie spice
1 3/4-oz. box powdered fruit pectin
4 1/2 c. sugar

Place pumpkin in a large saucepan. Add pumpkin pie spice and fruit pectin to pumpkin and mix well. Place over high heat; stir until mixture comes to a gentle boil. Immediately add the sugar and stir in well. Bring to a rolling boil and boil hard for one minute, stirring constantly. Remove from heat and ladle into jars with lids. Store in refrigerator 2 to 3 weeks. Makes about 5 1/2 cups.

*Elenna Firme
Haxtun, CO*

THE ULTIMATE FUDGE SAUCE

2 oz. unsweetened chocolate
3/4 c. sugar
1/4 t. salt
1/2 c. light corn syrup
1/2 c. milk
2 T. butter
1 T. vanilla

Combine first 5 ingredients over low heat ~ stir often. Add butter. Cool slightly, then add vanilla. oh boy!

IT'S A MIX, IT'S A GIFT!

Packaged with homespun style, recipe mixes make sweet and simple gifts that offer an extra helping of holiday fun.

Delight your favorite chocoholic with our Chunky Chocolate Cookie Mix! Photocopy the artwork below and glue to a jar label and recipe tag created from decorative card stock. Instructions are on page 131.

CHUNKY CHOCOLATE COOKIE MIX

a recipe from
Melanie Lowe ★ Dover, DE

1 ¼ c. all-purpose flour
1/2 t. baking soda
½ t. salt
½ c. brown sugar, packed
⅓ c. sugar
1 ⅓ c. semi-sweet chocolate chunks
1 c. chopped pecans

Blend together flour, baking soda & salt. Spoon into bottom of a wide-mouth, one-quart canning jar, pressing down well. Layer on the remaining ingredients in the order given, packing down tightly between each layer.

CHUNKY CHOCOLATE COOKIE MIX

2/3 c. butter, softened   1 t. water
1 egg   ½ t. vanilla extract

Cream together butter, egg, water & vanilla. Add cookie mix from jar and blend well. Drop by spoonfuls on ungreased cookie sheet and bake at 375 degrees for 7 to 10 minutes. Makes about 3 dozen cookies.

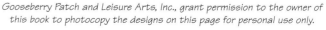

How to Eat Chocolate Chip Cookies Like A Child:

HALF-SIT, HALF-LIE on the bed, propped up by a PILLOW. Read a book. Place cookies next to you on the SHEET so that CRUMBS get in the BED. As you eat the COOKIES, remove each chocolate CHIP and place it on your STOMACH. When all the cookies are consumed, eat the CHIPS one by one, allowing two per PAGE.

— DELIA EPHRON

♥ Choose a favorite book, slip a bookmark inside the pages and drop inside a gift bag. Now slide a jar of Cookie Mix in there and tie a copy of ← this tag on the bag handle.
SILLY BUT FUN and FLAVORFUL!

WINTERTIME SPICE TEA

This is quite a favorite at our home. It's always a nice gift for teachers, friends and neighbors.

1³/₄ c. sugar
1 c. sweetened lemonade mix
1 c. powdered orange drink mix
¹/₂ c. instant tea
¹/₂ t. cinnamon
¹/₂ t. ground cloves

Mix all ingredients together and store in airtight container. Give recipe for serving. To serve, add 3 to 4 teaspoons to one cup of hot water; stir well.

Mary Beth Smith
St. Charles, MO

PANCAKES FROM THE PANTRY

These pancakes smell so good while they're cooking. Give with a jar of honey butter to make a really welcome gift!

4 c. quick-cooking oats, uncooked
2 c. all-purpose flour
2 c. whole-wheat flour
1 c. brown sugar, packed
1 c. dry milk
3 T. baking powder
2 T. cinnamon
5 t. salt
¹/₂ t. cream of tartar

Combine all ingredients together, mixing well. Add dry mix to an airtight container or to two one-quart canning jar. Add these instructions to your gift card: In a large mixing bowl, add 2 eggs; beat well. Gradually beat in ¹/₃ cup oil. Alternately add 2 cups of pancake mix and 1 cup of water to the egg mixture; blend well. Cook pancakes on a lightly greased griddle. Makes about 10 pancakes.

Margaret Scoresby
Mount Vernon, OH

Warm up an early bird's breakfast with gifts of tea and pancake mix. For a "short stack" with style, center a ribbon under the rim of the pancake mix lid and tie the jar of maple syrup on top. Instructions for the pancake label and the Wintertime Spice Tea Cup begin on page 131.

Simple and Speedy BASIC Bread Mix

You can use this basic mix to make 2 different breads!

a recipe from
Regina Vining
*
Warwick, RI

12 c. all-purpose flour
2 T. baking powder
2 T. baking soda
1 T. salt
3 c. sugar
3 c. brown sugar, packed

*

Sift together flour, baking powder, baking soda & salt. Stir in sugar & brown sugar until well blended. Store in a large airtight container. Place container in a cool, dry place and use within 6 months.

Feel free to copy these recipe cards and use colored pens to give them some ZING!

Orange~Berry Bread

¾ c. orange juice
1 c. fresh cranberries
2 eggs, beaten
3½ c. basic bread mix

⅓ c. applesauce
1 t. orange zest

Combine orange juice & cranberries in a food processor; pulse for 5 seconds. Blend together remaining ingredients; stir in orange juice mixture. Spoon into an oiled 9"x5" loaf pan ~ bake at 325 degrees for 1 hour or until center tests done.

Chocolate Chip·Zucchini Bread

3½ c. basic bread mix
⅓ c. applesauce
2 eggs, beaten
2 c. zucchini, grated

3 T. orange juice
1 t. orange zest
½ c. chocolate chips

Blend all ingredients together, stirring well. Pour batter into an oiled 9"x5" loaf pan. Bake at 325 degrees for 1 hour or until center tests done.

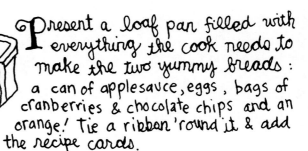

Present a loaf pan filled with everything the cook needs to make the two yummy breads: a can of applesauce, eggs, bags of cranberries & chocolate chips and an orange! Tie a ribbon 'round it & add the recipe cards.

HAZELNUT MOCHA MIX
Makes a great stocking stuffer!

1/4 c. plus 2 T. powdered non-dairy
    creamer
1/4 c. sugar
1/4 c. hazelnut-flavored instant
    coffee
2 T. baking cocoa

Combine all ingredients and mix thoroughly. Spoon into a plastic zipping bag and place in a fabric bag for gift giving. Add these serving instructions to your gift tag: Place 2 tablespoons plus 2 teaspoons of mix in a mug; add 3/4 cup hot water.

Mary Lou Traylor
Arlington, TN

CHOCOLATE CHIP PIE MIX
A sweet, chocolatey treat!

1 c. sugar
1/2 c. all-purpose flour
6-oz. pkg. semi-sweet chocolate
    chips
1/2 c. flaked coconut
1/2 c. chopped pecans

Blend together sugar and flour; place in a plastic zipping bag. Seal bag and tie closed with a festive ribbon and tag that says " dry ingredients." Combine chocolate chips, coconut and pecans in a second plastic zipping bag and label "chocolate packet." Tuck both in a holiday gift bag. Add the following instructions: In a bowl, combine 1/4 cup melted butter, 2 eggs and the contents of the "dry ingredients" bag; stir until just moistened. Stir in the contents of the "chocolate packet" bag. Spoon mixture into a 9" unbaked pie crust. Bake at 350 degrees for 35 to 40 minutes.

Kathy Grashoff
Ft. Wayne, IN

Relatives will enjoy opening country bags holding mixtures of Chocolate Chip Pie and Hazelnut Mocha. Fabric bag instructions begin on page 131.

HOT ORANGE CIDER MIX
Add an orange or apple slice to each mug before serving.

1 c. sugar
2 6-inch cinnamon sticks
1 whole nutmeg

Combine sugar, cinnamon sticks and nutmeg. Place in plastic-lined goodie bag. Add these instructions:

Give your coffee or cider mix in a pretty jar tucked in a tall, narrow paper bag tied with red raffia.

Place 2 cups apple cider and 6 cups orange juice in a slow cooker; stir in cider mix. Turn slow cooker to high for 2 to 3 hours or until cider is heated through. Remove spices before serving.

Coralita Truax
Loudonville, OH

83

JOLLY GINGERBREAD MEN MIX

Place a jar of this mix in a basket with a gingerbread man cookie cutter...a wonderful gift for a secret pal!

3^1/$_2$ c. all-purpose flour, divided
1 t. baking powder
1 t. baking soda
1 c. brown sugar, packed
2 t. ginger
1 t. cinnamon
1 t. allspice

Sift together 2 cups flour, baking powder and baking soda. Spoon into a one-quart canning jar, packing down tightly. Layer on brown sugar, pushing down well. Blend together remaining flour, ginger, cinnamon and allspice; layer over brown sugar and secure lid. Tie on the following instructions: Cream together ^{1}/$_2$ cup butter, ^{3}/$_4$ cup molasses and one egg; stir in dry mix. Dough will be stiff. Cover and refrigerate one hour. Roll dough to ^{1}/$_4$-inch thickness on a lightly floured surface, adding additional flour if dough is too sticky. Cut with a 4^1/$_4$"x3^1/$_2$" gingerbread boy cookie cutter and place on a lightly greased baking sheet. Bake at 350 degrees for 10 to 12 minutes. Makes about 22 cookies.

Kay Morrone
Des Moines, IA

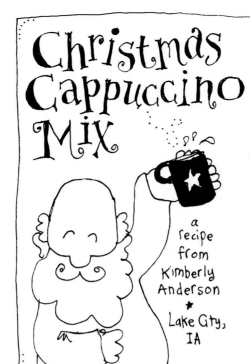

Christmas Cappuccino Mix

a recipe from Kimberly Anderson
Lake City, IA

2·^{1}/$_2$ c. instant chocolate drink mix
8 c. dry milk
2 c. powdered sugar
1 c. instant coffee granules
8-oz. jar French vanilla flavored non-dairy creamer

★

Combine all ingredients in a large bowl, then store in an airtight container.

Cappuccino:

^{1}/$_4$ to ^{1}/$_3$ c. cappuccino mix
6 to 8 oz. hot water

Combine mix and hot water; stir to blend.

Help someone catch the Christmas spirit with Jolly Gingerbread Men Mix. See page 131 to make the baking instruction card.

GRANDMA'S NOODLE SOUP MIX

Add a few ingredients to this mix and you have a soup that you can enjoy in no time at all.

4 to 5 oz. fine egg noodles
3 T. chicken bouillon
salt and pepper to taste
1/2 t. dried thyme
1/2 t. celery seed
3 bay leaves

In a large mixing bowl, carefully blend together all ingredients. Add to a one-quart wide-mount canning jar; add lid. Tie on the following cooking instructions: Combine noodle soup mix and 6 cups water in a large stockpot. Add 3 carrots, diced, 2 celery stalks, chopped, and one onion, chopped. Bring to a boil, reduce heat and simmer, covered, for 20 minutes. Stir in 3 cups chicken and simmer 5 minutes longer. Remove bay leaves. Makes approximately 2 quarts soup.

Connie Hilty
Pearland, TX

Tuck your jar of noodle soup in a basket with a farmhouse bowl, a loaf of freshly-baked bread and sweet, creamy butter.

· Soup and Hot Spicy Tea make a winter meal complete!

PIZZA BASKET

BUSY MOM SEAL OF APPROVAL

Line a basket (or deep-dish pizza pan) with a red-checked napkin. Add:

★ JARS OF PIZZA SAUCE
★ DRY DOUGH MIX (BELOW)
★ PACKAGES OF PEPPERONI & SHREDDED CHEESES
★ FRESH VEGGIES ~ PEPPERS, ONIONS, MUSHROOMS
★ PIZZA CUTTER
★ RECIPE CARD FOR FAVE PIZZA

DOUGH MIX
★

11·1/4 c. FLOUR, DIVIDED
3 PKGS. DRY YEAST
3 t. SUGAR
1·1/2 t. SALT
...
Add the following to 3 plastic zipping bags:
3·3/4 c. flour, 1 pkg. dry yeast, 1 t. sugar, 1/2 t. salt. Combine well.

Recipe for Homemade ★ DOUGH ★

To 1 bag of dough mix (left), add 1·1/2 c. very warm water & 2 T. oil. Stir well 'til dough forms. Knead dough on lightly-floured surface for 5 minutes - cover & rest 10 minutes. Divide dough in half - place in 2 lightly-oiled 12" pizza pans. Let rise 30 minutes in warm place. Bake at 425° for 10 minutes. Remove from oven, cover with sauce & toppings ~ cook 10 more minutes in 425° oven.

PATCHWORK BEAN SOUP MIX

This colorful soup mix would be great paired with crazy quilt potholders or oven mitts!

1/2 c. dried kidney beans
1/2 c. dried black-eyed peas
1/2 c. dried black beans
1/2 c. dried red beans
1/2 c dried split green peas
1/2 c. dried Great Northern beans
1/2 c. dried kidney beans
1/2 c. dried lima beans
3 T. chicken bouillon
1 T. dried, minced onion
salt and pepper to taste
1/2 t. garlic powder
1 T. dried parsley flakes
1 t. celery seeds
1/4 c. brown sugar, packed

Layer each type of bean in a one-quart jar. In a plastic zipping bag, blend together seasonings. For gift giving, attach the following instructions: Add beans to a large stockpot; cover with hot water and let soak overnight. Drain and add 2 quarts of water. Bring to a boil; reduce heat and simmer, covered, one to 2 hours or until beans are almost tender. Stir in two 14 1/2-ounce cans stewed tomatoes and seasoning mix. Simmer, uncovered, one to 1 1/2 hours or until beans are tender. Makes approximately 12 cups of soup.

Amy Butcher
Columbus, GA

Friends will love to get this colorfully layered Patchwork Bean Soup Mix. Instructions for the quilted country potholder and handmade recipe card are on page 132.

Soup mixes don't need to be layered in a jar if you're short on time. Give the mix in a no-sew bag for an easy and welcome gift!

BROWN SUGAR ROUNDS MIX

Delightful with a cup of chamomile tea.

1 1/2 c. all-purpose flour
1/2 t. baking soda
1/4 t. salt
1 1/4 c. brown sugar, packed and divided
1/2 c. chopped pecans

In a large bowl, blend together flour, baking soda and salt. Divide mixture in half and press approximately 1 1/4 cups into the bottom of a one-quart wide-mouth canning jar. Press down firmly so all ingredients will fit inside. Measure out 1/2 cup plus 2 tablespoons brown sugar and layer over flour mixture; pack down well. Add pecans, then layer on remaining brown sugar, packing tightly. Top with remaining flour mixture, pressing down until mixture fits completely into jar. Add a gift tag with the following instructions: Beat together 1/2 cup shortening and 1/2 cup butter until creamy. Add in jar mixture, stirring with a spoon until well blended. Beat together one egg and one teaspoon vanilla extract; stir into flour mixture. Shape dough in two, 10-inch rolls. Wrap in wax paper and chill for 48 hours. When ready to bake, slice cookies 1/4-inch thickness and place on an ungreased baking sheet. Bake at 375 degrees for 10 minutes or until firm. Make approximately 6 dozen cookies.

Kerry Mayer
Denham Springs, LA

White Chocolate Cocoa Mix

a recipe from Marian Buckley
— Fontana, CA —

1 t. vanilla powder
1 t. dried orange zest
½ c. white chocolate chips

Mix ingredients well and store in an airtight container or ½ pint glass canning jar.

✳ Slip a mitten over the top of the jar and pin this instruction tag on the mitten ... a charming little gift!

WHITE CHOCOLATE COCOA

1 ½ c. MILK
¼ c. COCOA MIX

Heat milk in saucepan, then blend in cocoa mix. Stir 'til chocolate chips melt. serves 2.

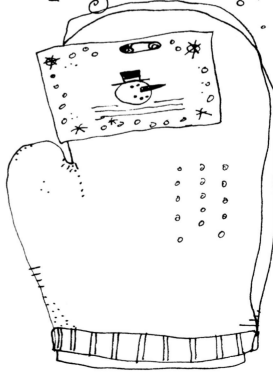

Christmas Favorites

SANTA'S KITCHEN

Kate, Holly & Mary Elizabeth have gathered this collection of hearty Christmas fare to help you season the holidays with the rich aromas and flavors of farmstyle cooking. Whether you're looking for a quick & easy dish for an office potluck, some delectable sweets to share with neighbors (or to nibble on yourself!) or the fixings for a fabulous family feast, you'll find lots of yummy choices among the savory, time-tested recipes that follow.

Honey-Roasted Pork Loin and Harvest Dressing are just a few of the delicious dishes on the menu for this country Christmas dinner. The easy-to-follow recipes begin on page 96.

Holiday Appetizers

Good food and good friends are special blessings we enjoy throughout the holidays. Whether you're hosting a gathering at your home or going to a friend's, you'll make a tasteful addition with one of the scrumptious appetizers in this handy collection. From a festive Patchwork Wheel of Brie to Sausage Stars and BLT Dip, each of our recipes is sure to be a hit. Most can even be made ahead of time, so there's more time to celebrate.

Mixed Fruit Ball, White Christmas Punch

MIXED FRUIT BALL

I like to make a pretty holiday presentation by surrounding this with clusters of red and green grapes and wedges of unpeeled apples.

2 8-oz. pkgs. cream cheese, softened
1/4 lb. Cheddar cheese, shredded
1 t. coriander
1/4 c. raisins, diced
1/4 c. dried apricots, diced
1/4 c. dried dates, diced
1/4 c. dried prunes, diced
1 c. chopped pecans

Mix cream cheese, Cheddar cheese and coriander until well blended. Add dried fruits and stir gently. Shape into a ball and roll in pecans. Refrigerate overnight.

Jane Williams
Austin, MN

WHITE CHRISTMAS PUNCH

Add a sprinkle of sliced almonds on top of each serving!

2 c. sugar
1 c. water
12-oz. can evaporated milk
1 T. almond extract
6 2-ltr. bottles lemon-lime carbonated drink
3 1/2-gal. cartons vanilla ice cream

In a saucepan, combine sugar and water. Stir constantly over medium heat until sugar dissolves. Remove from heat. Add evaporated milk and almond extract; let cool. Chill until ready to serve. Combine milk mixture and lemon-lime drink in punch bowl just before serving. Add ice cream; stir to break ice cream into small pieces.

Rebecca Boone
Olathe, KS

MUSHROOM TURNOVERS

A delicious appetizer to make ahead and freeze.

Crust:
8-oz. pkg. cream cheese
1 c. margarine, softened
2 c. all-purpose flour

Blend together and chill.

Filling:
4 c. sliced mushrooms,
   finely chopped
2/3 c. green onions, chopped
2 T. margarine, melted
1/3 c. sour cream
2 T. all-purpose flour
1/4 t. thyme
1/4 t. salt
1 egg white, beaten
sesame seeds

Sauté mushrooms and onions in margarine for about 3 minutes. Add next 4 ingredients, cooking for a few more minutes. Roll out half of dough at a time to 1/8-inch thickness and cut with a 2 1/2-inch biscuit cutter or a round cookie cutter. Place a heaping 1/4 teaspoon of mushroom mixture in the center of each circle. Fold over and press edges gently with fingers. Transfer turnovers to a lightly greased baking sheet using a spatula; finish sealing edges by pressing with a fork. Brush each turnover with egg white and sprinkle with sesame seeds. Bake at 350 degrees for 20 minutes. Makes about 65 turnovers.

Judy Borecky
Escondido, CA

CRANBERRY-ALMOND PUNCH

A refreshing and colorful punch.

16-oz. can jellied
   cranberry sauce
2 1/4 c. water
3/4 c. orange juice
1/2 c. lemon juice
1 t. almond extract
1 c. chilled ginger ale
Garnish: lemon slices and
   cranberries

With fork, crush cranberry sauce; beat until smooth with hand beater. Beat in water, orange juice, lemon juice and almond extract; chill. At serving time, stir in ginger ale. Garnish each serving with lemon slices and cranberries. Serves 4.

Susan Kennedy
Gooseberry Patch

Brown sugar B·I·T·e·S

a recipe from Barbara Briner ★ San Antonio, Tx

16-oz. pkg. bacon
1 lb. pkg. 2-inch smoked sausages
1/4 c. brown sugar, packed

—

Cut bacon into thirds. Wrap each sausage with a third of a slice of bacon and secure with a toothpick. Place in a baking dish in a single layer. Sprinkle with brown sugar. Bake for 35 to 45 minutes at 375 degrees. Serve warm. Makes about 48.

Mushroom Turnovers, Cranberry-Almond Punch

Cheesy Stuffed MUSHROOMS

STUFF YOUR- SELF!

a recipe from Sherry Barnhart ★ Portland, OR

20 to 25 lg. white mushrooms, with stems
2 T. butter
8-oz. pkg. Cheddar cheese, shredded

8-oz. pkg. cream cheese
garlic salt to taste
onion salt to taste
paprika to taste

Carefully remove mushroom stems. Dice stems ⌣ sauté them in butter until tender. Set aside to cool. Mix together Cheddar cheese & cream cheese until whipped. Season with garlic salt, onion salt & fold in the stems. Stuff mushrooms & place on a cookie sheet. Sprinkle tops with additional shredded cheese & paprika. Bake at 350 degrees for 15 to 20 minutes or 'til cheese is melted. Serve warm. Makes 20 to 25.

SONIA'S HOLIDAY SANGRIA

Use your favorite fresh fruit in this holiday treat!

1 qt. burgundy wine
2 c. lemon-lime carbonated drink
6-oz. can strawberry nectar
6-oz. can frozen orange juice
6-oz. can peach nectar
1/8 t. cinnamon
1 c. fruit, sliced

Combine all ingredients in a large container, adding fruit last so it will float on top. Cover and refrigerate for 24 hours, allowing flavors to blend. Serve chilled. Makes about 9 cups.

Sonia Bracamonte
Tucson, AZ

PATCHWORK WHEEL OF BRIE

A festive centerpiece for your appetizer table.

5 lb. round of Brie
1/2 c. sweetened dried cranberries or dried currants
1/2 c. walnuts, finely chopped
1/2 c. fresh dill, chopped
1/4 c. poppy seeds
1 c. sliced almonds, toasted

Remove the rind from the top of the cheese by cutting carefully with a sharp knife. Lightly score the top of the cheese into 10 equal pie-shaped sections. Sprinkle half of each of the toppings onto each wedge and press gently until you have decorated all 10 sections. Allow to stand at room temperature for at least 40 minutes before serving. Serve with water crackers or other light wafers. Serves 20 to 25.

Patchwork Wheel of Brie, Sonia's Holiday Sangria

SAUSAGE STARS

This is one of my favorite appetizers. To save time, I make the filling ahead and before serving, fill the wrappers and bake!

4 to 5 doz. won ton wrappers
1 lb. sausage, cooked and
    crumbled
1½ c. sharp Cheddar cheese,
    shredded
1½ c. Monterey Jack cheese,
    shredded
1 c. ranch-style salad dressing
½ c. sweet red pepper, chopped
2¼-oz. can sliced black olives

Press one won ton wrapper in each cup of a muffin tin; bake at 350 degrees for 5 minutes. Remove won tons and place on a baking sheet. Repeat with remaining won tons; set aside. Combine remaining ingredients well and fill baked wrappers. Bake at 350 degrees for an additional 5 minutes or until bubbly. Makes 4 to 5 dozen.

Geri Peterson
Pleasanton, CA

BLT DIP

Serve this with an assortment of crackers or sourdough rounds.

2 c. mayonnaise-style salad
    dressing
1 c. sour cream
2 lbs. bacon, crisply cooked and
    crumbled
1 tomato, chopped
2 green onions, chopped

Combine salad dressing and sour cream until well blended. Add bacon and refrigerate overnight. Fold in remaining ingredients.

Sandy Brinkmeier
Lena, IL

CHILI CON QUESO DIP

Serve with tortilla chips, crisp cold veggies and baked pita slices.

28-oz. can plum tomatoes,
    drained and chopped
2 4-oz. cans green chilies,
    drained and seeded
1 c. whipping cream
1 lb. Cheddar cheese, shredded
salt and pepper to taste

Over low heat, cook the tomatoes and chilies for about 15 minutes. Stirring constantly, add cream and cheese and continue cooking until mixture thickens. Season with salt and pepper and serve warm.

BROCCOLI & CHEESE HAM ROLLS

This recipe worked well for me served as a brunch for several people. I made the rolls a day ahead and poured the mixture on just before baking. I served fresh fruit and sweet rolls alongside.

2 10-oz. pkgs. frozen, chopped
    broccoli
8 slices Swiss cheese
8 slices cooked ham
10¾-oz. can mushroom soup
½ c. sour cream
1 t. mustard

Cook broccoli according to package directions; let cool. Place a slice of cheese on a slice of ham. Divide broccoli between the 8 ham-cheese slices. Roll slices and place, seam side down, in a buttered 13"x9" baking dish. Pour mixture of soup, sour cream and mustard over ham rolls. Bake, uncovered, at 350 degrees for 20 minutes.

Cheryl Ewer
Bismarck, ND

MARY ELIZABETH'S
Crabmeat Spread

6½-oz. can crabmeat
8-oz. pkg. cream cheese, softened
⅛ t. salt
¼ t. curry powder
¼ c. green onion, finely chopped
¼ c. green pepper, finely chopped
2 t. lemon juice
½ t. Worchestershire sauce
½ c. sour cream
1 bottle cocktail sauce
crackers

Rinse & remove cartilage from crabmeat. Refrigerate 'til serving. Combine cream cheese, salt, curry powder, onion, pepper, lemon juice, Worcestershire sauce & sour cream in mixing bowl at low speed with mixer 'til well blended. Spread mixture in a shallow dish ~ refrigerate at least 1 hour. Just before serving, pour cocktail sauce over cream cheese mixture & top with crabmeat.
Serve w/crackers.

Softened cream cheese is perfect for piping into cherry tomatoes and pea pods, or onto celery sticks. Garnish with a dash of paprika.

BARBEQUE MEATBALLS

This recipe was given to me by my mother, Nancy Campbell, and is a great appetizer or potluck dish...there are never any left over!

1 lb. ground beef
1/3 c. fine bread crumbs
1 egg, slightly beaten
1/2 t. poultry seasoning
1/2 c. catsup
2 T. brown sugar, packed
2 T. vinegar
2 T. soy sauce

Mix ground beef, bread crumbs, egg and poultry seasoning. Shape into about 2 dozen 1 1/2-inch balls. Brown balls slowly in a lightly oiled skillet over medium-high heat; pour off excess fat. In a small bowl, combine catsup, brown sugar, vinegar and soy sauce. Pour over meatballs. Cover and simmer over low heat, stirring constantly, for 15 minutes. Serve warm.

Suzanne Carbaugh
Mount Vernon, WA

Barbeque Meatballs

HOT MULLED PUNCH

During the holiday season, you will always find some of this punch brewing. It smells wonderful and tastes even better!

1 1/2 qts. cranberry juice
2 qts. apple juice
1/2 c. brown sugar, packed
4 cinnamon sticks, broken
1/2 t. salt
1 1/2 t. whole cloves

Pour juices into 30 to 36-cup coffee maker. Place remaining ingredients in basket of coffee maker and brew according to coffee maker instructions. When complete, remove basket and discard spices. Serve hot. Makes 28 punch cup servings.

Michelle Urdahl
Litchfield, MN

BAGEL CRISPS

Keep in an airtight container to have on hand for snacking during the holidays.

8 bagels, slightly frozen
6 T. margarine
3 t. dried oregano leaves or
    1 1/2 t. garlic powder

Slice the slightly frozen bagels 1/4-inch thick. Lightly butter and sprinkle with oregano or garlic powder. Bake at 250 degrees for 15 to 25 minutes or until crisp.

Peggy Gerch
Lincoln, NE

"The true essentials of a feast are only fun and feed."
— *Oliver Wendell Holmes*

¡Olé! A Spectacular Beginning!
Mexi★Chicken ROLL★UPS

a recipe from Joanne McDonald ★ British Columbia, Canada

8-oz. pkg. cream cheese
1 c. chicken, cooked & chopped
1 c. Monterey Jack cheese, shredded
⅓ c. red pepper, finely chopped
¼ c. fresh coriander
2 T. jalapeño pepper, chopped
2 t. cumin
4 10-inch flour tortillas
Garnish: salsa & sour cream

In a large bowl, combine cream cheese, chicken, cheese, red pepper, coriander, jalapeños & cumin. Spread mixture over tortillas. Roll up tightly. Slice into ½-inch pieces. Bake at 350 degrees for 10 to 15 minutes on lightly oiled baking sheet. Serve with salsa & sour cream. Makes 5 to 6 dozen.

Caponata

For a thoughtful party favor, write guests' names on glass Christmas balls with a gold or silver glitter pen.

CAPONATA
This rich, savory relish will keep for weeks in your refrigerator, if there's any left over!

2 eggplants, peeled
½ c. olive oil
2 onions, sliced
14½-oz. can tomatoes, drained and chopped
1 c. celery, chopped
¼ c. vinegar
2 T. sugar
salt and pepper to taste
¼ c. green olives, chopped
capers to taste

Slice eggplant and squeeze dry with paper towels. Dice into one-inch cubes. Brown in hot oil 10 minutes or until soft and brown, adding onions during last 3 minutes of browning. Add tomatoes and celery; simmer for 15 minutes. Add vinegar, sugar, salt, pepper, olives and capers. Simmer 20 minutes longer over low heat. Tastes best when served at room temperature on crackers or crusty Italian bread.

Santa's SNACK TIME!

Homestyle CHRISTMAS DINNER

Host a homestyle feast this Christmas! From soup to side dishes and dessert, these mouth-watering recipes will invite your family to linger and ask for extra helpings.

Herbed Celery Soup, Cheddar Shortbread

HERBED CELERY SOUP
A soup that's a terrific change of pace.

1/4 c. butter
4 c. celery, finely chopped
2 t. dried chives
1 1/2 t. dried tarragon
1/2 t. dried chervil
8 c. chicken broth
1/4 t. sugar
salt and pepper to taste
Garnish: fresh chives

In a medium saucepan, add butter, celery, chives, tarragon and chervil. Cover and cook for 5 minutes or until celery has softened. Add the chicken broth, sugar, salt and pepper; simmer over low heat for 20 minutes. Garnish with fresh chives. Makes about 9 cups.

Kathy Wyatt
Concord, CA

CHEDDAR SHORTBREAD
For a tasty variation, add sun-dried tomatoes and minced garlic.

2 c. sharp Cheddar cheese, shredded
1 1/2 c. all-purpose flour
3/4 t. dry mustard
1/4 t. salt
1/4 t. cayenne pepper
1/2 c. butter, melted
1 to 2 T. water, optional

Toss first 5 ingredients together; mix in butter. Mix with your hands to form a dough. Add water if dough feels too dry. On a floured surface, roll out half the dough to 1/4-inch thickness. Cut with a 2 1/2-inch star-shaped cookie cutter and place on an ungreased baking sheet. Repeat with the remaining dough. Bake at 375 degrees for 10 to 12 minutes. Remove to rack to cool. Makes 2 dozen.

Robin Sager
Hardin, KY

CORN CHOWDER

I make this soup with the last picking of corn from the garden, but it's just as good with frozen corn!

1 onion, chopped
2 T. butter
2 c. potatoes, diced
1 c. hot water
2 c. milk
2 T. all-purpose flour
10-oz. pkg. frozen whole kernel corn
1 t. salt
1/8 t. pepper
Garnish: fresh parsley, chopped

Sauté onion in butter until golden. Add potatoes and hot water; bring to a boil. Cover, reduce heat and simmer until potatoes are tender. Gradually stir milk into flour. Add to potatoes along with corn, salt and pepper. Bring to a boil. Reduce heat; stirring occasionally, simmer about 10 minutes. Garnish with parsley.

Barbara Bargdill
Gooseberry Patch

ALMOND PINE CONES

These cheese balls look so festive on your holiday table.

2 c. whole almonds
12 oz. cream cheese
1/2 c. mayonnaise
5 slices bacon, crisply cooked and crumbled
1 t. green onion, finely chopped
1/2 t. dried dill weed
1/8 t. pepper
Garnish: fresh rosemary sprigs

Spread almonds, in a single layer, in a shallow pan. Bake at 300 degrees for 15 minutes, stirring often, until almonds begin to turn color. Combine cream cheese and mayonnaise; mix well. Add bacon, onion, dill and pepper; mix well. Chill overnight. On a serving platter, form cheese mixture into 2 pine cone shapes. Beginning at narrow end, press almonds at slight angle into the cheese mixture in rows. Continue overlapping rows until all cheese is covered. Garnish with fresh rosemary. Serve with crackers.

Laurie Keep
Medina, OH

BACON TREATS

This is always a crowd pleaser.

1 lb. sliced bacon
8-oz. can water chestnuts
1/2 c. mayonnaise-type salad dressing
1 c. brown sugar, packed
1/2 c. chili sauce

Slice bacon and water chestnuts in half. Wrap water chestnut with a slice of bacon; secure with a toothpick. Place in a 13"x9" baking dish. Mix all other ingredients together; pour over water chestnuts. Bake at 350 degrees for 45 minutes.

Marsha Downs
Ypsilanti, MI

MARINATED MUSHROOMS

This lightly seasoned salad gives color to your plate without competing with other dominant flavors.

1/2 lb. mushrooms, halved
12 cherry tomatoes
1/2 c. oil-free sweet and sour dressing
1 T. fresh parsley, minced

In medium bowl, combine all ingredients. Cover and refrigerate several hours or overnight. Makes 4 servings.

Amy Schueddig
Imperial, MO

Grease the lip of your cream pitcher with butter at that holiday gathering...it will prevent gravy from dripping all over your favorite tablecloth, and it will be easier to clean up for you!

Almond Pine Cones

THREE ♥ FRIENDS
THREE Layer RUBY RED SALAD
...PERFECT FOR THE HOLIDAYS!

BOTTOM LAYER:

3-oz. package raspberry gelatin
1 c. boiling water
10-oz. package frozen raspberries in syrup

Dissolve gelatin in boiling water. Add frozen berries and stir until thawed & separated. Pour into a lightly oiled 9" square pan. Place in refrigerator for gelatin to thicken.

Middle LAYER:

1 c. sour cream
3-oz. package cream cheese, softened
2 T. sugar
1/2 c. pecans, chopped

Mix all ingredients together and carefully spread on top of thickened raspberry gelatin. Chill.

Top LAYER:

3-oz. package cherry gelatin
1 c. boiling water
8¼-oz. can crushed pineapple, drained
16-oz. can whole-berry cranberry sauce

Dissolve cherry gelatin in boiling water. Stir in drained pineapple and cranberry sauce. Allow to thicken slightly at room temperature. Carefully spoon over sour cream mixture. Chill until firm. Cut into squares and serve on spinach or lettuce leaves. Garnish with a dollop of whipped cream and a fresh raspberry.

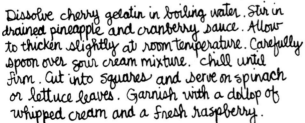

BETTER a GOOD DINNER than a Fine coat.
— French Proverb

Each year, for our Christmas dinner table, we put a special favor at each person's place that they get to keep. Usually it's a handmade ornament for the tree.

— Jan Ertola

SALMON WITH DILL SAUCE
This salmon tastes best when served warm or at room temperature.

2 to 3-lb. salmon fillet
1/2 c. soy sauce
1 t. pepper

Dill Sauce:
1/2 c. whipping cream
1/4 c. water
1/4 c. olive oil
1/2 c. brown mustard
1/2 c. fresh dill weed, chopped
4 t. sugar

To prepare salmon, rinse and pat dry. Place, skin side down, on aluminum foil-lined pan and rub with soy sauce. Season with pepper and broil for 12 to 15 minutes. To prepare dill sauce, whisk all ingredients together. To serve, pour sauce over individual servings of salmon.

WILD RICE CASSEROLE
A warm and hearty side dish.

1 to 1¼ c. wild rice, uncooked
1 T. salt
1/2 c. butter
1 onion, finely chopped
1 lb. sliced mushrooms
1/2 c. slivered almonds
1 c. chicken broth
Garnish: sliced almonds

Place rice in a saucepan, adding enough water to cover; soak overnight. When ready to prepare, add salt to rice and water; simmer for 45 to 50 minutes. Drain rice and sauté in butter with onion and mushrooms until onion is soft, but not brown. Mix cooked rice mixture, almonds and chicken broth in a large casserole dish. Cover tightly and cook at 325 degrees for one hour. If it starts to dry out, add more broth. Garnish with sliced almonds.

Mickey Johnson

HONEY-ROASTED PORK LOIN

A wonderful, old-fashioned main dish when served with homemade stuffing or noodles.

2 to 3-lb. boneless pork loin roast
1/4 c. honey
2 T. Dijon mustard
2 T. mixed or black peppercorns, crushed
1/2 t. dried thyme
1/2 t. salt

Place roast on a lightly greased rack in a shallow roasting pan. Combine honey and remaining ingredients; brush half of mixture over roast. Bake at 325 degrees for one hour; brush with remaining honey mixture. Bake 30 additional minutes or until thermometer inserted in thickest portion registers 160 degrees.

Sultana Purpora
Englewood, OH

HARVEST DRESSING

Not your ordinary dressing...delicious with pork or poultry!

2 apples, cored and chopped
1/2 c. golden raisins
3 T. butter
1/2 c. walnuts or pecans, coarsely chopped
1/4 c. brown sugar, packed
2 c. whole-wheat bread, cubed
apple juice or cider

Sauté apples and raisins in butter; add nuts, brown sugar and bread cubes. Add enough juice to moisten to desired texture. Bake in a 2-quart casserole dish at 400 degrees for 20 to 30 minutes.

Linda Lockwood
St. Louis, MO

Honey-Roasted Pork Loin, Harvest Dressing

PILGRIM SAUCE

A long-time favorite at our home.

1 c. frozen cranberry juice concentrate, thawed
1/3 c. sugar
12-oz. pkg. cranberries
1/2 c. dried cranberries
3 T. orange marmalade
2 T. orange juice
2 t. orange zest
1/4 t. allspice

Combine cranberry juice concentrate and sugar in saucepan. Boil, stirring constantly, until sugar dissolves. Add cranberries and cook for about 7 minutes or until fresh berries pop and dried berries soften. Remove from heat; stir in orange marmalade, orange juice, orange zest and allspice. Chill until ready to serve.

Barbara Etzweiler
Millersburg, PA

ASPARAGUS & TOMATO SALAD

This salad has a tasty combination of flavors.

16 stalks asparagus
1 lb. Roma tomatoes, diced
1 1/2 T. fresh basil, chopped
1 t. salt
1/2 t. pepper
1/2 lb. Feta cheese, crumbled
1/3 c. balsamic vinegar

Cut the stems from asparagus stalks; discard. Slice asparagus on the diagonal and blanch in boiling water for 5 minutes. Remove from boiling water and immediately immerse in cold water to stop the cooking. In a large serving bowl, combine asparagus and tomatoes. Add basil, salt and pepper. Stir in Feta cheese; toss and refrigerate. Before serving, toss with balsamic vinegar.

Barbara Rannazzisi
Elk Grove, CA

"It's a lovely thing…everyone sitting down together, sharing food."

— Alice May Brock

Asparagus & Tomato Salad, Vanilla-Glazed Sweet Potatoes

VANILLA-GLAZED SWEET POTATOES

This heavenly dish is always on our holiday table! It is rich, delicious and there are never any leftovers.

3 lbs. sweet potatoes, peeled
1/4 c. butter
1/4 c. brown sugar, packed
3 T. orange juice
1 T. vanilla extract
1 t. salt
1 t. orange zest
1/4 t. pepper
1/2 c. chopped pecans

Boil sweet potatoes in water until tender; drain. Cool slightly, then cut into 1/4-inch slices. Arrange the slices in a greased, broiler-proof 13"x9" baking dish, overlapping slightly. In a small saucepan, melt butter over low heat. Add brown sugar, orange juice, vanilla, salt, orange zest and pepper, stirring until combined. Heat, but do not allow to boil. Remove from heat and brush sauce evenly over potato slices. Broil 6 inches from heat until golden, about 6 or 7 minutes. Sprinkle with pecans. Makes 6 servings.

Teri Lindquist
Gurnee, IL

Savory Mashed Potatoes

"We hath no better thing to eat under the sun than these mashed potatoes." -Kate

5 large potatoes, peeled & diced
1/4 c. milk
1/2 t. seasoned salt
3 T. margarine
1 c. sour cream

3-oz. package cream cheese, softened
1 t. dried chives
1/2 c. butter-flavored crackers, crushed
1/4 c. cheddar cheese, shredded

Cook potatoes in salted water 'til tender ~ drain. Beat potatoes, milk, seasoned salt & 2 tablespoons margarine in a mixing bowl until fluffy.

Mix in sour cream, cream cheese & chives. Turn into buttered casserole dish. Combine remaining tablespoon of margarine with crushed cracker crumbs ~ Sprinkle on top of potato mixture. Bake for 30 minutes in a 350° oven. Top with shredded cheese during last 10 minutes of baking time. ~ Serves 5. (This recipe can be prepared a day in advance if you wish.)

BAKED BROCCOLI

You can add sliced water chestnuts if you want a little more crunch...very good.

1/2 c. celery, chopped
1/2 c. onion, chopped
2 T. butter
10-oz. pkg. frozen, chopped broccoli
2 c. rice, cooked
10 3/4-oz. can cream of chicken soup
8-oz. jar pasteurized process cheese sauce
1/2 c. milk
1/4 c. bread crumbs, buttered

Sauté celery and onion in butter. Add broccoli and stir until broken up and slightly cooked. Mix together remaining ingredients, except bread crumbs, in a separate bowl. Add to broccoli mixture. Place in a casserole dish coated with non-stick vegetable spray. Cover with buttered crumbs. Bake at 350 degrees for 20 to 30 minutes.

Judy Borecky
Escondido, CA

GOLDEN BUTTER ROLLS

I'm very blessed to have a wonderful mom, and doubly blessed that she's also a great cook. This recipe may seem like a lot of work, but it's well worth the effort. Our entire family loves these delicious rolls!

1 c. milk
1/2 c. butter
1 pkg. active dry yeast
1/2 c. plus 1 t. sugar, divided
1/2 c. lukewarm water
1 t. salt
3 eggs, beaten
1 c. whole-wheat flour
3 1/2 to 4 cups all-purpose flour
3/4 c. butter, softened and divided

In a heavy saucepan, scald milk and butter. Remove from heat and cool. In a small bowl, dissolve yeast and one teaspoon sugar in lukewarm water. When mixture foams, add to a large mixing bowl with remaining sugar, salt, eggs, whole-wheat and all-purpose flour. Add the cooled milk mixture and blend until smooth. Knead on a lightly floured board until shiny, then place in a large oiled bowl; brush the top of dough with 1/4 cup softened butter. Cover and let dough rise until double in size. Divide dough into 3 portions. Using a rolling pin, roll each portion in a 1/2-inch-thick circle. Cut each circle into 10 or 12 pie-shaped wedges. Roll each up from the large end and place one inch apart on a greased baking sheet. Repeat with remaining portions of dough. Brush the tops of each roll with 1/4 cup softened butter; let rise until double. Bake at 375 degrees for 15 to 20 minutes or until golden. Remove and brush with remaining butter while rolls are still warm.

Susan Ingersoll
Gooseberry Patch

RICE PUDDING

This old-fashioned side dish brings back memories of the love and laughter shared at my grandparents' house. Their home was always filled with the sights and smells of many old favorite Swedish dishes.

1/2 c. long-grain rice, uncooked
6 c. milk, divided
1/4 t. salt
3 eggs, beaten
1/3 c. sugar
1 t. vanilla extract
1 c. raisins
Garnish: nutmeg

Rinse rice well; set aside. Scald 4 cups milk, skim off foam and add rice. Add salt and cook over medium heat until mixture thickens, stirring constantly. Add eggs, sugar, vanilla and remaining milk. Stir in raisins; mix well. Transfer mixture to a greased 2-quart casserole dish; sprinkle with nutmeg. Bake at 325 degrees for one hour. Serves 8 to 10.

Janice Carpentier
Aurora, IL

HOLIDAY HOT FUDGE DESSERT

Serve with vanilla ice cream or whipped cream.

1 c. all-purpose flour
2 t. baking powder
3/4 c. sugar
1/4 t. salt
6 T. cocoa, divided
1/2 c. chopped nuts
1/2 c. milk
2 t. oil
1 t. vanilla extract
1 c. brown sugar, packed
1 1/2 c. hot water
Garnish: whipped cream and peppermint candies, crushed

Mix flour, baking powder, sugar, salt, 2 tablespoons cocoa and nuts. Add milk, oil and vanilla. Spread into an 8"x8" baking pan. Combine brown sugar and remaining cocoa and sprinkle on top of mixture in pan. Pour hot water over entire batter. Do not stir. Bake at 350 degrees for 45 to 50 minutes. Garnish with whipped cream and peppermint candies. Serves 6 to 8.

Kim Dubay
Freeport, ME

PUMPKIN ICE CREAM PIE

A quick and easy pie to make for the holidays.

1/2 gal. vanilla ice cream
1 c. canned pumpkin
1/2 c. brown sugar, packed
1 T. orange juice
1/2 t. ginger
1/4 t. cinnamon
1/4 t. nutmeg
9-inch graham cracker crust
Garnish: whipped cream and cinnamon sticks

Place ice cream in a large bowl; cut up and allow to soften. Mix pumpkin, brown sugar, orange juice, ginger, cinnamon and nutmeg, using an electric mixer. Add to the softened ice cream and mix well. Spoon into graham cracker crust. Freeze until firm. Garnish with whipped cream and whole cinnamon sticks. Serves 8.

Brenda Umphress
Colorado Springs, CO

Rice Pudding, Holiday Hot Fudge Dessert

HOLIDAY FRUITCAKE

There have been lots of jokes about inedible and tasteless fruitcakes that nobody in their right mind would eat, but this fruitcake is always greeted with cheers and devoured.

2½ c. all-purpose flour
1 t. baking soda
2 eggs, beaten
27-oz. jar mincemeat
14-oz. can sweetened condensed
   milk
¼ c. apricot brandy, optional
1 lb. mixed candied fruit
½ lb. red candied cherries
1½ c. walnuts, coarsely chopped
Garnish: walnut halves and
   red and green candied cherries

Sift together flour and baking soda; set aside. Combine eggs, mincemeat, sweetened condensed milk and brandy, if desired. Stir in fruit and nuts. Stir in flour mixture. Turn into three 7³/₈"x3⁵/₈" loaf pans lined with wax paper coated with non-stick vegetable spray. Decorate tops of cakes with walnut halves and red and green candied cherries. Bake at 300 degrees for one hour and 25 minutes or until center springs back when touched and top is golden; cool. Turn out and remove wax paper. When completely cool, wrap in new wax paper and then in aluminum foil. Store in a cool place for up to 6 weeks.

Kathy-Leigh Russo

*Can one desire too much
of a good thing?
— Shakespeare, "As You Like It"*

Pumpkin Ice Cream Pie, Holiday Fruitcake

Sweet Treats

*Crispy, creamy, moist & dreamy…
every delightful morsel of these homemade
holiday treats will melt in your mouth!*

Christmas Morning Almond Pound Cake

CHRISTMAS MORNING ALMOND POUND CAKE

*Serve while the presents are being opened,
or make it as a gift for a family you love.*

2/3 c. butter, softened
8 oz. almond paste
1 t. almond extract
1 t. vanilla extract
1 1/4 c. sugar
4 eggs
1 t. baking powder
1/4 c. sour cream
2 1/2 c. all-purpose flour
3/4 c. milk
Garnish: powdered sugar, whipped
    cream and maraschino
    cherries with stems

In a bowl, blend together butter, almond paste and extracts until smooth. Slowly add sugar and beat again. Add eggs, one at a time, beating after each addition. Add baking powder to sour cream; beat together and add to above mixture. Slowly add flour alternately with milk until you have a nice smooth batter. Pour into a greased and floured 12-cup Bundt® pan. Bake at 325 degrees for 50 to 55 minutes or until the top is golden brown and it springs back when touched. Turn off oven and open oven door. Let sit about 30 minutes and then remove to counter on rack or cutting board. When cool, remove to a serving dish. Garnish with powdered sugar, dollop of whipped cream and maraschino cherries.

Wendy Paffenroth
Pine Island, NY

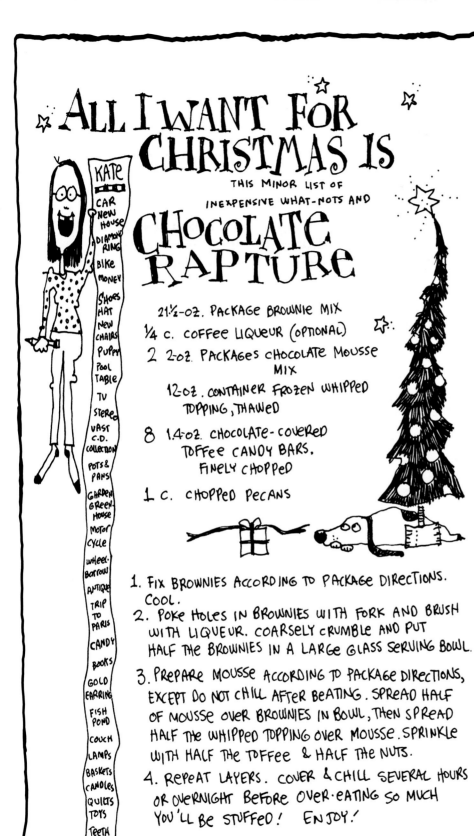

ALL I WANT FOR CHRISTMAS IS

THIS MINOR LIST OF INEXPENSIVE WHAT-NOTS AND

CHOCOLATE RAPTURE

KATE
CAR
NEW HOUSE
DIAMOND RING
BIKE
MONEY
SHOES
HAT
NEW CHAIRS
PUPPY
POOL TABLE
TV
STEREO
VAST C.D. COLLECTION
POTS & PANS
GARDEN GREENHOUSE
MOTOR CYCLE
WHEEL BARROW
ANTIQUE
TRIP TO PARIS
CANDY
BOOKS
GOLD EARRING
FISH POND
COUCH
LAMPS
BASKETS
CANDLES
QUILTS
TOYS
TEETH

21½-oz. PACKAGE BROWNIE MIX

¼ c. COFFEE LIQUEUR (OPTIONAL)

2 2-oz. PACKAGES CHOCOLATE MOUSSE MIX

12-oz. CONTAINER FROZEN WHIPPED TOPPING, THAWED

8 1.4-oz. CHOCOLATE-COVERED TOFFEE CANDY BARS, FINELY CHOPPED

1 c. CHOPPED PECANS

1. FIX BROWNIES ACCORDING TO PACKAGE DIRECTIONS. COOL.
2. POKE HOLES IN BROWNIES WITH FORK AND BRUSH WITH LIQUEUR. COARSELY CRUMBLE AND PUT HALF THE BROWNIES IN A LARGE GLASS SERVING BOWL.
3. PREPARE MOUSSE ACCORDING TO PACKAGE DIRECTIONS, EXCEPT DO NOT CHILL AFTER BEATING. SPREAD HALF OF MOUSSE OVER BROWNIES IN BOWL, THEN SPREAD HALF THE WHIPPED TOPPING OVER MOUSSE. SPRINKLE WITH HALF THE TOFFEE & HALF THE NUTS.
4. REPEAT LAYERS. COVER & CHILL SEVERAL HOURS OR OVERNIGHT BEFORE OVER-EATING SO MUCH YOU'LL BE STUFFED! ENJOY!

FONDANT

While I was growing up, our family would begin making candy on the first Sunday afternoon in December and continue each Sunday until Christmas. It was such a wonderful "together" time. Dad always cracked the nuts and my two brothers licked the pans!

2 c. sugar
1 c. milk
2 T. margarine
1 t. vanilla extract
Garnish: pecan halves

Combine sugar and milk in a saucepan and cook to a soft-ball stage or 238 degrees on a candy thermometer. Remove from heat. Add margarine and vanilla; cool. Using a heavy-duty mixer, or kneading by hand, mix until stiff enough to shape into balls. Using approximately one teaspoonful, roll fondant into balls and top each ball with a pecan half. Makes approximately 40 pieces of fondant.

Marjorie Foland
Wilmington, OH

CARAMEL CORN

Great for slumber parties or whenever you have a houseful of munchers!

1/2 c. margarine
2 c. brown sugar, packed
1/2 c. corn syrup
1/2 t. salt
1 t. vanilla extract
1 t. baking soda
6 qts. popped popcorn

Heat margarine, brown sugar, corn syrup and salt until it comes to a boil. Continue to boil for 5 minutes without stirring. Remove from heat. Add vanilla and baking soda; stir. Pour over freshly popped popcorn. Bake one hour at 250 degrees, stirring every 20 minutes.

Judy Borecky
Escondido, CA

105

ANNIE'S SOFT MOLASSES COOKIES

Madge's aunt used to make these yummy cookies 4 inches in size and bake them in a woodstove!

1 c. sugar
1 c. shortening, melted
1 c. molasses
1 egg, beaten
4 t. baking soda
2/3 c. hot water
1 T. vanilla extract
5 c. all-purpose flour
1 1/2 t. cream of tartar
1 1/2 t. ginger
1 1/2 t. cinnamon
1/2 t. ground cloves
3/4 t. salt
1/2 c. vanilla frosting

Mix sugar, shortening and molasses; add egg. Dissolve baking soda in the hot water and add vanilla; mix well and set aside. Sift together flour, cream of tartar, spices and salt. Add water mixture. Combine thoroughly with molasses mixture. Chill dough for at least 3 hours. Roll out dough to 1/4-inch thickness and cut out with desired 2 3/4-inch cookie cutter. Place on greased baking sheet. Bake at 375 degrees for 7 minutes; let cool. Place frosting in a small microwave-safe bowl; microwave on high for 20 seconds. Stir well. Microwave 5 additional seconds, if needed to make a good dipping consistency. Dip tips of cookies in frosting. Makes about 4 dozen cookies.

Madge Bowman
Shreve, OH

Annie's Soft Molasses Cookies, Cheesecake Cookies

CHOCOLATE-PEANUT BUTTER CUPCAKES

A treat for any celebration! Make them extra special by dusting tops with powdered sugar using lace paper doilies or heart cut-outs.

Filling:
2 T. whipping cream
2 oz. semi-sweet baking
    chocolate, grated
2 t. sugar
1/4 c. creamy peanut butter

Cupcakes:
6 T. butter
6 oz. semi-sweet baking
    chocolate
2 eggs
2/3 c. sugar
1 t. vanilla extract
3/4 c. all-purpose flour
1/4 t. baking soda
1/4 t. salt

To prepare filling, heat cream in small saucepan until boiling. In a mixing bowl, pour cream over chocolate and sugar; stir until combined and chocolate melts. Add peanut butter and mix well. Refrigerate filling for 35 to 40 minutes or until slightly firm. In double boiler over low heat, melt butter and chocolate. In mixing bowl, beat eggs until foamy, adding sugar and vanilla; beat until fluffy. Beating at low speed, add melted chocolate mixture. Beat in flour, baking soda and salt; mix until just combined. Pour batter into muffin tins coated with non-stick vegetable spray, filling 2/3 full. Roll rounded teaspoonfuls of filling and press one ball lightly into the center of each cupcake. Bake at 350 degrees for 15 to 20 minutes.

CHEESECAKE COOKIES

These are my favorite cookies because they're so moist and tasty. I remember they were considered a special treat, usually made for company, but once in awhile we'd come home from school and a pan of them, warm from the oven, would be waiting for us!

1/3 c. butter
1/3 c. brown sugar, packed
1 c. all-purpose flour
1/2 c. walnuts, finely chopped
1/4 c. sugar
8-oz. pkg. cream cheese
1 egg
2 T. milk
1 T. lemon juice
1/2 t. vanilla extract

Cream butter with brown sugar in a small mixing bowl. Add flour and walnuts; blend together. Mixture will be crumbly. Reserve one cup for topping. Press remainder of mixture into the bottom of an 8"x8" baking pan. Bake at 350 degrees for 12 to 15 minutes or until lightly browned. Blend sugar with cream cheese until smooth. Add egg, milk, lemon juice and vanilla; beat well. Spread over baked crust and sprinkle with reserved topping. Bake for 25 minutes. Cool; cut into 2-inch squares.

Mary Walsh
Valencia, CA

WHITE CHOCOLATE MACADAMIA BROWNIE PIE

The crunchy macadamia nuts combine with the creamy white chocolate to create a fabulous taste sensation.

1/2 c. unsalted butter, softened
1 c. sugar
2 eggs
1/2 c. all-purpose flour
1/4 c. cocoa
1 t. vanilla extract
1/2 c. macadamia nuts, chopped
3 oz. white chocolate chips

Cream butter and sugar together and beat in the eggs. Add flour, cocoa and vanilla. Fold in the nuts and chips. Pour into a greased 9" pie pan. Bake at 325 degrees for 35 minutes. Pie should be moist; toothpick will not come out completely clean. Let cool, but serve slightly warm, if possible, with a scoop of vanilla ice cream on the side.

PECAN FINGERS

Using real butter gives these cookies a rich flavor.

1 c. butter, softened
2 c. all-purpose flour
1/2 c. powdered sugar
2 t. vanilla extract
2 c. pecans, finely chopped
Garnish: powdered sugar

Cream butter; mix in flour, powdered sugar and vanilla. Add pecans, mixing well. Chill dough until firm. Roll into finger lengths and place on a greased baking sheet. Bake at 250 degrees for one hour. Roll in powdered sugar while still warm.

Jane Keichinger

ROCKY ROAD FUDGE

★ 4   4 1/2-ounce milk chocolate bars
★ 3 c. miniature marshmallows
★ 3/4 c. coarsely broken walnuts

PARTIALLY MELT CHOCOLATE BARS OVER LOW HEAT IN SMALL PAN. REMOVE FROM HEAT ᴧ BEAT SMOOTH. STIR IN NUTS & MARSHMALLOWS. LET COOL AND SNARF DIRECTLY FROM PAN ᴧ OR SPREAD IN BUTTERED 8"x 8" PAN, CHILL & CUT WHEN SET.

*Now I lay me down to sleep,
a pan of fudge here
at my feet;
If I should die
before I wake,
you'll know I died
of stomach ache.*

*– COUNTRY FRIENDS' VARIATION
OF OLD RHYME*

Every year, each of my children selects one old favorite cookie recipe and one new one for us to prepare. It's amazing how favorites change, and how they "remember" who discovered the new favorite.
— Kathy Christianson

THE PEANUT BUTTER BARS

Many years ago when I was in elementary school, our "Lunch Lady," Mrs. Hopkins, made these for us once a week. The aroma filled the school as they were baking and we knew we were in store for the best possible treat. I've never had anything that tasted so good! Now I make these for my own family and they agree...they are THE Peanut Butter Bars.

1½ c. plus 2 T. butter, softened
¾ c. peanut butter
¼ c. corn syrup
1 c. sugar
1¾ c. all-purpose flour
2 eggs
1 t. salt

Cream butter and peanut butter; add corn syrup, sugar, flour, eggs and salt. Mix about 5 minutes. Spread in greased 13"x9" baking pan. Bake at 350 degrees for 25 minutes, watching carefully. Cool, ice and cut into squares.

Icing:
¼ c. shortening, melted and
    cooled
½ c. cocoa
¼ t. salt
⅓ c. milk
1½ t. vanilla extract
3½ c. powdered sugar

Combine shortening, cocoa and salt. Add milk and vanilla. Stir in powdered sugar in three parts; beat well.

Carol Bull
Delaware, OH

Mom's Candy Apple Walnut Pie

MOM'S CANDY APPLE WALNUT PIE

The red hots add the spice.

2 frozen 9-inch deep-dish
    pie crusts
6 c. cooking apples, thinly sliced
⅔ c. chopped walnuts
½ c. cinnamon red hot candies
⅓ c. plus 2 T. sugar, divided
⅓ c. all-purpose flour

If desired, let one pie crust thaw, and reshape edges into a fluted design. Set aside. In a large bowl, toss together apples, walnuts, cinnamon candies, ⅓ cup sugar and flour. Pour into fluted pie crust. Break and crumble second frozen crust into very small pieces; toss with remaining 2 tablespoons sugar. Sprinkle over apples. Bake at 375 degrees on a baking sheet for 55 to 60 minutes or until candies melt and bubble up through the crumbled crust. Cool completely before serving. Makes 8 servings.

Juanita Williams
Jacksonville, OR

CRUSTLESS PUMPKIN PIE

A great alternative to pumpkin pie!

16-oz. can pumpkin
12-oz. can evaporated milk
1½ c. sugar
4 eggs
2 t. pumpkin pie spice
1 t. salt
18¼-oz. pkg. yellow cake mix
1 c. chopped nuts
2 sticks butter, melted
Garnish: whipped topping and
    nutmeg

Combine pumpkin, milk, sugar, eggs, pumpkin pie spice and salt, blending well. Pour into an ungreased 13"x9" baking dish and sprinkle cake mix over top. Sprinkle on nuts. Drizzle butter onto cake mix; do not stir. Bake at 350 degrees for 45 minutes to an hour, testing for doneness. Serve with whipped topping and a sprinkle of nutmeg.

Linda Webb
Delaware, OH

CINNAMON PUDDING CAKE

A terrific dessert for a chilly winter evening! Serve with a mug of homemade cocoa.

1 c. sugar
2 T. butter, softened
1 c. milk
2 c. all-purpose flour
2 t. baking powder
2 t. cinnamon
¼ t. salt

Mix all ingredients together and blend well. Pour into a greased 13"x9" baking pan; add topping.

Topping:
2 c. brown sugar, packed
2 T. butter
1¼ c. water

Combine all ingredients in a saucepan; bring to a boil. Pour mixture over the cake batter; do not stir. Bake at 350 degrees for 25 minutes. Makes 12 servings.

Phyllis Peters
Three Rivers, MI

Pecan Pie Mini Muffins

a recipe from Kathy Mentink
★ Elgin, IL

YUM!

1 c. brown sugar, packed
½ c. all-purpose flour
1 c. pecans, chopped
⅔ c. butter, melted
2 eggs, beaten

*

In a bowl, combine first three ingredients; set aside. Combine butter & eggs~ mix well. Stir into flour mixture until just moistened. Fill paper-lined miniature muffin cups ⅔ full. Bake at 350 degrees for 20 to 25 minutes or until tested done. Remove immediately to cool on wire racks. Makes 3 dozen muffins.

Crustless Pumpkin Pie, Pecan Pie Mini Muffins

"Nine out of 10 people like chocolate. The tenth person always lies."
— John G. Tullius

109

Fireside Breads and Muffins

No one can resist piping hot, crusty breads and delicious muffins fresh from the oven!

DAMASCUS BRICK SWEET ROLLS

There's nothing like the smell of fresh breads baking to welcome guests. The memories and smells of their childhood soon warm their hearts.

1 c. plus 2 T. milk, divided
1 c. butter, divided
2 t. salt
1/2 c. plus 1 t. sugar, divided
2 pkgs. active dry yeast
1 c. warm water
1 egg, beaten
6 to 7 c. bread flour
cinnamon-sugar to taste
2 c. powdered sugar
1/2 t. vanilla extract

Combine one cup milk, 1/2 cup butter, salt and 1/2 cup sugar in a large saucepan until just warm. In a small mixing bowl, combine yeast and water until yeast is dissolved; add remaining sugar. When yeast mixture begins to foam, add to milk mixture; mix well. Fold in egg. Add flour and knead just until smooth. Roll dough out on a floured surface to a 16"x12" rectangle. Sprinkle with cinnamon-sugar mixture to taste; dot with remaining butter. Roll up dough lengthwise and cut into one-inch slices. Place on a lightly greased baking sheet; cover and let rise 25 minutes or until double. Bake at 375 degrees for 12 to 15 minutes. Combine powdered sugar, remaining milk and vanilla; drizzle over rolls. Makes 1 1/2 dozen rolls.

The Damascus Brick
Junction City, OH

Damascus Brick Sweet Rolls

MACADAMIA MINI-LOAVES
A delicious coconut-flavored bread.

3 1/2-oz. jar macadamia nuts
1/3 c. flaked coconut
1 1/2 c. plus 1 T. sugar, divided
1 lemon
3/4 c. butter, softened
3 c. all-purpose flour
1/2 c. milk
1 1/2 t. vanilla extract
1 t. baking powder
2 eggs

Finely chop enough macadamia nuts to measure 1/3 cup; set aside. Coarsely chop remaining nuts; place in a small bowl and stir in coconut and one tablespoon sugar. Grate 2 teaspoons lemon zest and squeeze 3 tablespoons juice. Grease and flour four 5 3/4"x3 1/4" loaf pans or one 9" tube pan. In a large bowl, with mixer at high speed, beat butter and remaining sugar until light and fluffy. At low speed, beat in flour, milk, vanilla, baking powder, eggs, lemon zest and juice until just mixed, constantly scraping the bowl. Stir in reserved macadamia nuts. Spoon batter into pans. Sprinkle coconut mixture evenly over batter, then lightly press into batter. Bake small loaves at 350 degrees for 60 minutes or tube cake for one hour 10 minutes or until toothpick inserted in center comes out clean. If topping begins to brown too quickly, loosely cover pans with aluminum foil. Cool cakes in pans on wire racks for 10 minutes; remove from pans. Cool completely on racks. Makes 4 loaves, 4 servings each or 1 ring, 16 servings.

Terri Rasmussen
Orange, CA

Angel Biscuits

Heavenly!

Light and Fluffy!
Make the dough the night before for fresh hot biscuits on Christmas morning!

☆ 2 3/4 c. flour
☆ 2 T. sugar
☆ 1 1/2 t. baking powder
☆ 1/2 t. baking soda
☆ 1/2 t. salt
☆ 1 stick margarine
☆ 2 T. warm water
☆ 1 c. buttermilk
☆ 1 pkg. active dry yeast

Combine flour, sugar, baking powder, baking soda & salt in large mixing bowl. With a pastry blender or 2 knives, cut in margarine until mixture resembles coarse meal. Place yeast in small bowl & dissolve with 2 T. of warm water. Mix dissolved yeast & buttermilk into coarse flour mixture. Do not overmix! Dough should just cling together. Knead dough gently (about 12 strokes) on well-floured surface. Grease a bowl with shortening or oil. Place dough in bowl & cover with plastic wrap. Chill overnight. The next morning, roll dough to 1/2" thickness on floured surface. Cut with a 2-to-3" cookie or biscuit cutter. Place on baking sheet. Cover with clean towel ∼ let rise in a warm place for about 30 minutes. Bake for 10 to 12 minutes at 400° or until golden brown. Serve warm with butter & honey. Makes 18-to-24 biscuits.

Bread is the warmest and kindest of words. ∼ RUSSIAN SAYING

BRAZIL NUT LOAF

Enjoy one loaf and take the other to a party.

1½ c. all-purpose flour
1½ c. sugar
1 t. baking powder
1 t. salt
10-oz. pkg. whole pitted dates
2 c. chopped walnuts
1 c. Brazil nuts
10-oz. jar maraschino cherries, drained
5 eggs, beaten
1 t. vanilla extract

Sift together dry ingredients and add dates, nuts and cherries. Stir to coat with flour mixture. Add eggs and vanilla. Blend everything well. Spoon into two 8½"x4½" greased loaf pans. Bake at 325 degrees for one hour 15 minutes to one hour 20 minutes. Cool.

Judy Borecky
Escondido, CA

EASY ORANGE ROLLS

So easy to make, and what a wonderful aroma while they're baking!

½ c. butter
¾ c. sugar
2 T. frozen orange juice
zest of 2 oranges
3 12-oz. tubes refrigerated biscuits

In a small saucepan, combine butter and sugar. Heat until sugar dissolves. Blend in frozen orange juice and orange zest. Dip individual biscuits in orange mixture and layer in a lightly oiled Bundt® pan; repeat with all biscuits. Pour any remaining orange mixture over biscuits. Bake at 375 degrees for 20 minutes.

Robyn Wright
Delaware, OH

Brazil Nut Loaf

PUMPKIN NUT BREAD

Easy snacking for the Christmas crowd.

3¼ c. all-purpose flour
¾ c. quick-cooking oats, uncooked
2 t. baking soda
1½ t. pumpkin pie spice
½ t. baking powder
½ t. salt
3 eggs
15-oz. can pumpkin
1½ c. sugar
1½ c. brown sugar, packed
½ c. water
½ c. oil
½ c. evaporated milk
1 c. chopped walnuts

Combine flour, oats, baking soda, pumpkin pie spice, baking powder and salt in a large bowl. Beat together eggs, pumpkin, sugars, water, oil and evaporated milk on medium speed until combined. Beat flour mixture into pumpkin mixture until blended; stir in nuts. Fill 2 greased 9"x5" loaf pans and bake at 350 degrees for one hour and 5 minutes to one hour and 10 minutes or until toothpick comes out clean. Cool in pans 10 minutes; remove from pans to cool completely.

CRUSTY CORNMEAL ROLLS

A delicious roll that's worth the time...prepare a good vegetable soup while you're waiting for the dough to rise!

2 c. milk
1/2 c. shortening, melted
1/2 c. sugar
1/3 c. cornmeal
1 1/2 t. salt
2 eggs, beaten
1 pkg. active dry yeast
1/4 c. lukewarm water
4 1/2 to 5 c. all-purpose flour
3 T. butter, melted

In a double boiler, combine milk, shortening, sugar, cornmeal and salt. Stir the mixture often, cooking until thick. Allow to cool; add eggs. Dissolve yeast in water and add to batter. Beat well; cover and let rise in a greased bowl for about 2 hours. After batter has risen, add flour to form a soft dough. Knead dough lightly and let rise again for another hour; knead again. Roll dough out to one-inch thickness with a floured rolling pin and use a 2 1/2-inch biscuit cutter to cut out dough. Brush with butter. Place on a greased baking sheet. Cover and let rise for another hour. Bake at 375 degrees for 13 to 15 minutes or until golden. Makes 20 rolls.

Crusty Cornmeal Rolls, Honeybee Butter

HONEYBEE BUTTER
• 1 STICK BUTTER
• 6 T. HONEY
• Beat ingredients together 'til fluffy.

WHOLE-WHEAT BREAD

A lady in our church has been making this bread for us for more years than I am allowed to mention! It's delicious and easy to make.

3 c. warm water
3 pkgs. active dry yeast
1/4 c. honey
5 c. whole-wheat flour
5 t. salt
5 c. all-purpose flour
5 T. oil

Mix together water, yeast and honey. Add whole-wheat flour and salt; mix well. Stir in all-purpose flour. Pour oil over the dough and knead 2 to 3 minutes. Cover dough and let rise for 45 minutes. Punch down and knead slightly. Shape into 2 loaves and place in 2 greased 9"x5" loaf pans. Let rise until double in size. Bake at 400 degrees for 20 minutes, then loosely cover with a tent of aluminum foil. Bake 10 minutes longer. Makes 2 loaves.

Diann Fox
Lewisberry, PA

DILLY ONION BREAD

An easy-to-make quick bread that's full of flavor!

3 c. all-purpose flour
1/2 c. plus 2 T. sugar
1 1/2 T. baking powder
2/3 c. butter
1 c. milk
4 eggs
5 t. dill seed
2 t. dried, minced onion

Oil four 6-inch loaf pans; set aside. Using a large bowl, combine flour, sugar and baking powder well; cut in butter. In a separate bowl, blend milk, eggs, dill seed and onion. Add to flour mixture and stir. Pour equal amounts into prepared loaf pans and bake at 350 degrees for 30 minutes or until a knife inserted in the center comes out clean. Cool on a rack and serve warm.

Apricot Crescents

APRICOT CRESCENTS

Serve these with a steaming mug of chamomile tea and fresh fruit. Perfect for breakfast or a light brunch.

1 c. butter
2 c. all-purpose flour
1 egg yolk
1/2 c. sour cream
1/2 c. sugar, divided
1/2 c. apricot preserves
1/2 c. flaked coconut
1/4 c. pecans, finely chopped
sugar

Cut butter into flour until mixture resembles coarse crumbs. Beat egg yolk with sour cream; add to crumb mixture and blend well. Divide into fourths; shape into balls and flatten into 1/2-inch thickness between layers of plastic wrap. Chill several hours or overnight. Remove dough from refrigerator and let stand 10 minutes. Combine preserves, coconut and pecans, stirring well. Working with one portion of dough at a time, roll into a 10 1/2-inch circle on a floured surface. Sprinkle with 2 tablespoons sugar. Place 3 tablespoons of filling on circle; gently spread filling over dough with a pastry brush. Cut each circle into 12 pie-shaped wedges and roll into a crescent shape, beginning at the wide end. Sprinkle each rolled crescent with additional sugar. Place one inch apart on greased baking sheet. Repeat with remaining dough, sugar and filling. Bake at 350 degrees for 15 to 17 minutes or until lightly browned. Immediately remove from oven and place on wire racks to cool. Makes 4 dozen.

Rene Smith
Shawnee, OK

OATMEAL APPLE MUFFINS

Muffins with a fresh apple flavor.

1 c. quick-cooking oats, uncooked
3/4 c. milk
1/2 c. raisins, optional
1 1/4 c. all-purpose flour
2 t. baking powder
1/2 t. salt
1/2 t. cinnamon
1 egg
1/2 c. brown sugar, packed
1/4 c. oil
1 to 2 apples, peeled, cored and chopped

In a small bowl, combine oats and milk; set aside. Soak raisins in a little hot water to "plump" them; drain. Combine in a medium bowl, flour, baking powder, salt and cinnamon; mix well. Beat egg, brown sugar and oil until blended. Add egg mixture to dry ingredients; stir until well blended. Stir in oat mixture, apples and raisins. Stir together until blended. Grease and fill muffin tins 3/4 full. Bake at 400 degrees for 15 to 20 minutes.

Kathleen Griffin
N. Charleston, SC

BROWN SUGAR & CINNAMON BUTTER

1 STICK OF BUTTER, softened
4 t. BROWN SUGAR, packed
1/4 t. CINNAMON
1/8 t. NUTMEG
.....
In a small bowl, beat all ingredients together until fluffy.

FIELDSTONE FARM POPOVERS

Our daughter Emily loves these warm from the oven with butter and jam!

2 eggs
1 c. milk
1 c. all-purpose flour
1/2 t. salt

Butter 8 custard cups and place in oven on a baking sheet while preparing batter. Beat eggs slightly and add remaining ingredients. Beat mixture on medium speed for one minute, scraping sides of bowls. Batter should be smooth and thin. Remove custard cups from oven and fill each custard cup 1/3 full. Bake at 400 degrees for 50 minutes or until crisp and golden-brown. Do not open oven during baking time or popovers may fall.

Vickie

ENGLISH MUFFIN BREAD

The first time I made this bread we ate the whole loaf in one sitting!

2 pkgs. active dry yeast
1/2 c. warm water
5 c. all-purpose flour, divided
2 t. cinnamon
2 T. sugar
1 t. salt
1/4 t. baking soda
1 1/2 c. warm orange juice
1/4 c. oil
1/2 c. chopped walnuts or pecans
1/2 c. dried apricots, chopped
cornmeal to taste

Dissolve yeast in water; set aside. Combine 2 cups flour, cinnamon, sugar, salt and baking soda; stir in yeast mixture. Blend in orange juice and oil. Beat mixture on low until thoroughly combined. Increase speed to high and blend for an additional 3 minutes. Stir in nuts, apricots and remaining flour to form a stiff batter. Do not knead. Spoon batter into 2 lightly oiled 9"x5" loaf pans; sprinkle cornmeal over tops of loaves. Cover and let rise for 45 minutes. Bake at 350 degrees for 35 to 40 minutes. Makes 2 loaves.

Madge Bowman
Shreve, OH

Come for Brunch

Serve a basket-full!

Holly's Lemon Raspberry Yogurt Muffins

ingredients:
2 eggs, beaten
1/2 c. milk
1/2 c. lemon yogurt
4 T. butter, melted
1 t. vanilla
2 c. flour
1 T. baking powder
1 t. salt
1 t. lemon peel, finely grated

2/3 c. sugar
2 c. raspberries

Yields 12 Muffins

Combine eggs, milk, yogurt, butter & vanilla. In a medium bowl, stir together flour, baking powder, salt, lemon peel & sugar. Mix yogurt mixture into dry ingredients. In 2 to 3 strokes, fold in raspberries. Spoon into greased muffin cups. Bake at 350° for 18 to 20 minutes or when top springs back when touched. Serve plain or brush warm muffins with...

Lemon Glaze

2 T. lemon juice   1 t. lemon peel, finely grated
1/2 c. powdered sugar

Combine ingredients and brush over warm muffins.

"Bread cast upon the waters comes back eclairs."
— Bert Greene

You'll love these nutritious, oh-so-easy dishes for casual holiday meals and potlucks.

NANCY'S TURKEY PIE

A yummy main course that only needs a salad and a simple dessert for a complete meal.

1/2 c. butter, softened
1 c. sour cream
1 egg
1 c. all-purpose flour
1 t. salt
1 t. baking powder
1/2 t. dried sage

Combine butter, sour cream and egg. Beat at medium speed until smooth. Add flour, salt, baking powder and sage; blend at low speed, mixing well. Spread batter evenly over the bottom and up the sides of an ungreased 9 1/2" deep-dish pie plate.

Filling:
1/3 c. carrot, chopped
1/3 c. onion, chopped
1/3 c. green pepper, chopped
1/3 c. celery, chopped
1/3 c. red pepper, chopped
2 c. cooked turkey, chopped
10 3/4-oz. can cream of chicken
        soup
1/2 c. Cheddar cheese, shredded

Mix together vegetables, turkey and soup; place into pie crust and sprinkle with Cheddar cheese. Bake at 375 degrees for one hour. Let stand 15 minutes before serving.

Delores Hollenbeck
Omaha, NE

Nancy's Turkey Pie

HEARTY BEEF BRISKET

Slow-cooking makes the meat tender. Let it roast while you wrap packages or trim the tree!

16-oz. can stewed tomatoes, chopped
8-oz. can sauerkraut
1 c. applesauce
2 T. brown sugar, packed
3½ lb. beef brisket
2 T. cold water
2 T. cornstarch

Combine tomatoes, sauerkraut, applesauce and brown sugar in a Dutch oven. Bring to a boil; then reduce heat. Add brisket, spooning tomato mixture over top; cover and simmer on low 2 to 3 hours or until meat is tender. When brisket is thoroughly cooked, remove from Dutch oven and set aside. In a small bowl, combine cold water and cornstarch, whisking well. Blend into tomato mixture in Dutch oven. Cook until mixture thickens; continue to cook for 2 additional minutes. Spread sauce over top of brisket, reserving some as gravy.

Joanne West
Beavercreek, OH

SPINACH PIE

This is a terrific, light meal I like to serve with muffins and fresh fruit.

16-oz. carton cottage cheese
10-oz. pkg. frozen chopped spinach, thawed and drained
8 oz. Cheddar cheese, shredded
3 eggs, beaten
¼ c. butter, melted
3 T. all-purpose flour
salt blend to taste

Combine all ingredients. Pour into a 9" pie pan. Bake at 325 degrees for one hour. Cool slightly and cut into wedges.

Nancy Burton
Wamego, KS

Holly's Broccoli Ham and Cheese Strata

a perfect holiday brunch for those you love

14 slices white or wheat bread, crusts trimmed
1½ c. cheddar cheese, shredded
10-oz. pkg. chopped broccoli, thawed & drained
¼ c. onion, chopped
1 c. cooked ham, chopped
1 medium tomato, peeled, seeded & chopped
5 eggs
1 t. seasoned salt
½ t. garlic powder
½ t. prepared mustard
½ t. cayenne pepper
1½ c. milk

Butter a 13"x 9" baking dish. Layer 7 slices of bread on bottom of dish. Sprinkle half of cheddar cheese over bread slices. Next, layer thawed chopped broccoli, onion, ham & tomato over cheese & bread layers. Top with remaining cheese & bread slices. In mixing bowl, combine remaining ingredients; beat well. Pour egg mixture over layered ingredients in baking dish. Cover & refrigerate at least 3 hours or overnight. Bake in 350° oven for 40-50 minutes or until knife inserted in center comes out clean.

Mmmm! ∽ Serves 8-10 people (and one dog)

Why use everybody-has-'em, regular old cake pans and casserole dishes? Don't settle for boring...find something beautiful in stoneware or granite to cook in!

CHICKEN STEW

Let the cooker do all the work for you!

2 sweet potatoes, peeled and
   chopped
1 onion, sliced
6 boneless chicken breasts
$\frac{1}{2}$ t. dried thyme
$\frac{1}{4}$ t. pepper
2 bay leaves
3$\frac{1}{2}$ c. water, divided
2 3-oz. pkgs. chicken ramen
   noodles with seasoning
   packets

In a 3-quart slow cooker, layer
potatoes, onion and chicken.
Sprinkle with thyme and pepper.
Add bay leaves. Combine one cup
water and seasoning packets from
noodle soup, reserving noodles.
Pour seasoning over chicken; add
remaining water to stockpot. Cover
and cook on low heat 7 hours. Stir
in reserved noodles; turn heat to
high and cook 10 minutes. Remove
bay leaves before serving.

Joanne West
Beavercreek, OH

I'm in SUCH a Stew!

Reuben Casserole

REUBEN CASSEROLE

*A favorite sandwich turned into
a casserole!*

2 14$\frac{1}{2}$-oz. cans sauerkraut,
   drained
2 12-oz. cans corned beef,
   crumbled
4 c. Swiss cheese, shredded
   and divided
1 c. mayonnaise
1 c. Thousand Island dressing
4 T. butter, melted
$\frac{1}{2}$ c. soft rye bread crumbs
$\frac{1}{2}$ t. caraway seeds

Layer sauerkraut, corned beef and
half the cheese in a 13"x9" baking
dish. Mix mayonnaise and dressing
together; pour over casserole
mixture. Sprinkle with remaining
cheese. Mix together butter and
bread crumbs; sprinkle over top.
Sprinkle with caraway seeds. Bake
at 375 degrees for 30 minutes.

Phyllis Laughrey
Mount Vernon, OH

SOUR CREAM TACOS

A wonderful way to use leftover turkey.

1 onion, chopped
2 T. oil
1 to 2 c. chicken broth
4 to 6 canned jalapeño peppers,
    chopped
1 t. salt
1/2 t. pepper
3 c. cooked turkey or chicken,
    diced
2 c. sour cream
1 lb. American cheese, shredded
2 14 1/2-oz. cans tomatoes,
    chopped
12 corn tortillas, torn
1 c. Cheddar cheese, shredded

Sauté onion in oil; add chicken
broth, jalapeño peppers, salt and
pepper. Mix turkey, sour cream,
American cheese and tomatoes
together. Add onion mixture
to turkey mixture, along with
the torn tortillas; mix well.
Place in a 13"x9" baking pan.
Bake at 350 degrees for
30 to 40 minutes. The last
10 minutes of baking, top with
the Cheddar cheese. Serves 6.

Neta Liebscher
El Reno, OK

*"One makes one's own
happiness only by taking care
of the happiness of others."*
— Saint-Pierre

SPAGHETTI CASSEROLE

*Feeds a crowd and can be made ahead
and refrigerated before baking.*

1 c. onion, chopped
1 c. green pepper, chopped
1 T. butter
28-oz. can tomatoes, undrained
4-oz. can mushrooms, drained
3.8-oz. can sliced, black olives,
    drained
2 t. dried oregano
1 lb. ground beef, browned and
    drained
12 oz. spaghetti, cooked and
    drained
2 c. Cheddar cheese, shredded
10 3/4-oz. can condensed cream of
    mushroom soup
1/4 c. water
1/4 c. grated Parmesan cheese

In a large skillet, sauté onion and
green pepper in butter until tender.
Add tomatoes, mushrooms, olives
and oregano. Add ground beef and
simmer, uncovered, for 10 minutes.
Place half of the spaghetti in a
greased 13"x9" baking dish. Top
with half of the vegetable mixture.
Sprinkle with one cup of Cheddar
cheese. Repeat layers. Combine
soup and water; stir until smooth.
Pour over casserole. Sprinkle with
Parmesan cheese. Bake, uncovered,
at 350 degrees for 30 to
55 minutes or until heated
through. Makes 12 servings.

Laura Strausberger
Cary, IL

SPOTTY'S SPEEDY SPANISH SKILLET

...a one-pan wonder!

1 small green pepper, cut in strips
1 T. butter
2 15-oz. cans Spanish rice
12-oz. can whole kernel corn, drained
1 1/2 t. minced dried onion
3/4 c. canned black beans, rinsed
16-oz. can Mexican-style
    tomatoes, chopped

1/2 t. Worcestershire sauce
dash ground red pepper
few dashes of hot sauce
3/4 c. sharp Cheddar cheese,
    grated

★

Cook green pepper in butter
until tender. Stir in remaining
ingredients except cheese. Heat
through. Sprinkle cheese on top
just before serving.

¡ole!

HOLIDAY ETIQUETTE:
Please Remove Antlers before being seated at Christmas dinner.

*Clean up as you go. Table
salt poured on an oven spill
will make it easier to clean up
later. A damp sponge makes
a great spoon rest.*

INSTRUCTIONS

PHOTO ORNAMENTS
(shown on pages 8 and 9)

- old photographs
- photo transfer paper
- white fabric
- print homespun fabric
- fusible interfacing
- scraps of muslin
- permanent fine-point markers
- decorative-edge craft scissors
- medium-weight cardboard
- low-loft polyester batting
- hot glue gun
- fabric-covered welting
- black felt
- fabric glue
- $^3/_4$-inch wide grosgrain ribbon
- charms
- greenery sprigs

Use fabric glue for all gluing unless otherwise indicated.

1. Have a copy shop transfer your photos onto photo transfer paper.

2. Follow manufacturer's instructions to transfer photos onto white fabric...fuse interfacing to wrong side of transferred photos and to the back of muslin pieces for nameplates.

3. Use markers to write names or dates on nameplates; draw "stitched" borders around names, then draw wavy borders around photos. Use craft scissors to cut out photos and nameplates just outside borders.

4. For each ornament, cut a piece from cardboard to accommodate photo and nameplate. Cut a piece from batting the same size as cardboard piece and a piece from homespun one inch larger on all sides than cardboard piece. Place fabric wrong side up on a flat surface. Center batting, then cardboard on fabric; fold fabric edges to the back of cardboard and hot glue to secure. Beginning and ending at top center, hot glue flange of welting to back side of ornament along edges.

5. Arrange and glue photos and nameplates on ornaments. Cut triangles from felt for picture corners; glue corners to photos and allow to dry.

6. For hanger, hot glue ends of a 6-inch length of ribbon to back of ornament. Hot glue charms, a ribbon bow and greenery to ornament as desired.

7. Cut a piece from fabric $^1/_2$ inch smaller than ornament. Glue fabric over back of ornament.

PHOTO PILLOW ORNAMENT
(shown on page 10)

- photograph
- photo transfer paper
- scrap of muslin
- fusible interfacing
- red and green print fabrics
- red and green embroidery floss
- polyester fiberfill
- one yard of $^3/_4$-inch wide grosgrain ribbon

Use a $^1/_2$-inch seam allowance for all sewing unless otherwise indicated. Refer to Embroidery Stitches, page 133, before beginning project.

1. Have a copy shop transfer your photo onto photo transfer paper.

2. Following manufacturer's instructions and aligning edges with grain of muslin, transfer photo onto muslin. Cut a piece of interfacing $^1/_4$ inch larger than photo. Center and fuse interfacing to back of transferred photo. Cut out photo $^1/_4$ inch outside edge of interfacing; pull threads to fringe edges.

3. For pillow top, cut four 5-inch squares from print fabrics. Matching wrong sides, sew squares together to form a 9-inch square pillow top.

4. Pin photo at center of pillow top. Using 3 strands of floss, work one red *French Knot* berry and 2 green *Lazy Daisy* leaves at each corner of photo. Trim pillow top 2$^1/_2$ inches outside edges of photo. For backing, cut a piece of fabric the same size as pillow top.

5. Matching wrong sides and leaving an opening for turning, sew pillow top and back together...clip corners and turn right side out. Stuff pillow with fiberfill; tack opening closed.

6. Tie a bow at center of ribbon. Sew knot of bow to back of pillow at top and sew streamers to back of pillow at bottom.

SHUTTER CARD DISPLAY
(shown on page 13)

- spray primer
- red spray paint
- set of wooden shutters
- white acrylic paint
- old toothbrush
- homespun fabrics
- craft glue
- assorted buttons

Allow primer, paint and glue to dry after each application.

1. Apply primer, then red spray paint to shutters. *Spatter Paint*, page 134, shutters with white paint.

2. Tear strips of homespun to fit edges and center supports of shutters; glue strips in place. Glue buttons along strips as desired.

3. Arrange card holder with slates opening upward; place cards on holder.

PHOTO TRAY
(shown on page 14)

- wooden frame with glass and back (we used a 15"x18" frame)
- drill and bits
- 2 drawer pulls
- black spray paint
- paste floor wax
- ivory acrylic paint
- paintbrushes
- fine-grit sandpaper
- tack cloth
- wood-tone spray
- clear acrylic spray sealer
- assorted fabrics
- paper-backed fusible web
- spray adhesive
- photograph 4 inches smaller than opening of frame
- staple gun
- craft glue
- assorted buttons

Allow paint, wood-tone spray, sealer and glue to dry after each application.

1. Remove glass and back from frame. Drill holes on short sides of frame, spaced to fit pulls.

2. Spray paint frame black. Apply a thin layer of wax over frame, then paint frame ivory. Lightly sand frame for a slightly aged look, then wipe with tack cloth. Apply wood-tone spray, then 2 to 3 coats of sealer to frame.

3. Attach pulls to frame.

4. Cut pieces from fabric and web the same size as backing from frame…fuse web to wrong side of fabric. Cut another piece of fabric one-inch smaller on all sides than backing and a piece of web 1¼ inch smaller on all sides than backing. Center and fuse the web to the wrong side of the fabric…pull threads to fringe edges. Centering smaller fabric piece on top, fuse fabric pieces to backing.

5. Apply spray adhesive to back of photo. Center and smooth photo on backing. Place glass and backing in frame, then staple along edges on back of frame to secure backing. Glue buttons to frame as desired.

MEMORY ALBUM
(shown on page 15)

Capture treasured memories in a handcrafted photo album. Start with pages of card stock for the photo pages; glue on photos backed with festive papers. Then, use a pencil to draw fun pictures and write memories from the day…don't forget to add the date. Use a permanent marker to go over your work.

For the cover, embellish embossed card stock with corrugated craft cardboard cut-outs and card stock banners. Stack the pages and covers together and punch holes for the binding. For each hole, place a button on each side of the hole and use floss to sew through the holes of the buttons; knot the floss ends on the back to secure.

TICKING CANDY CANES
(shown on pages 16 and 17)

- tracing paper
- red & white ticking
- assorted white buttons
- pinking shears
- polyester fiberfill

1. Trace candy cane pattern, page 136, onto tracing paper. Matching wrong sides, fold one edge of ticking over 10 inches. For each candy cane, pin pattern to folded area of fabric so stripes on fabric run diagonally across pattern; cut out ½ inch outside pattern.

2. Sew buttons down center of one candy cane shape if desired.

3. Using a ½-inch seam allowance and leaving an opening for stuffing, sew pieces together. Use pinking shears to trim seam to ⅛ inch. Firmly stuff candy cane with fiberfill, then sew opening closed.

POPCORN GARLAND
(shown on pages 16 and 17)

Quick & easy…that's what this old-fashioned tree trimming is. Use a needle to string popped corn (stale popcorn doesn't break as easily) and artificial cranberries on heavy thread.

FELT REDBIRDS
(shown on pages 16 and 17)

- tracing paper
- red felt
- fabric for wings
- gold embroidery floss
- assorted buttons
- polyester fiberfill
- hot glue gun
- ¾-inch long twigs for feet
- 4-inch long twigs for legs
- white acrylic paint
- stiff paintbrush

1. Trace bird and wing patterns, page 136, onto tracing paper.

2. For each bird, use patterns to cut 2 bodies from felt and one wing from fabric.

3. On one body piece, use floss to sew on a button for an eye and sew through a button to secure wing to body. Aligning body pieces and leaving an opening for stuffing, use 3 strands of floss to work *Blanket Stitches*, page 133, along edges of bird; lightly stuff with fiberfill and sew opening closed.

4. Glue feet to bottom of legs. Follow *Dry Brush*, page 134, to paint legs white; allow to dry. Glue tops of legs between body pieces on bottom of bird.

SNOWFLAKE DOOR BASKET
(shown on page 19)

- 4-inch dia. paper doilies
- small sharp scissors
- craft glue
- hot glue gun
- close-up photographs
- brown paper-covered wire
- medium-weight cardboard
- fabric
- white card stock
- red corrugated craft cardboard
- decorative-edge craft scissors
- button
- permanent fine-point marker
- grapevine door basket
- fresh greenery

Use craft glue for all gluing unless otherwise indicated.

1. For each snowflake, use at least 3 plies of doily (several plies usually stick together). Use scissors to carefully cut away doily sections as desired to create snowflakes (our snowflakes are all made from identical doilies).

2. Trim photo and glue to center of snowflake. Hot glue one end of wire to back of snowflake.

3. For sign, cover a 4½"x5½" piece of cardboard with a 5"x6" piece of fabric; glue edges to back of cardboard. Center and glue a 2½"x3¼" piece of card stock onto craft cardboard; use craft scissors to trim cardboard to ¼ inch outside edges of card stock. Glue craft cardboard to center of fabric-covered cardboard. Tie an 8-inch long fabric strip into a bow; glue bow to tag and a button to knot of bow. Use marker to write message on the tag.

4. Arrange greenery, snowflakes and sign in basket as desired.

FRAMED AND WINDOW SNOWFLAKES
(shown on pages 20 and 21)

- white paper for snowflakes
- tracing paper
- transfer paper
- craft knife or small sharp scissors
- spray adhesive
- iridescent micro-glitter
- mat board
- wooden picture frames
- red and green plaid fabrics
- craft glue
- white buttons
- clear nylon thread

1. Begin with a 6¹/₂-inch square of white paper for each framed snowflake and a 9¹/₂-inch square of paper for each window snowflake; refer to Figs. 1 through 5 to fold your paper into a triangle shape.

Fig. 1

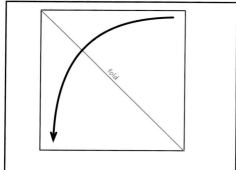

Fig. 2

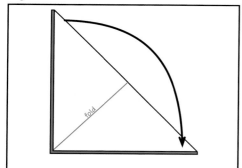

Fig. 3

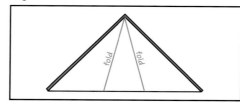

Fig. 4

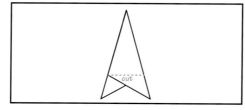

Fig. 5

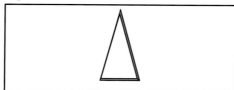

2. Trace desired snowflake pattern, page 148, onto tracing paper (if making framed snowflakes, enlarge the patterns 50% on a photo copier, then trace onto tracing paper). Aligning solid red line on pattern with folded edge of triangle, use transfer paper to transfer design to triangle; use craft knife or scissors to cut away black areas of pattern. Gently unfold snowflake and press.

3. Apply spray adhesive to one side of snowflake, then cover snowflake with glitter. Gently shake snowflake to remove excess glitter.

4. To mount snowflake for framing, cut a piece from mat board to fit in frame. Cut a piece of fabric the same size as mat board. Apply spray adhesive to wrong side of fabric…smooth fabric onto mat board. Apply spray adhesive to wrong side of snowflake; carefully center and smooth snowflake onto fabric side of mat board. Glue buttons to snowflake. Secure snowflake in frame.

5. To mount snowflakes in window, use thread to make desired length hanger for each snowflake.

EMBROIDERED MUSLIN STOCKING
(shown on page 34)

- tracing paper
- muslin
- cream, green and brown pearl cotton
- assorted buttons

Refer to Embroidery Stitches, page 133, before beginning project.

1. Trace stocking, star and tree patterns, page 139, onto tracing paper. Pin the pattern to 3 layers of muslin; cut out 3 stocking shapes.

2. Remove pattern and baste 2 stocking pieces together for stocking front. Pin pattern to stocking front. Referring to floss color on pattern and using pearl cotton, work *French Knots* over dots and *Straight Stitches* for snowflakes, then *Couch* pearl cotton along tree, star and stocking cuff. *Couch* pearl cotton over center of each large snowflake. Carefully tear away pattern.

3. Sew buttons along top of stocking and down tree.

4. Matching right sides and leaving top open, sew stocking front and back pieces together; clip curves and turn stocking right side out.

5. Press top of stocking ¹/₄ inch to the wrong side; *Blind Stitch* in place.

6. For hanger, braid two 6-inch lengths of each color pearl cotton together; knot and fray ends. Tack ends of hanger to heel seam of stocking.

KNIT STOCKINGS
(shown on page 35)

Abbreviations

K	knit
mm	millimeters
P	purl
PSSO	pass slipped stitch over
st(s)	stitches
tog	together

( ) – worked enclosed instructions **as many times** as specified by the number immediately following **or** work all enclosed instructions in the stitch or space indicated **or** contains explanatory remarks.

SANTA STOCKING

Materials

- Worsted Weight Yarn:
  Beige Heather - 3 ounces, (90 grams, 190 yards)
  Red - 1¼ ounces, (40 grams, 95 yards)
  Winter White - 15 yards
  Green - 10 yards
  Blue - 5 yards
  Black - 5 yards
  Gold, Peach & Brown - small amount of **each**
- straight knitting needles, size 7 (4.50 mm) or size needed for gauge
- bobbins
- 3 stitch holders
- markers
- yarn needle

Gauge: In Stockinette Stitch, 20 sts and 26 rows = 4 inches

Top

With Red, cast on 68 sts **loosely**.

Rows 1-6: Beginning with a **knit** row, work in Stockinette Stitch (knit one row, purl one row).

Row 7 (Eyelet row): K1, (YO, K2 tog) across to last st, K1.

Rows 8-14: Work in Stockinette Stitch for 7 rows.

Leg

Rows 15-88: Starting with a **knit** row and working even in Stockinette Stitch, follow Santa chart, page 140.
Cut yarn.

Left Heel

When instructed to slip a stitch, always slip as if to **purl** *unless otherwise specified.*

Row 1: Slip 16 sts onto st holder (Right Heel), slip 36 sts onto second st holder (top of Foot), slip 1, with Red, knit across: 16 sts.

Row 2: Purl across.

Row 3: Slip 1, knit across.

Rows 4-15: Repeat Rows 2 and 3, 6 times.

Short Rows (form corner of Heel): P2, P2 tog, P1, turn; slip 1, K3, turn; P3, P2 tog, P1, turn; slip 1, K4, turn; P4, P2 tog, P1, turn; slip 1, K5, turn; P5, P2 tog, P1, turn; slip 1, K6, turn; P6, P2 tog, P1, turn; slip 1, K7, turn; P7, P2 tog, P1, turn; slip 1, K8, turn; P8, P2 tog; cut yarn: 9 sts.

Slip remaining sts onto st holder.

Right Heel

With **right** side facing, slip sts from Right Heel st holder onto empty needle.

Row 1: With Red, knit across.

Row 2: Slip 1, purl across.

Rows 3-14: Repeat Rows 1 and 2, 6 times.

Short Rows: K2, slip 1 as if to **knit**, K1, PSSO, K1, turn; slip 1, P3, turn; K3, slip 1 as if to **knit**, K1, PSSO, K1, turn; slip 1, P4, turn; K4, slip 1 as if to **knit**, K1, PSSO, K1, turn; slip 1, P5, turn; K5, slip 1 as if to **knit**, K1, PSSO, K1, turn; slip 1, P6, turn; K6, slip 1 as if to **knit**, K1, PSSO, K1, turn; slip 1, P7, turn; K7, slip 1 as if to **knit**, K1, PSSO, K1, turn; slip 1, P8, turn; K8, slip 1 as if to **knit**, K1, PSSO; cut yarn: 9 sts.

Gusset and Instep Shaping

Row 1: With Beige Heather, pick up 7 sts on inside of Right Heel, slip 36 sts from next st holder (top of Foot) onto empty needle and knit across, pick up 7 sts on inside edge of Left Heel, slip 9 sts from Left Heel st holder onto empty needle and knit across: 68 sts.

Row 2 AND ALL WRONG SIDE ROWS: Purl across.

Row 3: K 15, K2 tog, K 34, slip 1 as if to **knit**, K1, PSSO, K 15: 66 sts.

Row 5: K 14, K2 tog, K 34, slip 1 as if to **knit**, K1, PSSO, K 14: 64 sts.

Row 7: K 13, K2 tog, K 34, slip 1 as if to **knit**, K1, PSSO, K 13: 62 sts.

Row 9: K 12, K2 tog, K 34, slip 1 as if to **knit**, K1, PSSO, K 12: 60 sts.

Row 11: K 11, K2 tog, K 34, slip 1 as if to **knit**, K1, PSSO, K 11: 58 sts.

Row 13: K 10, K2 tog, K 34, slip 1 as if to **knit**, K1, PSSO, K 10: 56 sts.

Rows 14-40: Work in Stockinette Stitch for 27 rows.
Cut yarn.

Toe Shaping

Row 1: With Red K 11, K2 tog, K1, place marker, K1, slip 1 as if to **knit**, K1, PSSO, K 22, K2 tog, K1, place marker, K1, slip 1 as if to **knit**, K1, PSSO, K 11: 52 sts.

Row 2: Purl across.

Row 3: (Knit across to within 3 sts of marker, K2 tog, K2, slip 1 as if to **knit**, K1, PSSO) twice, knit across: 48 sts.

Row 4: Purl across.

Rows 5-18: Repeat Rows 3 and 4, 7 times: 20 sts.

Bind off remaining sts.

Finishing

With Blue, add French Knots for eyes.

With a double strand of Winter White, add French Knot pom-pom to hat.

With **right** sides together, sew seam.

For stocking top, fold top edge to **wrong** side along Eyelet Row and sew in place.

For hanging loop, braid three 6-inch lengths of Red yarn and attach to seam.

SNOWMAN STOCKING

Materials

- Worsted Weight Yarn:
  Beige Heather - 2¼ ounces, (70 grams, 140 yards)
  Red - ¾ ounces, (20 grams, 45 yards)
  Blue - ¾ ounces, (20 grams, 45 yards)
  Green - 10 yards
  Winter White - 15 yards
  Gold, Black & Brown - small amount of **each**
- straight knitting needles, size 7 (4.50 mm) or size needed for gauge
- bobbins
- 3 stitch holders
- markers
- yarn needle

Gauge: In Stockinette Stitch, 20 sts and 26 rows = 4 inches

Top

With Red, cast on 68 sts **loosely**.

Rows 1-6: Beginning with a **knit** row, work in Stockinette Stitch (knit one row, purl one row).

Row 7 (Eyelet row): K1, (YO, K2 tog) across to last st, K1.

Rows 8-14: Work in Stockinette Stitch for 7 rows.

Leg

Rows 15-84: Starting with a **knit** row and working even in Stockinette Stitch, follow Snowman chart, page 141.
Cut yarn.

(continued on page 124)

123

Left Heel

When instructed to slip a stitch, always slip as if to **purl** *unless otherwise specified.*

Row 1: Slip 16 sts onto st holder (Right Heel), slip 36 sts onto second st holder (top of Foot), slip 1, with Blue, knit across: 16 sts.

Row 2: Purl across.

Row 3: Slip 1, knit across.

Rows 4-15: Repeat Rows 2 and 3, 6 times.

Short Rows (form corner of Heel): P2, P2 tog, P1, turn; slip 1, K3, turn; P3, P2 tog, P1, turn; slip 1, K4, turn; P4, P2 tog, P1, turn; slip 1, K5, turn; P5, P2 tog, P1, turn; slip 1, K6, turn; P6, P2 tog, P1, turn; slip 1, K7, turn; P7, P2 tog, P1, turn; slip 1, K8, turn; P8, P2 tog; cut yarn: 9 sts.

Slip remaining sts onto st holder.

Right Heel

With **right** side facing, slip sts from Right Heel st holder onto empty needle.

Row 1: With Blue, knit across.

Row 2: Slip 1, purl across.

Rows 3-14: Repeat Rows 1 and 2, 6 times.

Short Rows: K2, slip 1 as if to **knit**, K1, PSSO, K1, turn; slip 1, P3, turn; K3, slip 1 as if to **knit**, K1, PSSO, K1, turn; slip 1, P4, turn; K4, slip 1 as if to **knit**, K1, PSSO, K1, turn; slip 1, P5, turn; K5, slip 1 as if to **knit**, K1, PSSO, K1, turn; slip 1, P6, turn; K6, slip 1 as if to **knit**, K1, PSSO, K1, turn; slip 1, P7, turn; K7, slip 1 as if to **knit**, K1, PSSO, K1, turn; slip 1, P8, turn; K8, slip 1 as if to **knit**, K1, PSSO; cut yarn: 9 sts.

Gusset and Instep Shaping

Row 1: With Beige Heather, pick up 7 sts on inside of Right Heel, slip 36 sts from next st holder (top of Foot) onto empty needle and knit across, pick up 7 sts on inside edge of Left Heel, knit 9 sts from Left Heel st holder onto empty needle and knit across: 68 sts.

Row 2 AND ALL WRONG SIDE ROWS:
Purl across.

Row 3: K 15, K2 tog, K 34, slip 1 as if to **knit**, K1, PSSO, K 15: 66 sts.

Row 5: K 14, K2 tog, K 34, slip 1 as if to **knit**, K1, PSSO, K 14: 64 sts.

Row 7: K 13, K2 tog, K 34, slip 1 as if to **knit**, K1, PSSO, K 13: 62 sts.

Row 9: K 12, K2 tog, K 34, slip 1 as if to **knit**, K1, PSSO, K 12: 60 sts.

Row 11: K 11, K2 tog, K 34, slip 1 as if to **knit**, K1, PSSO, K 11: 58 sts.

Row 13: K 10, K2 tog, K 34, slip 1 as if to **knit**, K1, PSSO, K 10: 56 sts.

Rows 14-40: Work in Stockinette Stitch for 27 rows.
Cut yarn.

Toe Shaping

Row 1: With Blue K 11, K2 tog, K1, place marker, K1, slip 1 as if to **knit**, K1, PSSO, K 22, K2 tog, K1, place marker, K1, slip 1 as if to **knit**, K1, PSSO, K 11: 52 sts.

Row 2: Purl across.

Row 3: (Knit across to within 3 sts of marker, K2 tog, K2, slip 1 as if to **knit**, K1, PSSO) twice, knit across: 48 sts.

Row 4: Purl across.

Rows 5-18: Repeat Rows 3 and 4, 7 times: 20 sts.

Bind off remaining sts.

Finishing

With Black, add French Knots for eyes, nose, and buttons.

With **right** sides together, sew seam.

For stocking top, fold top edge to **wrong** side along Eyelet Row and sew in place.

For hanging loop, braid three 6-inch lengths of Red yarn and attach to seam.

BUTTON WREATH
(shown on pages 36 and 37)

- white spray paint
- 18-inch dia. plastic, flat-backed wreath
- hot glue gun
- lots of assorted white buttons
- iridescent glitter paint
- paintbrush
- pinking shears
- gingham fabric
- embroidery floss to match fabric

1. Glue lots and lots of white buttons to wreath, overlapping as necessary for desired coverage.

2. Paint buttons and wreath with glitter paint as desired; set aside to dry.

3. For bow loop, use pinking shears to cut a 4"x22" strip from fabric. Matching wrong sides and overlapping ends one inch, fold ends of strip to the center. Tie floss tightly around overlapped area. For knot, cut a 2¼"x5" strip from fabric; press long edges ¼ inch to wrong side. Overlapping ends at back, glue strip over gathers of loops. For streamers, cut a 2½"x17½" strip from fabric: glue center of strip to back of bow. Glue bow to the wreath…notch streamer ends.

TICKING TREE
(continued from page 41)

Star Ornaments
- tracing paper
- tan ticking
- round and heart-shaped buttons
- embroidery floss
- rattail cord
- polyester fiberfill
- pinking shears

Refer to Embroidery Stitches, page 133, before beginning project. Use 3 strands of floss for all stitching.

1. Trace small star pattern, page 142, onto tracing paper. For each star, use pattern to cut 2 stars from ticking.

2. If desired, lightly pencil a favorite word of the season on the right side of one star shape, Work Backstitches over the word, or add a bow-tied button or heart button at the center of the star.

3. For the hanger, knot the ends of a 7-inch length of cord together. Matching wrong sides of star, pin knot of hanger between star front and back at top point. Leaving an opening for stuffing, work Running Stitches along the edges of the star to sew pieces together.

4. Lightly stuff star with fiberfill, then sew opening closed. Use pinking shears to trim edges of stars.

Tree Skirt
- 28-inch square of gingham fabric
- string
- chalk pencil
- thumbtack
- pinking shears
- lace
- tissue paper
- embroidery floss

1. Matching right sides, fold fabric in half from top to bottom and again from left to right.

2. Tie one end of string to chalk pencil. Insert thumbtack through string 15 inches from the pencil. Insert thumbtack through the fabric as shown in Fig. 1; mark the outside cutting line.

Fig. 1

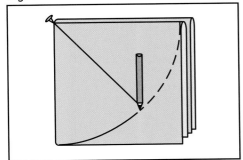

3. Repeat Step 2, inserting thumbtack 2 inches from pencil; mark inner cutting line. Use pinking shears to cut along drawn lines through all layers of fabric.

4. Draw a straight line from inner circle to outer edge…use pinking shears to cut skirt open along line.

5. Sew lace along outer edges of circle.

6. Trace words, page 143, onto tissue paper desired of number times. Arrange and pin patterns along outer edge of skirt. Use 3 strands of floss to work Backstitches over words. Carefully tear away patterns.

TICKING STOCKING
(shown on page 42)

- tracing paper
- 15"x22" pieces of tan ticking and lining fabric
- vintage crocheted lace
- jute
- embroidery floss
- assorted buttons

Use a 1/4-inch seam allowance for all sewing unless otherwise indicated.

1. Following *Making Patterns*, page 134, and using the stocking pattern on page 146, draw a complete stocking pattern on tracing paper. Cut out pattern 1/4 inch outside drawn lines. Matching right sides and long edges, fold ticking

and lining in half; stack fabrics together. Pin pattern to fabrics; cut out stocking and lining pieces.

2. Sew stocking pieces together; clip curves and turn right side out. Repeat to sew lining pieces together; do not turn. Press top edge of stocking and lining 1/4 inch to wrong side. Matching seams and top edges, place lining in stocking. *Blind Stitch*, page 133, top edges together to secure.

3. For cuff, cut a 16-inch piece from lace; match short edges and sew together. Matching cuff seam with heel seam on stocking, pin cuff to stocking. *Blind Stitch* cuff to top edge of stocking.

4. For hanger, knot ends of an 8-inch length of jute together. Sew knot of hanger to inside of stocking at heel seam.

5. Use 3 strands of floss to sew buttons to cuff as desired.

CHICKEN FEEDER CANDLEHOLDER
(shown on page 51)

- trough-style chicken feeder
- household cement
- craft steel
- tracing paper
- utility scissors
- white spray primer
- white spray paint
- wood-tone spray
- clear acrylic spray sealer
- homespun fabric
- hot glue gun
- fresh greenery
- fresh red pears
- fresh red and green apples
- taper candles
- birdseed

Allow cement, paint, wood-tone spray and sealer to dry after each application.

1. Using household cement to piece strips as necessary, cut 2 one inch wide strips of craft steel to fit long edges of feeder. Trace the scallop pattern, page 139, onto tracing paper; cut out. Beginning at the center and working outward, use pattern to mark scallops along top edge of steel strips. Use utility scissors to cut along scallops. Use household cement to glue strips along inside edges of feeder.

2. Spray feeder with primer, then white paint. Lightly spray feeder with wood-tone spray, then 2 to 3 coats of sealer.

3. Piecing as necessary, tear a strip of homespun to go around feeder…glue strip around feeder.

4. Tie a strip torn from homespun into a bow. Glue bow to center front of feeder. Glue greenery to knot of bow.

5. Hollow out some of the fruit for candleholders and insert tapers. Fill the feeder with birdseed; arrange fruits and candleholders in the feeder.

CUT-OUT TAGS AND CARDS
(shown on pages 54 and 55)

Tags
- smooth and embossed card stock
- decorative-edge craft scissors
- assorted buttons
- permanent fine-point markers
- craft glue
- craft knife and cutting mat
- fabric scraps
- tracing paper
- brown kraft paper
- rickrack

Use straight-edge or decorative-edge scissors, as desired, to cut out tags.

1. Photocopy tag designs, page 135, onto card stock; cut out tags.

2. For heart tag, sew buttons to tag, then write name on tag. Glue tag to embossed card stock. Trim card stock to 1/4 inch outside edge of tag.

3. For sewn star tags, use craft knife to cut out large star from tag. Glue fabric over star on back side of tag; sew a button at center of star. Place tag on card stock and sew along edges. Trim background card stock close to tag.

4. For sewn heart tag, trace the heart from tag onto tracing paper; cut out. Using pattern, cut heart from red card stock; glue heart to tag. Place tag on card stock and sew along edges. Trim background card stock close to tag.

(continued on page 126)

5. For block name tag, write name on small squares of kraft paper; trim squares to fit on tag. Glue name to tag, then embellish with rickrack and sewn-on buttons. Glue tag to card stock, then draw a "stitched" border. Trim background card stock close to border.

6. For hanging tag, write name on a strip of kraft paper. Draw sprinkles of stars and dots around name; cut out. Glue strip to a piece of card stock. Draw a "stitched" border around strip; cut out. Catching the ends of a piece of rickrack, sew a button at top of tag. Glue tag to another piece of card stock and cut out.

Cards
- 8¹/₂"x 11" card stock with envelopes to fit bi-fold cards
- craft knife and cutting mat
- fabric scraps
- craft glue

1. Photocopy card designs, page 147, onto card stock. Cut out card fronts along outer lines. Use a craft knife to carefully cut shapes from card fronts.

2. Cut pieces from fabric scraps large enough to cover cut out shapes; glue over cut-outs on back of card front.

3. Fold another piece of card stock in half; unfold. Center and sew card front on front of card stock.

COPPER-TOP GIFT BOXES
(shown on page 57)

- desired colors of acrylic paint
- paintbrushes
- paper maché box with lid to fit desired design from page 137 or 148
- clear acrylic spray sealer
- tracing paper
- removable tape
- craft-weight copper sheet
- corrugated cardboard
- stylus
- stencil brush
- black stencil cream
- soft cloth
- decorative-edge craft scissors
- craft glue

Allow paint, sealer and glue to dry after each application.

1. Paint box and lid as desired. Apply sealer to box and lid.

2. Trace truck or snowman pattern, pages 137 or 148, onto tracing paper. Tape pattern to copper, then tape copper to cardboard. Use stylus to draw over pattern lines; remove pattern.

3. Use stencil brush to apply stencil cream over design…leaving cream in lines, wipe off excess cream with a soft cloth.

4. Remove copper from cardboard. Use craft scissors to trim edges of copper piece. Center and glue copper piece on lid.

KITCHEN ANGEL
(shown on page 58)

- craft saw
- 13-inch wooden spoon
- ¹/₂-liter plastic bottle
- flesh-tone acrylic paint
- paintbrushes
- tracing paper
- transfer paper
- red and black permanent fine-point markers
- hot glue gun
- curly doll hair
- sand
- fabric
- embroidery floss to coordinate with fabric
- utility scissors
- 2 small metal measuring spoons
- craft wire
- lace scraps
- star-shaped button
- brown card stock
- 3-inch dia. grapevine wreath
- small basket with handle
- miniature kitchen utensils

1. For head, use a saw to trim handle of wooden spoon so spoon rests on bottle opening when handle is placed in bottle. Paint spoon flesh color and allow to dry.

2. Trace face pattern, page 149, onto tracing paper; use transfer paper to transfer face to back of spoon. Use red marker to draw over lips and black marker to draw over remaining lines…lightly color cheeks red.

3. Arrange and glue hair on head.

4. Fill bottle with sand. Insert handle of spoon in bottle; fill opening of bottle with hot glue to hold head in place.

5. For dress, tear an 11"x12" piece from fabric. Matching wrong sides and short edges and using a ¹/₄ inch seam allowance,

sew back of dress together; turn right side out. Using floss, work *Running Stitches*, page 133, along top edge of dress. Place dress over bottle. Pull floss ends to gather dress at neck; knot and trim floss ends.

6. For sleeves, cut a 3"x12" piece from fabric. Press, then sew short edges of fabric piece ¹/₄ inch to the wrong side. Matching right sides and long edges, use a ¹/₄-inch seam allowance to sew edges together to form a tube; turn right side out. For hands, use utility scissors to trim handles of measuring spoons to 3 inches. Cut a 14-inch length of wire for arms. Wrap 2 inches of one end of wire around the handle of one measuring spoon. Thread arms through sleeves, then wrap 2 inches of end of wire around handle of remaining measuring spoon. Glue center of arms at back of neck.

7. Overlapping ends at back, glue a length of lace around neck for a collar. Tie a ³/₄"x8" strip torn from fabric into a bow; glue bow and a button to collar.

8. Photocopy wing pattern, page 149, onto card stock; cut out. Glue wings to back of angel.

9. Glue wreath to head for halo. Fill basket with utensils and place in angel's hands; glue to secure.

PRIMITIVE EMBROIDERED SWEATER
(shown on page 62)

- green, brown and gold embroidery floss
- tissue paper
- cotton knit sweater
- seven ³/₈-inch dia. ecru buttons
- seven ³/₄-inch dia. blue, green or gold star-shaped buttons
- eight ¹/₂-inch dia. red buttons

Work stitches through nearest "hole" in knit of sweater. Refer to Embroidery Stitches, page 133, before beginning project.

1. Trace pattern, page 152, onto tissue paper. Position and pin pattern on sweater.

2. Stitching through tissue paper and using 2 strands of floss, work brown *Running Stitches* for tree trunk and branches, green *Straight Stitches* for needles and gold *Cross Stitches* for tree base. Carefully remove tissue paper.

3. Use 2 strands of gold floss to sew buttons on tree as desired.

SNOW KID SWEATSHIRTS
(shown on page 63)

- paper-backed fusible web
- white fleece
- fabric for hat
- orange and black felt
- child-size sweatshirt
- clear nylon thread
- $^3/_4$-inch dia. black buttons for eyes
- white, orange, red and black embroidery floss
- $^1/_2$-inch dia. red buttons for mouth
- scraps of lace and ribbon (for snow girl only)
- $^3/_4$-inch dia. red button for hat or bow tie
- assorted white buttons

1. For each snow kid, use snowman pattern, page 153, and follow *Making Appliqués*, page 134, to make one head appliqué from fleece, hat appliqué from fabric and mouth and nose appliqués from felt. If making snow boy, make bow tie and hatband appliqués from fabric.

2. Arrange and fuse appliqués on sweatshirt. Using nylon thread, follow *Machine Appliqué*, page 134, to sew along edges of head, hat, hatband, and bow tie to secure. Sew black buttons to snow kid for eyes. Use 3 strands of white floss to make a *French Knot*, page 133, through one hole in each button for highlight in eye.

3. Using 3 strands of floss, work orange *Running Stitches*, page 133, along edges of nose, and black *Running Stitches* along mouth. Use 2 strands of red floss to sew $^1/_2$-inch dia. red buttons at ends of mouth.

4. For snow girl, sew a length of lace or fabric along bottom of hat. Tie 2 bows from ribbon. Sew one bow and a button to top of hat and one bow under chin.

5. For snow boy, sew a red button to center of bow tie.

6. Sew assorted white buttons to shirt for snowflakes.

STAR PILLOW
(shown on page 64)

- tracing paper
- 2 coordinating fabrics
- paper-backed fusible web
- fabric for pocket trim
- pinking shears
- embroidery floss
- assorted buttons
- polyester fiberfill

Use 3 strands of floss for all stitching.

1. Using patterns, page 154, and referring to the Assembly Diagram, page 154, make a whole star pattern and one pocket pattern from tracing paper. Using patterns, cut 2 stars from first fabric and one pocket from remaining fabric. Piecing as necessary, cut a 3"x61" strip from same fabric as stars.

2. Follow manufacturer's instructions to fuse web to fabric for pocket trim. Use pinking shears to cut a $^3/_4$"x4$^3/_4$" strip. Press edges of pocket $^1/_4$ inch to the wrong side; top stitch top edge of pocket. Center and fuse trim $^1/_4$ inch below top of pocket. Use floss to sew 3 buttons across trim.

3. Trace words pattern, page 154, onto tracing paper. Pin pattern on pocket; work *Back Stitches*, page 133, over words. Carefully remove pattern.

4. Pin pocket at center on right side of one star piece (pillow front); use floss to work *Running Stitches*, page 133, along sides and bottom of pocket to secure.

5. Matching right sides and using a $^1/_2$-inch seam allowance, baste ends of strip together. Matching right sides and raw edges, pin strip along edges of pillow front. Using a $^1/_2$-inch seam allowance, sew strip to pillow front. Repeat for pillow back. Remove basting threads along strip seam; turn pillow right side out.

6. Sew buttons along edges of pillow front.

7. Stuff pillow with fiberfill, then sew opening closed.

THROW PILLOWS
(continued from page 65)

3. Cut a 5$^1/_2$"x7$^1/_2$" piece from burlap; remove threads to fray edges $^1/_2$ inch.

4. Using tree and trunk patterns, page 136, follow *Making Appliqués*, page 134, to make 3 tree appliqués from green felt and 3 trunk appliqués from brown felt. Arrange and fuse appliqués on burlap.

5. Pin burlap on pillow top. Using 3 strands of floss, work *Running Stitches*, page 133, along burlap edges to secure. Sew a button at each corner of burlap.

6. For welting, measure around edges of pillow top; add 4 inches. Piecing as necessary, cut a 2-inch wide bias fabric strip determined measurement. Cut a piece of cord determined measurement.

7. Press one end of fabric strip $^1/_2$ inch to wrong side. Beginning $^1/_2$ inch from pressed end, center cord on wrong side of strip. Fold strip over cord. Beginning $^1/_2$ inch from pressed end, use a zipper foot to baste close to cord along length of strip. Trim seam allowance to $^1/_2$ inch.

8. Beginning with pressed end of welting and matching raw edges, pin welting to right side of pillow top (Fig. 1). Trimming to fit, insert unfinished end of welting into folded end of welting (Fig. 2). Using a zipper foot, baste welting in place close to cord.

Fig. 1

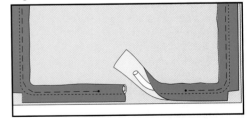

Fig. 2

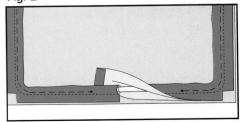

(continued on page 128)

9. Matching right sides and leaving an opening for turning, sew pillow top and pillow back together. Clip corners and turn right side out. Stuff pillow with fiberfill and sew opening closed.

Heart Pillow

1. For pillow top, cut four 10-inch squares from different fabrics. Refer to **Step 2** of **Tree Pillow** to make pillow top and pillow back.

2. Cut an 8¹⁄₂-inch square from burlap; remove threads to fray edges ¹⁄₂ inch.

3. Using heart patterns, page 136, follow *Making Appliqués*, page 134, to make one straight heart appliqué from red felt and one wavy heart appliqué from green felt. Arrange and fuse hearts on burlap. Sewing buttons to secure, cover red heart with buttons.

4. Follow **Steps 5 through 9** of **Tree Pillow** to complete pillow.

KID'S CHRISTMAS CARD KIT
(shown on page 66)

Bag
- homespun fabric
- ¹⁄₄-inch wide red grosgrain ribbon
- muslin
- fusible interfacing
- paper-backed fusible web
- tracing paper
- transfer paper
- black permanent fine-point marker
- red, green and gold acrylic paint
- paintbrushes
- pinking shears
- card making supplies (we used cookie cutters, markers, tubes of glitter, decorative-edge craft scissors, craft glue sticks and crayons)

1. Cut two 8¹⁄₄"x11³⁄₄" pieces from homespun. Press, then stitch all edges of each piece ¹⁄₄ inch to the wrong side.

2. For casing, press top edge of each piece ³⁄₄ inch to the wrong side; stitch in place.

3. Matching right sides, using a ¹⁄₄-inch seam allowance and stitching side seams below casing, sew sides and bottom of bag together. Turn bag right side out.

4. For drawstrings, cut two 22-inch lengths from ribbon. Refer to Fig. 1 to thread the drawstrings through the casings at top of bag; knot ends of each drawstring together.

Fig. 1

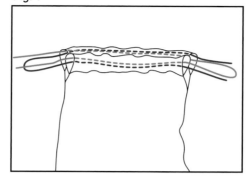

5. For bag label, cut one 3¹⁄₂"x6¹⁄₂" piece each from muslin, interfacing and web. Fuse interfacing to muslin and web to interfacing; do not remove paper backing.

6. Trace label design, page 137, onto tracing paper. Use transfer paper to transfer design to label. Use black marker to draw over transferred lines.

7. Paint design as desired; allow to dry. Use marker to go over detail lines, if necessary. Use pinking shears to trim edges of label.

8. Remove paper backing from label; fuse label to front of bag.

9. Fill bag with card-making supplies for your favorite young crafter to use for making Christmas cards.

Paper Pad
- tablet of construction paper
- pinking shears
- homespun fabric
- spray adhesive
- muslin
- fusible interfacing
- paper-backed fusible web
- tracing paper
- transfer paper
- black permanent fine-point marker
- white, flesh, red, green, gold, brown, gray and black acrylic paint
- paintbrushes

1. Measure the cover of the tablet up the front, around the spine and down the back; add 2 inches. Measure across the front of the cover; add 2 inches. Using pinking shears, cut a piece from homespun the determined measurements.

2. Apply spray adhesive to wrong side of fabric piece. With one inch of fabric extending past edges of tablet, smooth fabric onto cover. Clip fabric away at spine and cut fabric diagonally across corners; smooth edges to inside of cover.

3. For tablet label, cut one 7¹⁄₂"x10¹⁄₂" piece each from muslin, interfacing and web. Fuse interfacing to muslin and web to interfacing; do not remove paper backing.

4. Trace angel design, page 155, onto tracing paper. Use transfer paper to transfer design to label. Use a black marker to draw over transferred lines.

5. Paint design as desired; allow to dry. Use marker to go over detail lines, if necessary. Use pinking shears to trim edges of label.

6. Remove paper backing from label; fuse label to front of tablet.

DOGGIE BED
(shown on page 71)
- 3⁷⁄₈ yards of 44-inch wide heavyweight fabric for cover
- string
- fabric marking pencil
- thumbtack
- dimensional fabric paint
- 1³⁄₈ yards of 90-inch wide muslin
- 12-inch metal zipper
- cedar chips

Use a ¹⁄₂-inch seam allowance for all sewing unless otherwise indicated.

1. Cut a 42-inch square from cover fabric. Fold square in half from top to bottom and again from right to left. To mark cutting line for circle, tie one end of string to fabric marking pencil. Insert thumbtack through string 20¹⁄₂ inches from pencil. Refer to Fig. 1 to insert thumbtack in corner of fabric and mark cutting line. Cutting through all layers, cut out circle along line. Fold circle in half to use as a pattern in Step 2.

Fig. 1

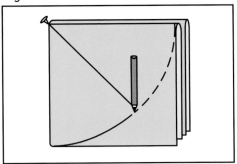

2. Cut two 27"x42" pieces from cover fabric; place fabric pieces together. Referring to Fig. 2, pin folded fabric circle on fabric pieces 5 inches from one edge and mark extended edges. Cutting through both layers, cut out half circles.

Fig. 2

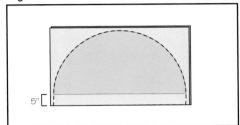

3. Press straight edge of each half circle 1/4 inch to the wrong side; press 1 3/4 inches to wrong side again. Top stitch along pressed edges.

4. For bottom of bed, place half circles right sides up with straight edges overlapped 3 inches; pin in place. Baste overlapped edges to secure.

5. Piecing as necessary, cut two 4"x65 1/2" strips from cover fabric. Matching right sides, sew ends of fabric strip together to form a loop. Press seam allowances to one side.

6. Matching right sides and raw edges, pin one edge of fabric strip to edge of bottom of bed. Easing in fullness, sew along curved edge. Repeat to sew top of bed to strip. Clip curves and remove basting threads along bottom; turn right side out. If desired, use dimensional paint to write name on side of bed; allow to dry.

7. For lining, cut two 45-inch squares from muslin. Inserting thumbtack 22 inches from pencil, repeat Step 2 to cut 2 circles from muslin squares. Place muslin circles together.

8. Use fabric marking pencil to mark a 12-inch zipper opening along edge of one muslin circle. Beginning and ending 5 inches beyond marks, baste along zipper line; press seam open. Center zipper, right side down, along seam between zipper marks on wrong side of muslin. Using a zipper foot, sew 1/4 inch from zipper along sides, bottom and top. Remove all basting threads and open zipper.

9. Matching right sides and raw edges and leaving open at zipper, sew muslin circles together. Turn right side out through zipper opening.

10. Fill lining with cedar chips, close zipper and place lining in cover.

CAT TOYS
(shown on page 72)

Fish
- tracing paper
- gold and red felt
- pinking shears
- two 1/2-inch dia. green buttons
- gold and red embroidery floss
- polyester fiberfill
- catnip (optional)
- rickrack

All buttons and trims should be sewn securely for animal safety.

1. Trace fish body and fin patterns, page 151, onto tracing paper. Using pattern, cut 2 bodies from red felt. Using pinking shears, cut 2 fins from gold felt.

2. Sew one body shape to right side of each fin shape. For eyes, sew one button to right side of each body piece. Matching wrong sides and leaving an opening for stuffing, use 3 strands of gold floss to sew edges together.

3. Firmly stuff fish with fiberfill...add catnip while stuffing, if desired. Sew opening closed.

4. Tucking ends under, use 3 strands of red floss and *Running Stitches*, page 133, to sew rickrack down sides of body and around head.

Mouse
- tracing paper
- pinking shears
- mustard and red felt
- paper-backed fusible web
- 1/4-inch dia. black shank buttons for eyes
- black baby rickrack
- 3/4-inch dia. button
- red and black embroidery floss
- polyester fiberfill
- catnip (optional)
- heavy-duty black thread

All buttons and trims should be sewn securely for animal safety.

1. Trace body pattern, page 151, onto tracing paper. Using pinking shears, cut 2 bodies from mustard felt.

2. Using ear pattern, page 151, follow *Making Appliqués*, page 134, to make 2 ears from red felt; fuse ears to mustard felt. Use pinking shears to cut out ears just outside edge of ear.

3. Sew one eye and one ear to each body piece...make sure one side is reversed.

4. For tail, tie a knot 3 inches from one end of a 10-inch length of rickrack. Thread 3-inch end through one hole in the 3/4-inch diameter button; knot the end to secure.

5. Matching wrong sides, securing button of tail between layers and leaving an opening for stuffing, use 3 strands of red floss to sew edges together.

6. Firmly stuff mouse with fiberfill...add catnip while stuffing, if desired. Sew opening closed. Trim tail to desired length, then tie a knot in end of tail.

7. For whiskers, make a stitch on one side of the nose using 2 strands of heavy-duty thread...knot the threads together to secure and trim the ends to desired length. Repeat for the opposite side.

Bell Ball
- tracing paper
- red felt
- green baby rickrack
- embroidery floss to coordinate with felt
- polyester fiberfill
- one inch dia. jingle bell
- catnip (optional)

(continued on page 130)

All trims should be sewn securely for animal safety.

1. Trace ball pattern, page 151, onto tracing paper. Use pattern to cut 3 shapes from red felt.

2. Placing rickrack between edges, match and pin one rounded edge of two pieces together. Use 3 strands of floss to sew edges together. Repeat to attach third piece to one edge. Leaving an opening for stuffing, repeat to sew remaining edges together. Firmly stuff ball with fiberfill and bell…add catnip while stuffing, if desired. Sew opening closed.

3. Tie a 12-inch length of ribbon into a bow; sew bow to top of ball.

BUTTON-RIMMED BASKET
(shown on pages 74 and 75)

- basket (we used an 8"x9" basket)
- 2 homespun fabrics
- low-loft polyester batting
- paper-backed fusible web
- hot glue gun
- lots of assorted buttons

1. For front panel, measure height and width of front of basket; cut 2 pieces from fabric determined measurements. Cut one piece from batting 1/2 inch smaller than the fabric pieces. Layer batting between wrong sides of fabric pieces. Sew pieces together 1/4 inch from edges; pull threads to fray edges.

2. Using tree pattern, page 143, follow *Making Appliqués*, page 134, to make enough tree appliqués from fabric to fit across panel. Fuse appliqués to panel, then glue one button at top of each tree. Glue panel to basket.

3. Glue buttons along rim of basket.

FABRIC WRAPPER
(shown on page 75)

Using jute to tie the ends, wrap a block of fudge in a pinked piece of fabric…glue sprigs of artificial greenery to the top. Add a hand-lettered tag made from ecru card stock on red embossed card stock, backed with corrugated craft cardboard.

SNACK BAG
(shown on page 75)

- tracing paper
- decorative lunch-size paper bag
- cardboard
- craft knife and cutting mat
- clear tape
- clear cellophane
- black permanent fine-point marker
- hot glue gun
- assorted buttons
- hole punch
- fabric
- ecru card stock
- craft glue stick
- red corrugated craft cardboard

1. Trace star pattern, page 143, onto tracing paper; cut out. Draw around pattern on front of bag desired number of times; place cardboard in bag under stars…use craft knife to cut out stars.

2. Tape a piece of cellophane large enough to cover stars on inside of bag. Use marker to draw "stitches" along edges of stars; hot glue buttons to bag.

3. Place gift in bag. Fold top of bag one inch to the front 2 times. Punch two holes one inch apart through center of folded portion of bag. Tear a 1"x12" strip from fabric; thread strip through holes and tie into a bow at front of bag.

4. Cut out a 1 1/4"x2" tag from card stock. Use marker to write name on tag. Use glue stick to glue tag on a piece of craft cardboard; cut out 1/4 inch outside edges of tag. Hot glue tag to bag.

SNOWFLAKE TIN
(shown on page 75)

Apply primer, then 2 to 3 coats of paint to outside of tin and lid; allow to dry. Use dimensional paint to paint "snowflakes" on tin as desired; paint a wavy line and a row of dots around edge of lid. Add a hand-lettered tag made from ecru card stock, backed with green corrugated craft cardboard.

CINNAMON CRUNCH BASKET
(shown on pages 74 and 75)

- basket (we used a 4"x8" red basket)
- fabric for liner
- pearl cotton
- assorted buttons
- spray adhesive
- 3 1/2"x5" fabric scrap
- 3 1/2"x5" piece of card stock
- decorative-edge craft scissors
- photocopy of tag design (page 157) on tan card stock
- 1/8-inch dia. hole punch

1. For basket liner, measure length of basket from top of rim, down side, across bottom and up opposite side; repeat to measure width of basket. Add 6 inches to each measurement; cut a piece from fabric the determined measurements.

2. Press edges of basket liner 1/4 inch to the wrong side…press 1/4 inch to wrong side again. Using 3 strands of pearl cotton, work *Running Stitches*, page 133, along pressed edges. Sew one button to each corner of liner. Place liner in basket.

3. Apply spray adhesive to wrong side of fabric scrap…smooth onto card stock piece. Use craft scissors to trim edges. Cut out tag design. Apply spray adhesive to wrong side of tag…smooth onto right side of fabric-covered card stock.

4. Punch 2 holes 1/2 inch apart at top center of tag. Use pearl cotton to attach tag to basket.

CRANBERRY BREAD BAG
(shown on page 77)

- fabrics for bag and trim
- paper-backed fusible web
- 1"x36" strip torn from fabric for bow
- photocopy of tag design (page 157) on ecru card stock
- tracing paper
- red paper
- craft glue stick
- corrugated craft cardboard
- black permanent fine-point marker

1. Cut a 17"x21" piece from fabric for bag and a 3"x21" strip from fabric for trim and fusible web. Matching long edges, fuse strip to wrong side of fabric for bag.

2. Matching right sides and short edges; fold fabric in half. Using a 1/4-inch seam allowance, sew side and bottom edges together to make bag...turn bag right side out.

3. Cut points in top of bag. Place gift in bag...tie fabric strip into a bow around top of bag.

4. Cut out tag. Trace heart shape from tag onto tracing paper. Using pattern, cut one heart from red paper; glue heart to tag. Glue tag to craft cardboard, then trim cardboard to 1/4 inch outside edges of tag. Use marker to write message on tag and draw "stitches" around heart. Glue tag to bag.

CAKE BOX
(shown on page 78)

Spruce up an ordinary cake box for the holidays. Unfold a cake box and apply spray adhesive to the right side...smooth the box onto the wrong side of a piece of wrapping paper. Use a craft knife to trim the paper around the box and cut through the slits. Refold the box and place your cake inside. Tie it up with a festive bow, add some greenery, then a handmade tag.

COOKIE MIX LABEL AND TAG
(shown on page 80)

- photocopy of label and instructions design (page 80) on ecru card stock
- craft glue
- white and red card stock
- decorative paper
- decorative-edge craft scissors
- 1/8-inch hole punch

Allow glue to dry after each application.

1. Cut out label, then glue to red card stock. Trim card stock to 1/8 inch outside edges of label. Glue label to decorative paper; use craft scissors to cut out 1/4 inch outside edges of red card stock. Glue label on jar.

2. For tag, glue instructions to wrong side of decorative paper. Use craft scissors to cut out just inside borders. Fold tag in half; punch a hole at top folded corner.

3. Tie several lengths of raffia into a bow around jar. Use raffia to attach tag to jar.

WINTERTIME SPICE TEA CUP
(shown on page 81)

- homespun fabric
- jute
- hot glue gun
- artificial holly with berries
- cinnamon sticks
- decorative-edge craft scissors
- photocopy of tag design (page 157) on ecru card stock
- craft glue stick
- red card stock
- black permanent fine-point marker

1. For bag, cut an 8 1/2"x15" piece from homespun. Matching right sides and short edges; fold fabric in half. Using a 1/4-inch seam allowance, sew side and bottom edges together to make bag...turn bag right side out. Pull threads to fray top edge of bag.

2. Place gift in bag and tie closed with a length of jute. Hot glue greenery and cinnamon sticks to knot of bow...save a little bit of greenery for the tag.

3. Use craft scissors to cut out tag 1/4 inch outside of edges of design. Using glue stick, center and glue tag to card stock...trim card stock to 1/4 inch outside edges of tag. Hot glue greenery to corner of tag...use marker to write message on tag.

PANCAKES FROM THE PANTRY
(shown on page 81)

For the tag, photocopy the tag design, page 156, onto card stock. Use decorative-edge craft scissors to cut out the tag, then glue it to embossed card stock. Trim the card stock to 1/8 inch outside the design...punch a hole in the top left corner and tie it to the gift.

MOCHA MIX BAG
(shown on page 83)

- pinking shears
- homespun fabric for bag
- embroidery floss
- 1"x20" pinked fabric strip for bow
- photocopy of tag design (page 153) on ecru card stock
- craft glue stick
- green embossed card stock
- decorative-edge craft scissors
- 1/8-inch dia. hole punch
- 1/16-inch dia. gold cord

1. For bag, use pinking shears to cut a 9"x12" piece from homespun. Matching right sides and short edges, fold piece in half. Using a 1/4-inch seam allowance, sew short edges together to form a tube; do not turn right side out.

2. Use floss to baste along bottom edge of tube. Pull threads tight to gather bottom of bag; knot threads to secure...turn bag right side out.

3. Place gift in bag; tie pinked strip into a bow around top of bag.

4. Cut out tag, then glue to card stock. Use craft scissors to trim card stock to 3/8 inch outside edges of design.

5. Punch a hole at top center of tag; use cord to attach tag to knot of bow.

HOUSE APPLIQUÉ BAG
(shown on page 83)

- pinking shears
- fabric for bag
- paper-backed fusible web
- fabric scraps
- black permanent fine-point marker
- recipe card

1. Use pinking shears to cut an 8"x21" piece from fabric for bag. Matching right sides and short edges and using a 1/4-inch seam allowance, sew long edges together for sides of bag.

2. Using patterns, page 157, follow *Making Appliqués*, page 134, to make 3 small window, 2 large window and one each chimney, roof, house, door, wreath and bow appliqués from fabric scraps.

3. Arrange and fuse appliqués on bag. Use marker to draw panes on windows.

4. Write recipe on recipe card. Place gift and recipe card in bag. Tear a 1"x12" strip from fabric scrap; tie strip into a bow around top of bag.

JOLLY GINGERBREAD MEN BASKET
(shown on page 84)

Embellish the handle of a basket with ribbon, greenery and bells...tear a piece of fabric to line the basket. Tuck in the cookie mix, a Gooseberry cookie cutter and a tag made from a photocopy of the recipe on page 156, glued to a piece of brown kraft paper.

131

PATCHWORK POTHOLDER AND TAG

(shown on page 86)

- red fabric scrap for heart
- paper-backed fusible web
- 2 coordinating fabrics for potholder
- polyester bonded batting
- photocopy of tag design (page 156) on brown card stock
- tracing paper
- red embossed card stock
- craft glue stick
- photocopy of instructions (page 156) on tan card stock

1. Using heart pattern, page 156, follow *Making Appliqués*, page 134, to make one heart appliqué from red fabric. Make two 3½-inch square appliqués from one potholder fabric.

2. Cut one 7-inch square from batting and two 7-inch squares from remaining potholder fabric. Arrange and fuse square appliqués, then heart appliqué on right side of one large potholder square. Follow *Machine Appliqué*, page 134, to sew over edges of appliqués.

3. Layer batting between wrong sides of 7-inch squares; baste in place.

4. Piecing as necessary, cut a 2¾"x30" strip from potholder fabric for binding. Press strip in half lengthwise; unfold. Press one long edge ¼ inch to wrong side, then one end ½ inch to wrong side. Beginning with unpressed end, matching raw edges and mitering corners, sew strip along edges on front of potholder.

5. Fold and pin binding to back of potholder, covering basting threads; stitch in place.

6. Cut out tag. Trace heart from tag onto tracing paper and cut out. Use pattern to cut one heart from red card stock...glue over heart on tag. Cut out instructions just outside border...glue to tag.

GENERALS

MAKING A BOW

Loop sizes given in project instructions refer to the length of ribbon used to make one loop of bow.

1. For first streamer, measure desired length of streamer from one end of ribbon; twist ribbon between fingers as shown in Fig. 1.

Fig. 1

2. Keeping right side of ribbon facing out, fold ribbon to front to form desired-size loop; gather ribbon between fingers (Fig. 2). Fold ribbon to back to form another loop; gather ribbon between fingers (Fig. 3).

Fig. 2   **Fig. 3**

3. If a center loop is desired, form half the desired number of loops, then loosely wrap ribbon around thumb and gather ribbon between fingers as shown in Fig. 4; form

remaining loops. Continue to form loops, varying size of loops as desired, until bow is desired size.

Fig. 4

4. For remaining streamer, trim ribbon to desired length.

5. To secure bow, hold gathered loops tightly. Fold a length of floral wire around gathers of loops. Hold wire ends behind bow, gathering all loops forward; twist bow to tighten wire. Arrange loops and trim ribbon ends as desired.

CROSS STITCH

Preparing floss: If your project will be laundered, soak floss in a mixture of one cup water and one tablespoon vinegar for a few minutes and allow to dry before using to prevent colors from bleeding or fading.

Counted Cross Stitch (X): Work one Cross Stitch to correspond to each colored square in chart. For horizontal rows, work stitches in two journeys (Fig. 1).

Fig. 1

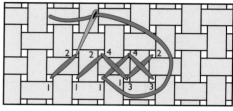

For vertical rows, complete stitch as shown in Fig. 2.

Fig. 2

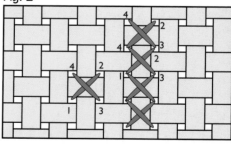

When working over 2 fabric threads, work Cross Stitch as shown.

Backstitch (B'ST): For outline detail, Backstitch (shown in chart and color key by black or colored straight lines) should be worked after all Cross Stitch has been completed.

Fig. 4

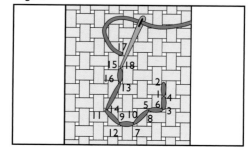

French Knot: Referring to Fig. 5, bring needle up at 1. Wrap floss once around needle and insert needle at 2, holding end of floss with non-stitching fingers.

Fig. 5

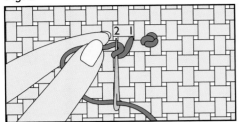

EMBROIDERY STITCHES

Preparing floss: If your project will be laundered, soak floss in a mixture of one cup water and one tablespoon vinegar for a few minutes and allow to dry before using to prevent colors from bleeding or fading.

Backstitch: Referring to Fig. 1, bring needle up at 1; go down at 2; bring up at 3 and pull through. For next stitch, insert needle at 1; bring up at 4 and pull through.

Fig. 1

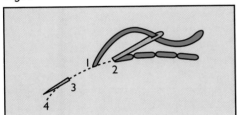

Blanket Stitch: Referring to Fig. 2a, bring needle up at 1. Keeping thread below point of needle, go down at 2 and come up at 3. Continue working as shown in Fig. 2b.

Fig. 2a   **Fig. 2b**

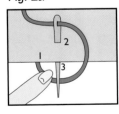 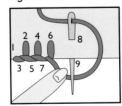

Blind Stitch: Come up at 1. Go down at 2 and come up at 3 (Fig. 3). Length of stitches may be varied as desired.

Fig. 3

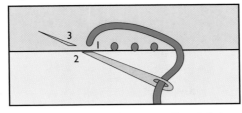

Couched Stitch: Referring to Fig. 4, bring needle up at 1 and go down at 2, following line to be couched. Work tiny stitches over thread to secure.

Fig. 4

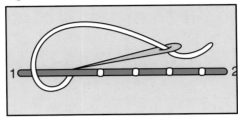

Cross Stitch: Bring needle up at 1 and go down at 2. Come up at 3 and go down at 4 (Fig. 5).

Fig. 5

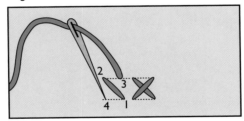

French Knot: Referring to Fig. 6, bring needle up at 1. Wrap floss once around needle and insert needle at 2, holding end of floss with non-stitching fingers. Tighten knot, then pull needle through fabric, holding floss until it must be released. For a larger knot, use more strands; wrap only once.

Fig. 6

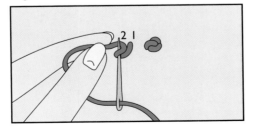

Lazy Daisy Stitch: Bring needle up at 1; take needle down again at 1 to form a loop and bring up at 2. Keeping loop below point of needle (Fig. 7), take needle down at 3 to anchor loop.

Fig. 7

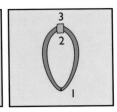

Running Stitch: Referring to Fig. 8, make a series of straight stitches with stitch length equal to the space between stitches.

Fig. 8

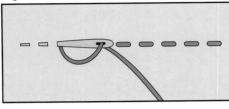

Straight Stitch: Referring to Fig. 9, come up at 1 and go down at 2.

Fig. 9

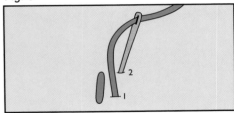

Whip Stitch: Referring to Fig. 10, bring needle up at 1; take thread around edge of fabric and bring needle up at 2. Continue stitching along edge of fabric.

Fig. 10

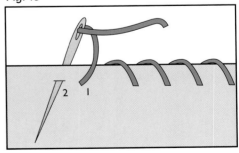

MAKING PATTERNS

When the entire pattern is shown, place tracing paper over the pattern and draw over lines. For a more durable pattern, use a permanent marker to draw over pattern on stencil plastic.

When patterns are stacked or overlapped, place tracing paper over the pattern and follow a single colored line to trace the pattern. Repeat to trace each pattern separately onto tracing paper.

When tracing a two-part pattern, match the dashed lines and arrows to trace an entire pattern onto tracing paper.

When only half of the pattern is shown (indicated by a solid blue line on pattern), fold the tracing paper in half. Place the fold along the solid blue line and trace pattern half; turn folded paper over and draw over the traced lines on the remaining side. Unfold the pattern; cut out.

MAKING APPLIQUÉS

To prevent darker fabrics from showing through, white or light-colored fabrics may need to be lined with fusible interfacing before being fused.

To make reverse appliqués, trace the pattern onto tracing paper; turn traced paper over and continue to follow all steps using the reversed pattern.

1. Trace the appliqué pattern onto paper side of web as many times as indicated for a single fabric. When making more than one appliqué, leave at least one inch between shapes.
2. Cutting 1/2 inch outside drawn shape, cut out web shape. Fuse to wrong side of fabric.
3. Cut out the appliqué shape along the drawn lines.

MACHINE APPLIQUÉ

Unless otherwise indicated in project instructions, set sewing machine for a medium-width zigzag stitch with a short stitch length. When using nylon or metallic thread, use regular thread in bobbin.

1. Pin or baste a piece of stabilizer slightly larger than design to the wrong side of background fabric under design.

2. Beginning on straight edge of appliqué if possible, position project under presser foot so that most of stitching will be on appliqué piece. Hold upper thread toward you and sew 2 or 3 stitches over thread to prevent raveling. Stitch over all exposed raw edges of appliqué and along detail lines as indicated in project instructions.
3. When stitching is complete, remove stabilizer. Pull loose threads to wrong side of fabric; knot and trim ends.

PAINTING TECHNIQUES

Transferring a pattern: Trace pattern onto tracing paper. Place transfer paper coated-side down between project and traced pattern. Use removable tape to secure pattern to project. Use a pencil to draw over outlines of design (press lightly to avoid smudges and heavy lines that are difficult to cover). If necessary, use a soft eraser to remove any smudges.

Painting basecoats: Use a medium round brush for large areas and a small round brush for small areas. Do not overload brush. Allowing to dry between coats, apply several thin coats of paint to project.

Transferring details: To transfer detail lines to design, reposition pattern and transfer paper over painted basecoats and use a pencil to lightly draw over detail lines of design.

Adding details: Use a permanent marker or paint pen to draw over detail lines.

Sealing: If an item will be handled frequently or used outdoors, we recommend sealing the item with clear acrylic sealer. Sealers are available in spray or brush-on form in several finishes. Follow the manufacturer's instructions to apply the sealer.

Dry Brush: Do not dip brush in water. Dip a stipple brush or old paintbrush in paint; wipe most of the paint off onto a dry paper towel. Lightly rub the brush across the area to receive color. Decrease pressure on the brush as you move outward. Repeat as needed.

Spatter Painting: Dip the bristle tips of a dry toothbrush into paint, blot on a paper towel to remove excess, then pull thumb across bristles to spatter paint on project.

Sponge Painting: Use an assembly-line method when making several sponge-painted projects. Place project on a covered work surface. Practice sponge-painting technique on scrap paper until desired look is achieved. Paint projects with first color and allow to dry before moving to next color. Use a clean sponge for each additional color.

For allover designs, dip a dampened sponge piece into paint; remove excess paint on a paper towel. Use a light stamping motion to paint item.

For painting with sponge shapes, dip a dampened sponge shape into paint; remove excess paint on a paper towel. Lightly press sponge shape onto project. Carefully lift sponge. For a reverse design, turn sponge shape over.

STENCILING

These instructions are written for multicolor stencils. For single-color stencils, make one stencil for entire design.

1. For first stencil, cut a piece from stencil plastic one inch larger than entire pattern. Center plastic over pattern and use a permanent pen to trace outlines of all areas of first color in stencil cutting key. For placement guidelines, outline remaining colored area using dashed lines. Using a new piece of plastic for each additional color in stencil cutting key, repeat for remaining stencils.
2. Place each plastic piece on cutting mat and use craft knife to cut out stencil along solid lines, making sure edges are smooth.
3. Hold or tape stencil in place. Using a clean, dry stencil brush or sponge piece, dip brush or sponge in paint. Remove excess paint on a paper towel. Brush or sponge should be almost dry to produce best results. Beginning at edge of cut-out area, apply paint in a stamping motion over stencil. If desired, highlight or shade design by stamping a lighter or darker shade of paint in cut-out area. Repeat until all areas of first stencil have been painted. Carefully remove stencil and allow paint to dry.
4. Using stencils in order indicated in color key and matching guidelines on stencils to previously stenciled area, repeat Step 3 for remaining stencils.

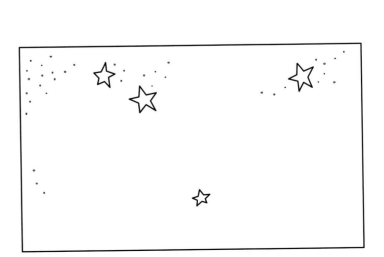

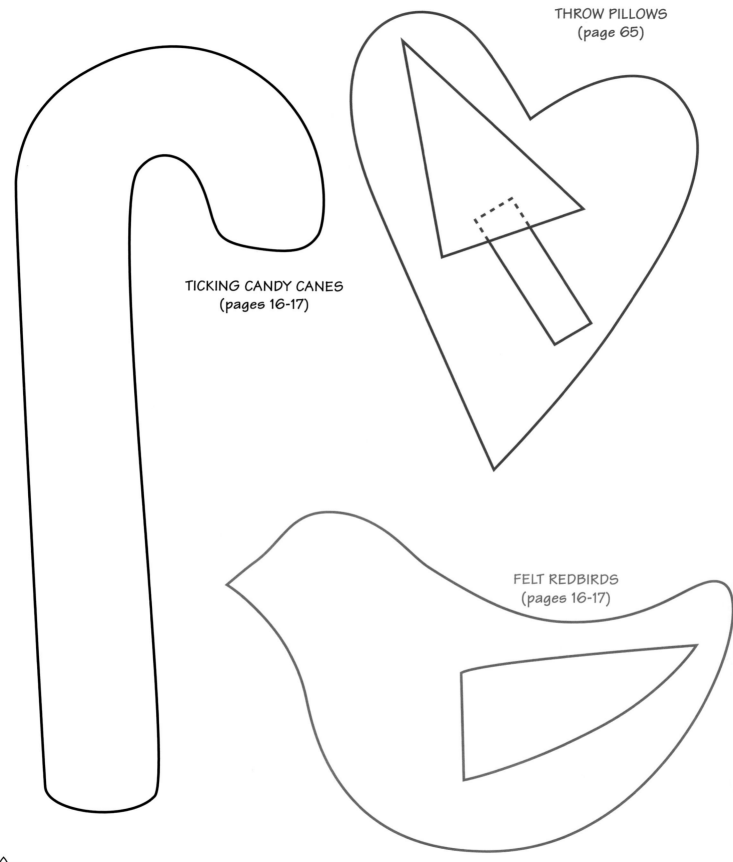

THROW PILLOWS
(page 65)

TICKING CANDY CANES
(pages 16-17)

FELT REDBIRDS
(pages 16-17)

KID'S CHRISTMAS CARD KIT
(page 66)

Gooseberry Patch and Leisure Arts, Inc., grant permission to the owner of this book to photocopy the designs on this page for personal use only.

COPPER-TOP GIFT BOXES
(page 57)

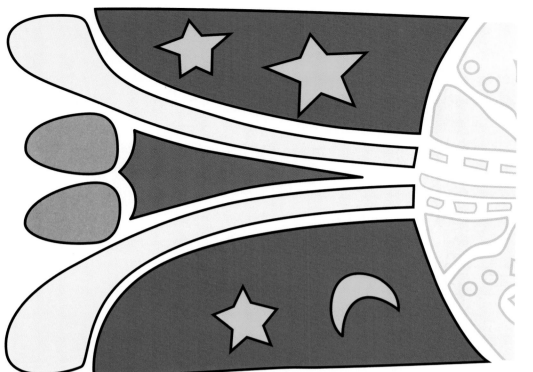

Stencil #	Paint Color
Stencil #1	flesh and brown
Stencil #2	red or green
Stencil #3	ivory
Stencil #4	grey
Stencil #5	gold

Mark each stencil with ● to match while painting.

STENCILED SANTAS
(pages 22-23)

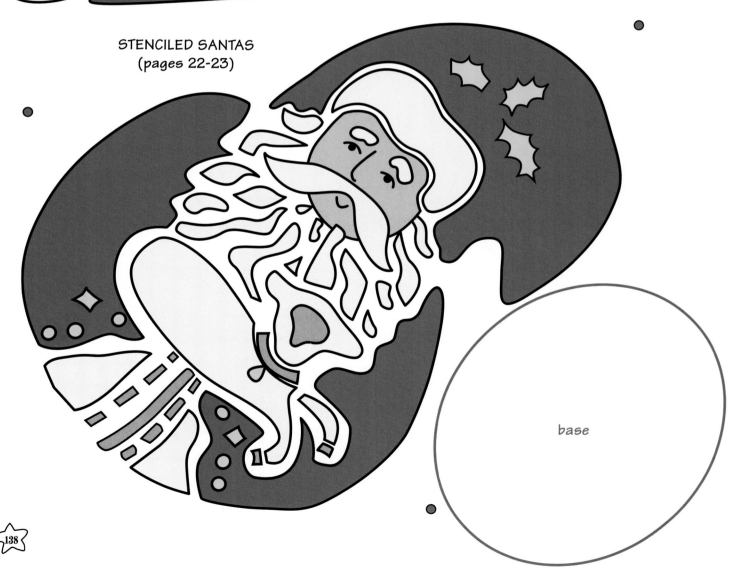

base

WARM THOUGHTS JAR
(page 29)

Warm thoughts

CHICKEN FEEDER CANDLEHOLDER
(page 51)

PATCHWORK POTHOLDER AND TAG
(page 86)

EMBROIDERED MUSLIN STOCKING
(page 34)

SANTA STOCKING
(page 35)

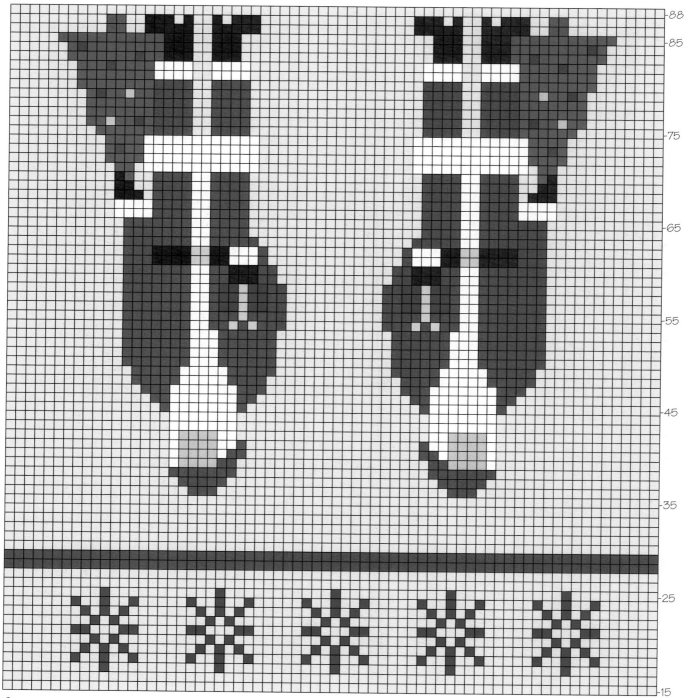

On **right** side rows, work chart from **right** to **left**; on **wrong** side rows, work chart from **left** to **right**.

■ Red	■ Blue	
■ Gold	■ Green	
□ Winter White	□ Beige Heather	
■ Black	■ Brown	

SNOWMAN STOCKING
(page 35)

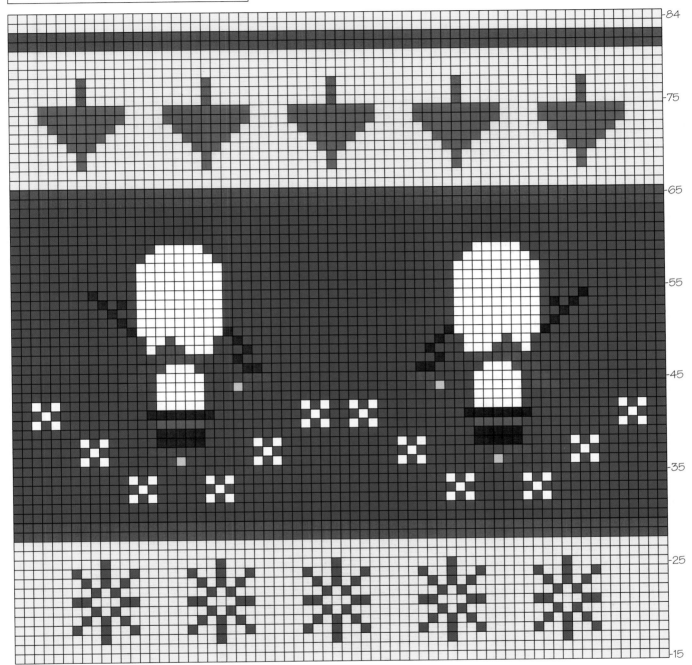

On **right** side rows, work chart from **right** to **left**; on **wrong** side rows, work chart from **left** to **right**.

141

Welcome Home

"WELCOME HOME" DOOR PILLOW
(page 18)

TICKING TREE
(page 40)

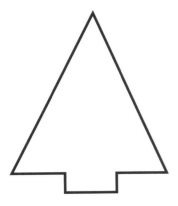

BUTTON-RIMMED BASKET
(pages 74-75)

PLAY DOUGH JARS
(page 68)

SNACK BAG
(pages 74-75)

TICKING TREE
(page 40)

Sparkles & wishes

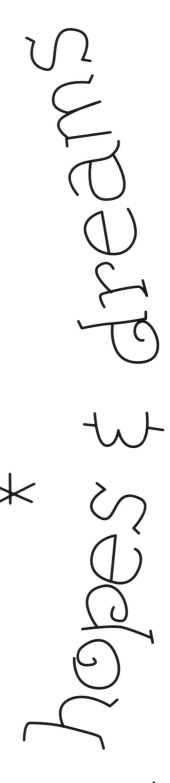

hopes & dreams

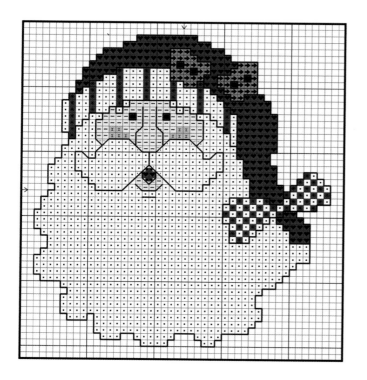

CROSS-STITCHED ORNAMENTS
(pages 44-45)

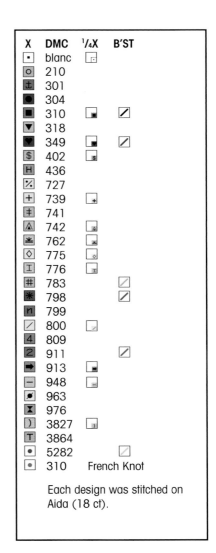

X	DMC	¼X	B'ST
·	blanc	□	
o	210		
‡	301		
●	304		
■	310	■	╱
▼	318		
▼	349	■	╱
$	402	$	
H	436		
⁒	727		
+	739	+	
‡	741		
⧍	742	⧍	
⋇	762	⋇	
◇	775	◇	
I	776	I	
⌗	783		╱
✳	798		╱
n	799		
╱	800	╱	
4	809		
2	911		╱
➡	913	■	
−	948	−	
✦	963		
⌶	976		
)	3827	)	
T	3864		
•	5282		╱
•	310	French Knot	

Each design was stitched on Aida (18 ct).

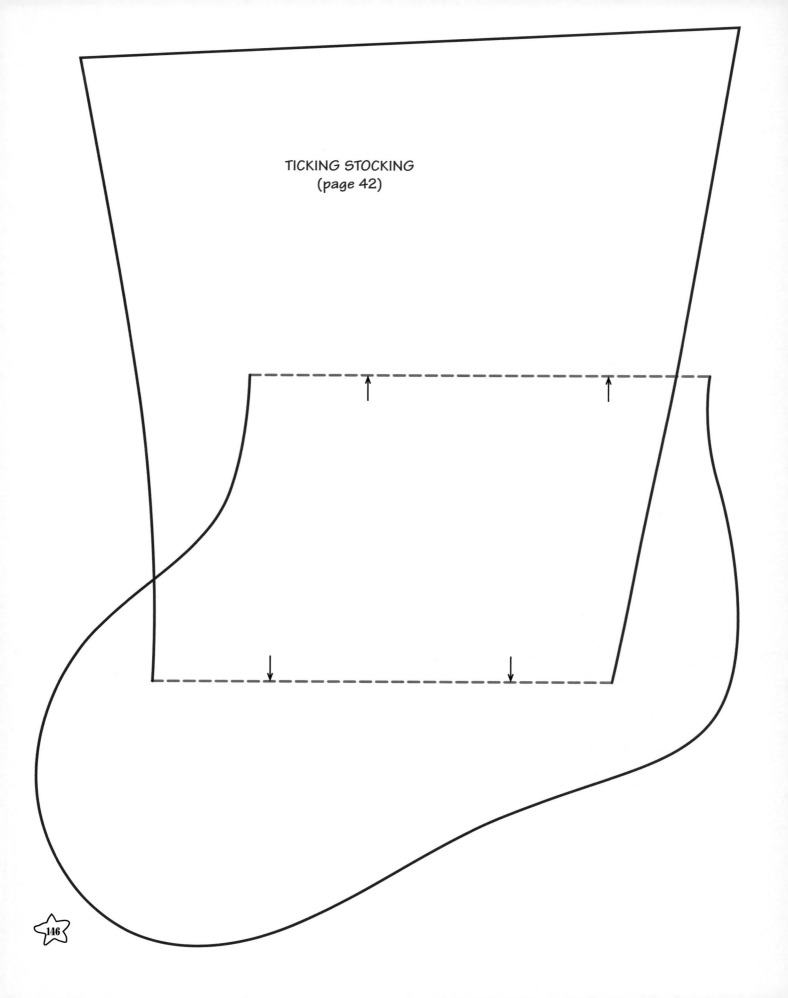

TICKING STOCKING
(page 42)

146

Christmas comes but once a year.....

Christmas comes but once a year.....

COPPER-TOP GIFT BOXES
(page 57)

FRAMED AND WINDOW SNOWFLAKES
(pages 20-21)

Good cookin'

is heaven-sent!

APPLIQUÉ TEA TOWELS
(page 61)

OVEN MITT AND APRON
(page 60)

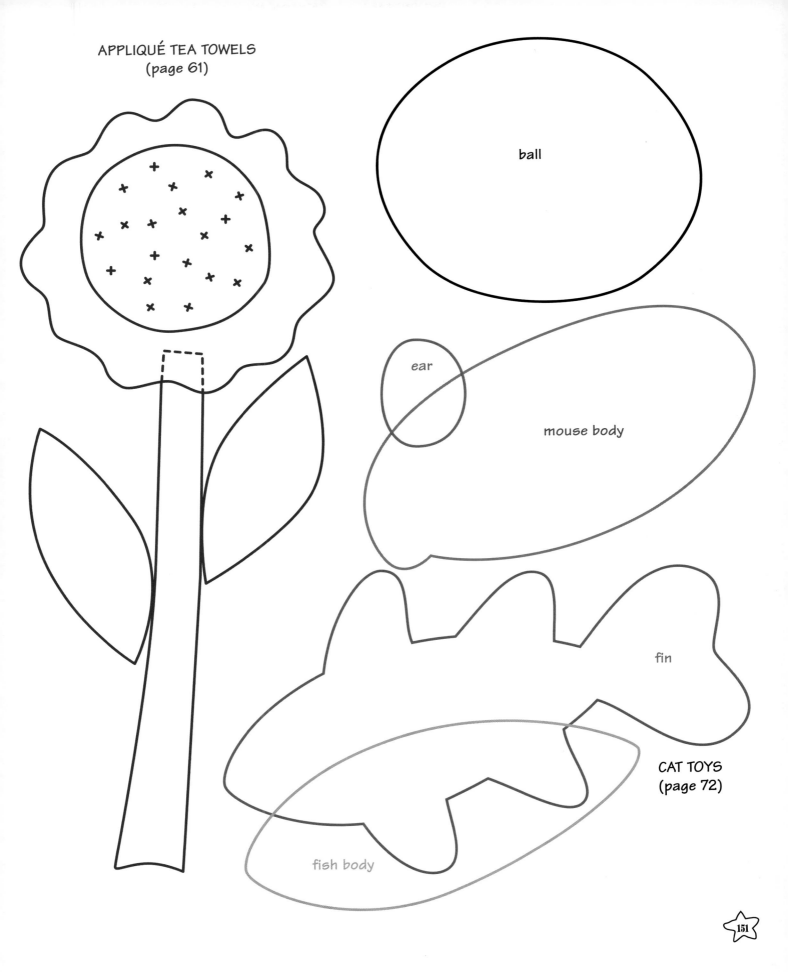

APPLIQUÉ TEA TOWELS
(page 61)

ball

ear

mouse body

fin

CAT TOYS
(page 72)

fish body

151

MOCHA MIX BAG
(page 83)

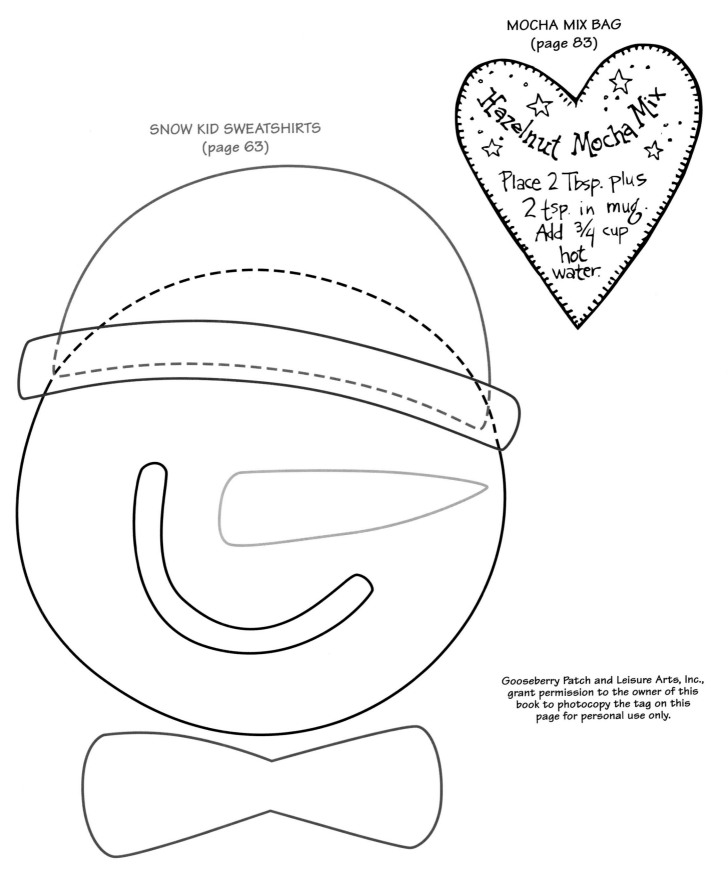

Hazelnut Mocha Mix
Place 2 Tbsp. plus
2 tsp. in mug.
Add 3/4 cup
hot
water.

SNOW KID SWEATSHIRTS
(page 63)

Gooseberry Patch and Leisure Arts, Inc.,
grant permission to the owner of this
book to photocopy the tag on this
page for personal use only.

ASSEMBLY
DIAGRAM

STAR PILLOW
(page 64)

Pocketful
of
Wishes

PATCHWORK POTHOLDER AND TAG
(page 86)

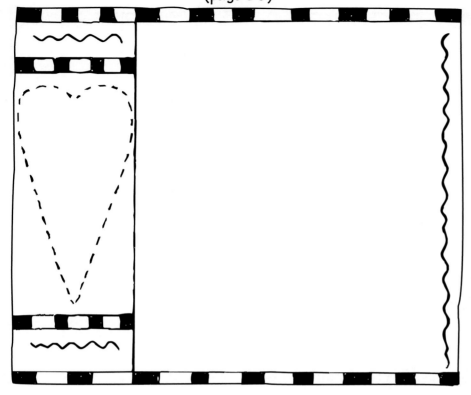

JOLLY GINGERBREAD MEN MIX
(page 84)

Cream together 1/2 cup butter, 3/4 cup molasses and one egg; stir in dry mix. Dough will be stiff. Cover and refrigerate one hour. Roll dough to 1/4-inch thickness on a lightly floured surface; add additional flour if dough is too sticky. Cut with a 4 1/4"x3 1/2" gingerbread boy cookie cutter and place on a lightly greased baking sheet. Bake at 350 degrees for 10 to 12 minutes. Makes about 22 cookies.

PANCAKES FROM THE PANTRY
(page 81)

In a large mixing bowl, add 2 eggs; beat well. Gradually beat in 1/3 cup oil. Alternately add 2 cups of pancake mix and 1 cup of water to the egg mixture; blend well. Cook pancakes on a lightly oiled griddle. Makes 10 pancakes.

Add beans to a large stockpot; cover with hot water and let soak overnight. Drain and add 2 quarts of water. Bring to a boil; reduce heat and simmer, covered, one to 2 hours or until beans are almost tender. Stir in two 14 1/2-ounce cans stewed tomatoes and seasoning mix. Simmer, uncovered, one to 1 1/2 hours or until beans are tender. Makes approximately 12 cups of soup.

PINE CONE FIRESTARTERS
(page 52)

CINNAMON CRUNCH BARS

CINNAMON CRUNCH BASKET
(pages 74-75)

WINTERTIME SPICE TEA CUP
(page 81)

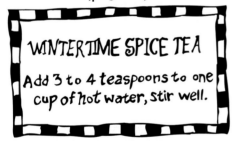

WINTERTIME SPICE TEA

Add 3 to 4 teaspoons to one cup of hot water, stir well.

CRANBERRY BREAD BAG
(page 77)

Cranberry Bread

HOUSE APPLIQUÉ BAG
(page 83)

PROJECT INDEX

RECIPE INDEX

BEVERAGES

Christmas Cappuccino Mix, 84
Cranberry-Almond Punch, 91
Hazelnut Mocha Mix, 83
Hot Mulled Punch, 94
Hot Orange Cider Mix, 83
Nutty Cocoa, 68
Santa Shakes, 69
Sonia's Holiday Sangria, 92
White Chocolate Cocoa Mix, 87
White Christmas Punch, 90
Wintertime Spice Tea, 81

BREADS, CRACKERS & MUFFINS

Angel Biscuits, 111
Apricot Crescents, 114
Brazil Nut Loaf, 112
Cheddar Shortbread, 96
Chocolate Chip-Zucchini Bread, 82
Cranberry Bread, 77
Crusty Cornmeal Rolls, 113
Damascus Brick Sweet Rolls, 110
Dilly Onion Bread, 113
Easy Orange Rolls, 112
English Muffin Bread, 115
Fieldstone Farm Popovers, 115
Golden Butter Rolls, 101
Lemon Raspberry Yogurt Muffins, 115
Macadamia Mini-Loaves, 111
Oatmeal Apple Muffins, 114
Orange-Berry Bread, 82
Pancakes From the Pantry, 81
Pecan Pie Mini Muffins, 109
Pizza Dough Mix, 85
Pumpkin Nut Bread, 112
Rainbow Toast, 69
Simple and Speedy Basic Bread Mix, 82
Whole-Wheat Bread, 113

CAKES

Chocolate-Peanut Butter Cupcakes, 106
Christmas Morning Almond Pound
    Cake, 104
Cinnamon Pudding Cake, 109
Holiday Fruitcake, 103
Sour Cream Breakfast Coffee Cake, 78

CANDIES & CONFECTIONS

Creamy Fudge, 76
Fondant, 105
Holly's White Chocolate Thrills, 77
No-Cook Mints, 76
Rocky Road Fudge, 107

CONDIMENTS

Brown Sugar & Cinnamon Butter, 114
Cranberry-Orange Chutney, 79
Honeybee Butter, 113
Pilgrim Sauce, 99
Red Pepper Jam, 79
Susan's Pumpkin Butter, 79

COOKIES & BARS

Annie's Soft Molasses Cookies, 106
Brown Sugar Rounds Mix, 86
Cheesecake Cookies, 107
Chunky Chocolate Cookie Mix, 80
Cinnamon Crunch Bars, 76
Jolly Gingerbread Men Mix, 84
One Cup of Everything Cookies, 76
The Peanut Butter Bars, 108
Pecan Fingers, 107
Simple Scottish Shortbread, 78

DESSERTS & TOPPINGS

Chocolate Rapture, 105
Holiday Hot Fudge Dessert, 102
Kate's Tortilla Treats, 69
Pizza Cobbler, 69
Rice Pudding, 102
The Ultimate Fudge Sauce, 79

DRY MIXES

Brown Sugar Rounds Mix, 86
Chocolate Chip Pie Mix, 83
Christmas Cappuccino Mix, 84
Chunky Chocolate Cookie Mix, 80
Grandma's Noodle Soup Mix, 85
Hazelnut Mocha Mix, 83
Hot Orange Cider Mix, 83
Jolly Gingerbread Men Mix, 84
Pancakes From the Pantry, 81
Patchwork Bean Soup Mix, 86
Pizza Dough Mix, 85
Simple and Speedy Basic Bread Mix, 82
White Chocolate Cocoa Mix, 87
Wintertime Spice Tea, 81

MAIN COURSES

Chicken Stew, 118
Hearty Beef Brisket, 117
Holly's Broccoli, Ham and Cheese
    Strata, 117
Honey-Roasted Pork Loin, 99
Nancy's Turkey Pie, 116
Pizza Basket, 85
Reuben Casserole, 118
Salmon with Dill Sauce, 98
Sour Cream Tacos, 119
Spaghetti Casserole, 119
Spinach Pie, 117
Spotty's Speedy Spanish Skillet, 119

PET TREATS

Braided Bird Wreath, 73
Healthy Dog Treats, 70
Kitty Kookies, 72

PIES

Chocolate Chip Pie Mix, 83
Crustless Pumpkin Pie, 109
Mom's Candy Apple Walnut Pie, 108
Pumpkin Ice Cream Pie, 102
White Chocolate Macadamia Brownie
    Pie, 107

SALADS

Asparagus & Tomato Salad, 100
Marinated Mushrooms, 97
Old-fashioned Candle Salad, 68
Three Friends Three Layer Ruby Red
    Salad, 98

SIDE DISHES

Baked Broccoli, 101
Harvest Dressing, 99
Savory Mashed Potatoes, 101
Vanilla-Glazed Sweet Potatoes, 100
Wild Rice Casserole, 98

SOUPS

Corn Chowder, 97
Grandma's Noodle Soup Mix, 85
Herbed Celery Soup, 96
Patchwork Bean Soup Mix, 86

Credits

We want to extend a warm *thank you* to the people who allowed us to photograph our projects at their homes: Carl and Monte Brunck, Tommy and Donna Harkins, Charles and Peg Mills, and Duncan and Nancy Porter.

We want to especially thank photographers Andy Uilkie and Ken West of Peerless Photography, Jerry R. Davis of Jerry Davis Photography, and Nancy Nolan of Nola Studios, all of Little Rock, Arkansas, for their excellent work. Photography stylist Jan Nobles also deserves a special mention for the high quality of her collaboration with these photographers.

To Wisconsin Technicolor LLC, of Pewaukee, Wisconsin, we say *thank you* for the superb color reproduction and excellent pre-press preparation.

We extend a special word of thanks to Linda Gillum of Kooler Design Studio, who created the Cross-Stitched Ornaments on pages 44-45.

Thanks also go to Kathleen Royal Phillips, who assisted Oxmoor House with some of the recipes in this book.

Hmmmmmmm....

The Healthful Hunger for A *great idea* is the beauty and blessedness of life.

— JEAN INGELOW —

Painting Rooms

HOW TO CHOOSE AND USE PAINT LIKE AN EXPERT

GLOUCESTER MASSACHUSETTS

ROCKPORT PUBLISHERS

Judy Ostrow

Contents

Portions of Section Two/Chapter Eight [pp. 108-113] were reprinted with permission from Gregor Cann and the *Boston Globe*, where this article first appeared in slightly different form on February 18, 2001. Photographs by Eric Roth.

First published in the United States of America by

Rockport Publishers, Inc.
33 Commercial Street
Gloucester, Massachusetts 01930-5089
Telephone: (978) 282-9590
Facsimile: (978) 283-2742
www.rockpub.com

ISBN: 1-56496-740-9
10 9 8 7 6 5 4 3 2

Design: Peter King & Company
Cover Image: Kevin Thomas
Cover Design: Francesco Jost

Printed in China.

The Power of Paint

FOR THE COST OF SEVERAL CANS OF COLOR AND A FEW SIMPLE TOOLS, YOU HAVE THE POWER TO TRANSFORM AN ORDINARY ROOM INTO SOMETHING MEMORABLE, BEAUTIFUL, AND COMFORTABLE. AVAILABLE IN AN ALMOST INFINITE RAINBOW OF COLORS, PAINT HAS BECOME THE MOST EASILY OBTAINABLE, VERSATILE, AND ECONOMICAL DECORATING MEDIUM.

Paint accomplishes myriad decorating tasks. It creates a unifying backdrop to harmonize an eclectic group of furnishings. It highlights a collection of prized possessions. It accentuates beautiful architectural features, making it easier to notice their detail. It brightens dull surroundings, or softens an austere setting. It can be manipulated to mimic many kinds of luxury materials – marble, precious metal, or exotic wood. With so much talent, paint has become an indispensable ingredient for home decoration. *Painting Rooms* is designed as a guidebook for using painted surfaces as a key component for decorating interiors.

section one

Choosing and Using Paint covers painting materials – the products, tools, and techniques that produce a range of looks and styles that readers can choose to duplicate in their personal spaces:

- Choosing the Right Paint
- Smooth Coatings
- Broken Color Effects
- Tools of the Trade
- Paint Practice

section two

How to Get the Perfect Color will demystify and unstress the process of bringing color home. It makes the transition from learning about the product and its capabilities to picking paint colors and effects that will complete a successful decorating plan:

- Painting with Blue
- Painting with Red
- Painting with Yellow
- Painting with Green
- Painting with Violet
- Painting with Orange
- Painting with Neutrals
- Change Color to Change the Mood

Often, when confronted with aisles of paint cans and thousands of color chips, we are seized by a kind of panic, a color identity crisis. We beat a retreat to white and beige – with so much choice, the potential for error seems great; color seems like a risky business.

To eliminate that sense of risk, the chapters in Section Two present images of finished rooms, grouped by color in the six hues of the spectrum, plus a section on neutrals – black, white, and brown. Selected not only for visual beauty, each photograph is also a hardworking tool to identify how paint color relates to its environment and acts with other furnishings to achieve beauty, harmony, and balance.

This section of the book follows no specific decorating dictum, no unbreakable rule. For, while such adages abound, the true test of a color and decorating plan is whether, finally, it is livable – and enjoyably so. We hope that *Painting Rooms* will help any reader learn many ways to live happily with color.

The Language of Color

- A *hue* is another name for a color.

- A *tint* is a color to which white has been added.

- A *tone* is a color to which gray has been added.

- A *shade* is a color to which black has been added.

- When talking about the *value* of a color, what is meant is its relative lightness or darkness compared to other colors. Think of a black-and-white photograph; colors of the same value will be perceived as the same shade of gray. To look at a room in terms of the values of its various colors, squint as you observe it. You will begin to see the values of objects in the room, and which are the same. Some objects fade into shadow (dark values) and some appear brighter than the others (light values).

- *Saturation* of a color relates to its darkness or density of color; a fully saturated color has a very dark, almost black, tone and will appear black or nearly so in a black-and-white photograph.

choosing the right paint

	WHAT IT DOES	WHAT IT'S GOOD FOR	THINGS TO CONSIDER
WATER-BASED PAINT:			
Latex	Spreads easily; cleans up with soap and water	All interior applications; may be diluted with water for broken color effects	Inexpensive brands may lack durability
Acrylic	Same as latex; higher quality solids	All interior applications; as above	Best quality are 100% acrylic
OIL-BASED PAINT:	Spreads evenly; durable finish; longer drying time than water-based products	All interior applications; dilute with its solvent (usually mineral spirits) for broken color application	Must be cleaned with mineral spirits or other solvents; produces fumes; requires excellent ventilation during application and drying
SPECIALTY PAINTS:			
Glazes	Clear or translucent coating for broken color effects; may be oil- or water-based; should be applied over opaque base.	Can be easily manipulated for many special effects	Relatively short drying time requires quick application; working this paint with a partner is helpful
Milk paints	Vintage recipe for paint that provides eco-friendly finish; available as a powder to be mixed with water	Provides a smooth, dead-flat finish; good for walls and furniture in colonial or other vintage rooms	Somewhat soft finish needs to be protected with clear polyurethane or wax; surfaces other than raw wood should be primed
Ecofriendly Paints	Few or no VOCs; many brands also formulated without harmful chemicals	Among the brands are products for most interior applications	Because many pigments contain VOCs, some brands only available in lighter colors

WHAT IT DOES	WHAT IT'S GOOD FOR	THINGS TO CONSIDER

Artists' Acrylics

| Fine arts paints, water-based; intensely pigmented | Good for broken color effects when small amounts of a color are needed | Intense colors mean these paints need to be diluted for lighter tints |

Universal tints

| Not a paint; these are pigments used for adding color | Good for adjusting to a specific custom color | Pigments are quite intense; should be added to paint drop by drop |

Metallic pigments

| Available as powder; mix with other paints | Add the sheen of various metals to a paint medium | Handle carefully; wear mask and gloves |

Crackling Medium

| Clear product applied over a base coat, then overpainted with a second opaque layer; this product makes the second layer crack to an antiqued, alligatored finish | For creating an aged, distressed appearance on woodwork, furniture, and walls | Best for use with decorative trim, paneling, doors, or cabinet surfaces; more difficult to get great results on large expanses of wall |

Textured paints

| Usually acrylics; mixed with a textured medium – small acrylic beads or sand – to produce a visibly textured finish | Produces a look that imitates suede or other textured material | Difficult to remove; application usually requires more paint than ordinary opaque coatings |

Primers

| Creates a smooth surface to which new layers of paint can adhere | Needed when changing colors, especially dark to light, to prevent bleed-through; provides surface integrity for any paint job | Match primers and paints from same manufacturer; ask for advice when painting special surfaces: glass, metal, plastic, etc. These may require special primers |

getting the effects you want

	WHAT IT DOES	WHAT IT'S GOOD FOR	THINGS TO CONSIDER
SMOOTH COATINGS:			
Flat finish	Provides a velvet smooth, non-reflective coating; hides wall defects	Authentic finish for vintage colonial style rooms; good background for art	Difficult to clean; sponge marks and fingerprints may show; use in low-traffic areas
Eggshell	Minimally reflective surface; acceptable base coat for broken color finishes	Same applications as flat finish	Easier to clean than flat finishes
Satin or Pearl	Slightly reflective; often chosen for trim, moldings in flat-finished rooms; excellent base for broken color finishes	Trim or walls where easy cleaning and low shine are important	Easy to clean; smooth surface may reveal wall flaws; requires good wall prep
Semigloss	Durable, somewhat glossy finish; good for trim, doors, molding	Good finish for high-traffic areas, as well as bathrooms and kitchens, where cleaning is an issue	Good wall preparation is key; walls must be clean and smooth for best results
High-gloss	Very glossy and durable finish	Same applications as semi-gloss; use where high shine is desirable	Glossy paint shows every wall flaw; smooth wall essential for best results
Textured finishes	Depending on degree of texture, gives impression of suede, sand, or nubby fabric	Use where texture makes sense; for the look of aged or rough walls, or to duplicate textured fabric	Requires more paint than other smooth coatings for effective coverage; once applied, can be difficult and messy to remove

WHAT IT DOES	WHAT IT'S GOOD FOR	THINGS TO CONSIDER

WHAT IT DOES	WHAT IT'S GOOD FOR	THINGS TO CONSIDER
Gives appearance of light texture; easy to apply	A method to apply color at less-than-full intensity for a softer look in rooms	For a uniform look, use consistent stroke; for freer looks, vary the stroking technique

Stippling

Provides a light, dappled appearance	Delicate and elegant effect for translucent color, for whole rooms or room features such as molding and trim	Somewhat difficult; execute this effect with a partner

Sponging

Easy effect for applying multiple layers of translucent color	Whole room treatments anywhere in the home; or use as accent treatment on a single wall or feature	Easiest of the broken color finishes; for most delicate looks, must use fine, evenly pored sponges

Ragging On

Provides an appealing, random texture	Lovely look for walls in formal rooms	Fairly easy; needs a light touch in applying

Ragging Off

Provides a beautiful, complex, and delicate texture	As above	Somewhat difficult; execute this effect with a partner

getting the effects you want

	WHAT IT DOES	WHAT IT'S GOOD FOR	THINGS TO CONSIDER
BROKEN COLOR EFFECTS:			
Dragging			
	Striated effect; looks rich and elegant	Use for cabinets, molding, wainscoting. Straight lines difficult to apply on full length walls	Not too difficult when working small areas
Combing Techniques			
	Like dragging, combing provides a striated effect that can be worked in many patterns	A great look for informal rooms and country houses	As above; take care to keep combing tool clean between strokes, so pattern stays clear
Stenciling			
	Easy way to apply a repeat pattern to walls	Use anywhere; great as a border device, or as an allover pattern–like wallpaper	Very easy
Reverse Stenciling			
	Requires multiple templates of same design	Can provide very subtle patterning when colors close in tone are used	Easy

WHAT IT DOES	WHAT IT'S GOOD FOR	THINGS TO CONSIDER	

Crackling

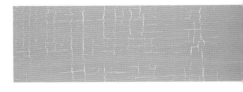

Provides the look of aged or distressed painted wood	Excellent for an antique look for small areas; doors, trim, cabinetry	Somewhat difficult as a total wall treatment; crackling will always create a random, not a uniform pattern

Marbling

The look of marble for the price of two or three cans of paint	Use anywhere marble is used; mantels, trim and woodwork, tabletops, etc. Whole marble walls are *only* for very luxurious environments	Somewhat difficult but a great deal of fun; practicing this technique is essential

Antiquing

Provides a softly aged look	Good for walls or details in period homes	Fairly easy technique

Parchment

Very beautiful and elegant wall finish	Superb for formal rooms	Somewhat difficult; technique requires lots of energy

Lace

Absolutely fabulous look of lace	Walls are difficult and the materials cost is somewhat high; use this technique for simpler projects – drawer fronts, tabletops	A great deal of work and quite expensive; must work with a partner for walls, and the results will be worth the effort

CHOOSING AND USING PAINT

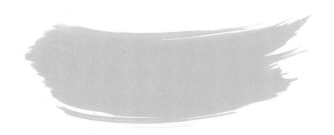

Welcome to the virtual paint aisle: In this section you can explore the different kinds of paint products — oil-based, water-based, specialty paints — their characteristics, and the types of projects best suited to their attributes.

▢ choosing the right paint

How to choose the right paint; examples of different applications on walls and in rooms.

▢ smooth coatings

Smooth applications, from matte walls that look like velvet to glossy, light-reflecting finishes.

▢ broken color effects

Techniques for manipulating paint, creating myriad impressions of light, pattern, and movement on walls by using a variety of special tools, techniques, and layers of color.

▢ tools of the trade

From brushes and rollers to gadgets, identifying the right equipment for the job.

▢ paint practice

The fine details of painting rooms: Tips from professional painting contractors make this chapter a must read for anyone striving for high-quality, long-lasting results.

CHAPTER ONE

Choosing the Right Paint

TODAY'S PAINT STORES OFFER SUCH A WIDE SELECTION OF PRODUCTS THAT COLOR BECOMES JUST ONE OF THE MAJOR DECISIONS TO BE MADE WHEN EMBARKING ON A PAINTING PROJECT. EVEN AFTER SELECTING THE TECHNIQUE — EITHER A SMOOTH OR A MANIPULATED FINAL FINISH — YOU MUST CHOOSE THE RIGHT PRODUCTS FOR EVERY LAYER.

The first choice is the carrier, or liquid base, of a paint product. Modern paints offer two choices for that portion of paint that makes it spreadable — oil or water. In general, whichever carrier is used for the first coat of paint will determine any and all layers that are applied on top of it. Water-base over water-base, oil-base over oil-base is the general rule, with few exceptions.

While almost infinite choice of color, texture, and overall effect of the final result is available from either oil- or water-based paint media, each has characteristics of application, drying time, ease of use, and environmental consequences that make this basic choice an important one.

In addition to the conventional choice between water-based latex and acrylic paints, and oil-based paints, there are other options in water-based products to meet environmental concerns or achieve a special decorative look. These are described later in the chapter.

water-based paints

▢ **LATEX**

Years ago, latex referred to a natural plant extract. It is now used to describe any of a number of mainly synthetic resins that maintain flexibility over time. The binders, which hold a latex, water-based paint to the painting surface, are made up of these synthetic resins, usually polyvinyl acetate, acrylic resins, or a combination of the two.

▢ **PURE ACRYLIC**

Pure acrylic paints are usually of higher quality and more expensive than other latex paints. The paint label will generally list ingredients, so read the label before buying.

▢ **LATEX ADVANTAGES:**

Constant improvements in paint technology have made water-based latex products the top-sellers in the paint aisle. They are easy to apply, and though they dry quickly, newer formulations eliminate brush marks in the glossier sheens, a problem with early latex paint. Many of these products have very little paint odor, and all clean up with soap and water, making them even more user-friendly.

▢ **LATEX DISADVANTAGES:**

On the downside, decorative painters warn that the quick drying time of latex products can wreak havoc with a broken color finish, since these paints may dry before a mistake can be corrected. However, there are several ways to diminish this disadvantage, covered later in this chapter.

oil-based paints

Oil-based paints have traditionally used a drying oil as their binder—the part that holds paint on a surface. While linseed, tung, or soy oils were the binders in early oil-based interior and exterior paints, these have been replaced in modern times with oils modified into a synthetic polymer, called an alkyd.

▢ **ALKYDS**

The alkyd resin is then dissolved into a petroleum-based solvent such as mineral spirits, which forms the liquid carrier of the oil-based paint. Thus alkyd has become a term that is generally synonymous with oil-based paint.

▢ **OIL-BASE ADVANTAGES:**

Oil-based paints have a long history of use by professional painters because of how smoothly they coat a surface and how long the finish endures. Their extended drying time allows brush marks to smooth out while the paint dries, and oil-based products cure to a desirably durable finish. When using oil-based products for manipulated, broken color finishes, the longer drying time (also known as "open" time) allows the decorative painter to correct mistakes before they dry, making the final finish less prone to flaws.

OIL-BASED ADVANTAGES:

While it is true that an oil-based finish makes a great looking wall covering, there are certain drawbacks to consider. Cleanup can be complex and messy, as equipment and spills must be cleaned with the appropriate solvent, usually mineral spirits or turpentine, both toxic (follow directions on the paint label regarding the appropriate cleaner.) Oil-based paints, made with petroleum-based solvent, have a long-lasting, sometimes noxious odor that requires excellent ventilation in any room where the paint is applied, until it dries. Prolonged exposure to these fumes is not advisable. Thus, children and pets (and you) will not be able to comfortably use a room while it is being primed, painted and/or decorated with a broken color finish executed in oil-based paints.

Second, the carrier in oil-based paint (petroleum-based solvent) is a volatile organic compound (VOC), which not only creates odors but also contributes to poor air quality indoors and outdoors. VOCs react with other pollutants to create ozone, contributing to a range of problems, including global warming.

OIL-BASED VS. LATEX

While these concerns may make the choice clear, bear in mind that a premium quality oil-base paint will not have to be applied as frequently as, for example, a bargain brand of latex paint. The premium oil finish may look beautiful for a decade or more, while the inexpensive latex brand keeps its good looks for three years or less. Water-based latex and acrylic paints contribute VOCs to the environment, though not in as great a quantity as oil paints, and using them every couple of years can add nearly as much ozone to the atmosphere as the once-a-decade application of oil finish. So, factor in the longevity of a paint finish in the final equation and decision.

other interior paints

Opaque oil-based and water-based latex and acrylic paints together represent a very high percentage of the paint market. Nonetheless, there remain many other types of coating with decorative interior applications. Some special effects require transparent glazing liquids, powdered pigments, and other less common materials; other products offer the consumer the opportunity to choose paint with very low toxicity and other ecofriendly attributes. Following is a roundup of these other varieties of paint.

▢ GLAZES
Liquid glazes, which come in all sheen levels and have a slippery texture, form the basic application medium for manipulated finishes. Glazes can be transparent, pre-tinted with pigments, or mixed by the decorative painter with paints or pigment powders. They can provide depth and luminosity to walls, as well as the decorative enhancement of applied effects. This decorative medium has become so popular that nearly every major paint manufacturer now offers a line of clear and colored glazes.

▢ OIL-BASED GLAZES
Oil-based glazes can be used with walls and surfaces base-coated with oil paint.

▢ WATER-BASED GLAZES
Water-based glazes are applied over water-based paint.

▢ GLAZE TIPS
Glazes differ from paint in that their drying time is quite short; when using them for walls, working quickly becomes an important part of the process, as unblended glaze on a wall can create unsightly lines in a painted effect. Decorative painters recommend that do-it-yourselfers work in tandem with a helper; one to apply glaze, one to work the effect. A bit of practice on a large piece of board can help perfect technique before the glaze is applied to large areas of wall. Some paint experts recommend using an extender product in the glaze to lengthen its "open" (drying) time.

▢ MILK PAINT
An age-old finish used by rural folk to add color to walls and furnishings, milk paint has enjoyed a recent comeback.

▢ MILK PAINT: BASICS
While the recipes may vary among milk paint manufacturers, the basic ingredients are casein (milk protein), lime, clay, and natural earth pigments. The paint is sold as a powder (once moistened with its carrier – ordinary water – it must be used quickly or the paint will sour).

▢ MILK PAINT: FINISH
Milk paint provides a warm, dead-flat finish with a slightly grainy appearance. Milk paint is an excellent choice for coating bare wood, as it needs no primer. On surfaces that have been previously finished, an acrylic additive can be mixed with the first coat; consult the manufacturer for additional advice on surface preparation.

▢ MILK PAINT DISADVANTAGES:
Milk paint does have one drawback; this natural, environmentally friendly product has no sealing qualities and is thus susceptible to water spotting and staining. It can be sealed with a coat of beeswax for an equally earth-friendly layer of protection, and many people with vintage homes or decor like the aged, distressed look of a worn finish. However, to preserve an unblemished appearance, the best protection is a topcoat of flat, clear acrylic finish.

ECOFRIENDLY PAINTS

Today, water-based paints are formulated with fewer volatile organic compounds (VOCs) than ever before; major manufacturers have also developed low- or no-VOC lines, driven by demand from health care facilities for paints that would not disrupt human traffic and habitation while they are being applied. Many small companies make paints with no or low VOCs, and they add to this feature a commitment to low or very minimally toxic ingredients. For those concerned about the environment, and people with special health concerns, these ecofriendly paints are worth investigating. Ask your paint dealer about major manufacturers' lines of low-VOC products; a listing of producers of ecofriendly paints can be found in the Resources section.

PAINT BOX

Getting a Consistent Metallic Look

SOME MANUFACTURERS NOW OFFER WALL PAINT WITH A LUMINOUS, METALLIC LOOK, ALTHOUGH MANY DO-IT-YOURSELFERS FIND IT DIFFICULT TO GET A PERFECT, SHIMMERING FINISH WITH THESE READY-MADE PAINTS.

TO IMPROVE SMOOTH COVERAGE AND FINISH MIX THE METALLIC PAINT WITH AN EQUAL QUANTITY OF OPAQUE PAINT IN A RELATED COLOR (GRAY WITH SILVER METALLIC, YELLOW WITH GOLD FINISHES).

ECOFRIENDLY: COLOR RANGE

Note, however, that since VOCs can be found in many commonly used colorants, many low-VOC paints from major producers are available only in light colors. The color ranges for each company differ, so request color charts and other information when consulting a local dealer or contacting these manufacturers.

ARTISTS' ACRYLICS

Sometimes only a small amount of a color is needed for a detail or decorative feature in a painting project, and less than a quart or pint of water-based paint is needed. Quarts are usually the smallest size available for major manufacturers' custom colors; stock colors are usually offered in pints. In this case, buy a tube of artists' acrylic paint. Since the paint colors are very intense, the color may be tinted with white, darkened with black, or toned down with a dab of its complement.

UNIVERSAL TINTS

These are the components used in the paint store to mix custom colors. Available in small bottles, the consumer may buy them for do-it-yourself tinting of paint. Keep in mind that universal tints cannot be used on their own (they are pigments, not paint); universal tints are also quite intense, so coloring your own paint should be a careful process, tinting drop by drop until the right color is achieved. Universal colorants can be used to tint both oil- and water-based paints.

METALLIC PIGMENTS

Metallic finishes can add drama or detail to a painted room. Create a metallic finish by mixing metallic powders—available for all the looks of metal, from chrome to gold—in the wall paint or glaze. The powders should be handled carefully; wear disposable gloves and a mask to protect skin and prevent inhalation of the powders; they are toxic.

CRACKLING MEDIUM

This water-based product creates an interesting, aged look when it is brushed on between two layers of paint or glaze, causing the top coat to crack and reveal the base coat. Do not use oil-based paint over this water-based medium.

primers

With few exceptions, walls and other surfaces require a coat of primer to promote a clean, smooth finish when the paint is applied. Use the manufacturer's recommended primer product for the best results. When painting in deep colors, a tinted primer coat is often recommended, though opinions vary as to whether this will affect the color of the final paint coating (some pros insist that a color primer will save additional coats of paint and not affect final appearance; others disagree.) For special surfaces – metal, plastic, painting over wallpaper, painting previously stained or waxed surfaces – your paint dealer can recommend an appropriate product.

paint quality

Not all paints are created equal; the quality of the final finish depends not only on the painter's skill, but also on the good chemistry and integrity of the coating. Browsing the paint store, it becomes apparent that paint is available at many price points, costing as little as ten dollars a gallon and as much as one hundred dollars. What is the meaning of such a discrepancy?

PIGMENTS AND COVERAGE

Quality ingredients are expensive, and the most expensive of these are the pigments used in paint formulation. Titanium dioxide is the portion of paint pigmentation that provides hiding power, and it is a costly substance. Good colorants also add to the price. Substituting inexpensive fillers for these ingredients brings down the cost of a can of paint, but the results can be disappointing, and worse, short-lived on the wall.

PREMIUM PAINTS

In the realm of super-premium paints (fifty dollars and more per gallon), complex approaches to color that use five, eight, or a dozen different pigments to create beautiful and luminous paint hues make up a big percentage of the purchase price. Full-spectrum coloring, as it is called, combined with the highest quality binders and, in the case of oil-based paints, superior grades of solvent, provide beautiful finished surfaces that will last far longer than ordinary bargain or mid-grade paints.

Of course, quick and inexpensive may be the road you finally choose. But consider that your time and effort are valuable commodities; for the best, longest-lasting results, use the finest paint your budget can manage.

CHAPTER TWO

Smooth Coatings

THE CLEAN LOOK OF A SMOOTH, UNBROKEN WALL FINISH HAS LONG BEEN THE MOST POPULAR

PAINT APPLICATION FOR INTERIORS. EVEN IF THE ROOM WILL BE DECORATED WITH ADDITIONAL

LAYERS OF MANIPULATED PAINT, A SMOOTH BASE OF A SINGLE COLOR COMPOSES THE UNDERLYING

WALL TREATMENT FOR MOST SPECIAL EFFECTS. Whatever final result a do-it-yourselfer wishes to

achieve, it becomes necessary to master the art of choosing and applying a smooth coat of paint.

To help readers decide on just the right smooth coat, this chapter explores and explains the

decorative benefits and the challenges of the many smooth looks of paint.

○ **SMOOTH COATINGS ADVANTAGES:**
Like a carpet, or coordinated window treatments, an unbroken expanse of colored wall becomes a distinctive feature that creates a mood, and at the same time functions as a unifying background for the furnishings and activity within a space. The right wall color can enliven and enhance a room's assets. A color that plays to a room's strengths, coordinating with its positive features – good light, spaciousness (or coziness), nice architectural detail – can positively affect the overall decorative impact and comfort level of a space.

○ **SMOOTH COATINGS DISADVANTAGES:**
Yet smooth coatings are demanding; with the exception of dead-flat paints, walls finished in layers of unbroken color must be thoroughly prepared, as any degree of gloss will reveal inherent flaws in the base surface. And, in spite of its effectiveness as a concealer, flat paint may be more difficult to clean and maintain than other coatings.

PAINT BOX

Base Coats for Broken Color Finishes

FLAT PAINTS ARE GOOD FOR MANY DECORATIVE APPLICATIONS, BUT DO NOT MAKE ACCEPTABLE BASE COATINGS FOR MANIPULATED LAYERS OF BROKEN COLOR FINISHES. WHEN APPLYING A **SMOOTH COATING AS A BASE COAT** FOR A MANIPULATED PAINT TECHNIQUE, USE A PAINT WITH SOME SHEEN. MANY DECORATIVE PAINTERS RECOMMEND SATIN (PEARL) AS AN UNDERCOAT.

---

what's in a paint?

All paints have three basic components.

- *Pigments* provide color and hiding power.
- *Binders* hold the pigment together, and provide the integrity and adhesion of the paint film.
- The *carrier* is the liquid that gives paint its consistency, so that pigment and binder can be applied to a surface.
- *Additives*. Many products also have additives, used to stabilize, thicken, defoam, or prevent the growth of bacteria in paint.

○ **SOLIDS AND SURFACE**
The pigment and binder are the components that remain on a surface when paint dries; together, they are the solids in paint.

○ **PIGMENT AND SHEEN**
Paint sheen – its degree of glossiness – is determined by the proportion of pigment to binder. High-gloss paints have a lower ratio of pigment to binder; matte finish paint has the highest proportion of pigment.

flat finish

Also called matte, flat paint has no shine and provides excellent coverage to most properly prepared surfaces. Because this coating does not reflect light, it conceals a multitude of flaws, so hairline cracks and dings seem to disappear. Many contractors like to paint new drywall with flat finish paint, since it does a good job of hiding taped drywall seams, and is easy to touch up.

◻ **FLAT FINISH: PAINT TYPES**
Matte finish paints can be oil- or water-based, and their formulas and consistencies vary with the manufacturer. In addition to latex and acrylic water-based paints, milk paint and other ecofriendly formulas also have a flat finish.

◻ **FLAT FINISH: COVERAGE AND QUALITY**
While every brand of flat-finish paint will provide a covering that looks smooth and hides wall defects, maintenance of these surfaces will vary according to each brand and its quality. Low-cost water-based paints do not clean up easily, often showing marks where a sponge has passed. The best quality, and thus the most expensive, flat-finish paints are the easiest to maintain.

◻ **FLAT FINISH: USES**
Because of maintenance issues, use flat-finish paints in low-traffic areas less susceptible to staining and spotting; flats are also the generally preferred finish for ceilings. Traditionally used in galleries and on theatre backdrops, flat finishes are highly desirable for wall finishes that serve as background for displaying art, sculpture, and textiles. Interior designers sometimes specify flat finishes for a room that is "busy" with furnishings, patterns, and accessories; the matte walls create an almost velvety, fabric-like canvas for the room.

◻ **FLAT FINISH: ANTIQUE LOOKS**
Matte-finished walls are also a natural treatment for antique homes, particularly old farmhouses and ancient cottages, which were originally decorated with flat-finish homemade paints made with earth pigments.

eggshell finish

Looking at paint chips finished with eggshell and matte paints side by side, it is often difficult to discern the difference. The very soft sheen of eggshell can usually be seen by holding the two chips at an angle and viewing them sideways, rather than straight on.

◻ **EGGSHELL FINISH: USES**
The low reflectivity of eggshell finish makes it desirable for the same uses as matte finish, with the additional benefit of easier maintenance. Most eggshell finish paints can be washed more satisfactorily than dead-flat finishes.

◻ **EGGSHELL FINISH: WEAR AND TEAR**
Nonetheless, this wall surface is still somewhat fragile; confine eggshell-finished surfaces to rooms where they will avoid constant wear and tear from errant fingerprints, moving furniture, and heavy traffic of people and pets. Because it does possess some very subtle sheen, eggshell can be used as a base coat for manipulated finishes.

satin finish

Satin finish paints have sufficient sheen to noticeably reflect the light in a room with a soft surface glow. Satin looks the way it sounds, a smooth covering for walls, like the gently shimmering fabric from which it gets its name.

◻ **SATIN FINISH: COVERAGE**
Because of its sheen, walls finished with satin paints require more preparation than flat or eggshell-finished walls. Light will detect flaws with uncanny precision, so walls must be adequately prepared; dents and cracks should be repaired, and bumps and lumps should be sanded smooth.

◻ **SATIN FINISH: USES**
Use a satin finish where increased light will enhance a space: in a dark hallway lit by wall sconces; in small rooms painted in deep colors, where lamplight can create a cozy feeling at night; in large, light spaces where the reflectivity will improve brightness, without glare. A satin finish provides the glow, without the shine.

◻ **SATIN FINISH: TRIM**
Satin finish can be used as a coating for trim when the walls are painted in flat or eggshell finish; satin's slight sheen will look marginally brighter than the walls when used in this way, thus accentuating details of molding and other woodwork.

semigloss finish

Quick cleanups and durability make semigloss paints a popular choice for high-
traffic and high-moisture areas. Available
in oil- and water-based products, a semigloss sheen provides a distinctly smooth
and reflective surface that is easy to
maintain.

☐ **SEMIGLOSS FINISH: SURFACE**
Repaired, sanded, and cleaned surfaces
create the base for a wall or trim treatment
in semigloss paint, as shiny surfaces will
accentuate flaws. While a finished semigloss treatment provides a delightfully
glowing surface and easy maintenance,
extra care in preparing the painting
base will ensure a beautiful, long lasting
paint job.

high-gloss finish

The hard, very shiny finish of high-gloss
paints makes them an excellent choice
wherever durability is a priority.

☐ **HIGH-GLOSS FINISH: USES**
Their high-polished look and easy maintenance make glossy enamels appropriate
for trim, doors, and cabinets, as all
of these surfaces get handled more
frequently than expanses of wall.

☐ **HIGH-GLOSS FINISH: SURFACE**
Applied to properly prepared, smooth
walls, a coating of high-gloss paint has a
glasslike surface. Use high-gloss products
on walls in places where their reflective
capability is desirable – dark rooms,
windowless hallways, and closets.

☐ **HIGH-GLOSS FINISH: PAINT TYPES**
High-gloss products are available in oil-
and water-based formulations. Because
of the sometimes noxious fumes, complicated cleanup, and longer drying times
of oil-based products, water-based gloss
paints are often preferred for interior
projects.

textured finishes

Paints premixed with ingredients that
provide texture – sand, for example – are
an easy way to create an interesting wall
finish with a coating that is applied in the
same manner as untextured smooth
paints.

☐ **TEXTURED PAINT: SURFACE**
Textured paints usually require two coats
for a smooth, seamless finish; for best
results, closely follow manufacturers'
instructions for application and drying
time between coats. Properly applied,
a textured paint will provide an interesting surface effect without manipulating
the paint.

☐ **TEXTURED PAINT: COVERAGE**
Because of the extra bulk of textured
paints, they will usually provide less
coverage per gallon than nontextured
products. Check the manufacturer's
spread rate, which is listed on the container, to gauge how many square feet
one gallon will cover, and figure paint
needs accordingly.

PAINT BOX

Enamel Paints

ENAMEL USED TO MEAN OIL-BASED
PAINTS WITH SHEEN. NOW, TO THE UNENDING
CONFUSION OF CONSUMERS, THIS WORD
REFERS TO ANY PAINT WITH SHEEN,
WHETHER WATER- OR OIL-BASED. THUS
ALL PAINTS WITH SHEEN, INCLUDING
EGGSHELL, CAN BE IDENTIFIED AS ENAMELS.

A Sheen by Any Other Name...

WHILE FLAT, EGGSHELL, SATIN, SEMIGLOSS,
AND HIGH-GLOSS ARE STANDARD NAMES
FOR THE VARYING SHEEN LEVELS OF
PAINT, SOME MANUFACTURERS OFFER
INTERMEDIATE SHEENS, OR CALL THEIR
PRODUCTS BY DIFFERENT NAMES. **GLOSS**
CAN SOMETIMES MEAN A SHEEN LEVEL
BETWEEN SEMIGLOSS AND HIGH-GLOSS.

PEARL CAN BE FOUND BETWEEN SATIN
AND SEMIGLOSS; IN SOME CASES, IT IS THE
NAME FOR THE WATER-BASED VERSION OF
SATIN. ASK THE PAINT DEALER FOR A CARD
OR CHIP SAMPLE THAT SHOWS PRODUCT
SHEEN LEVELS FOR A PARTICULAR MANU-
FACTURER BEFORE PURCHASING THE PAINT.

CHAPTER THREE

Broken Color Effects

THE TRANSFORMING POTENTIAL OF PAINT DOES NOT END WITH A CHOICE OF COLOR OR SHEEN.

BECAUSE OF ITS VISCOSITY, PAINT CAN EASILY BE MANIPULATED WITH A VARIETY OF TOOLS, FROM

CRUNCHED-UP PLASTIC BAGS TO GOOSE FEATHERS. Applied over a smooth base coat, these

manipulated layers are known as broken color effects. They offer the home painter the oppor-

tunity to add pattern, texture, and layers of color to the painted wall.

Like walls finished with wallpaper or fabric, walls treated with a broken color technique provide

an additional dimension to a scheme. Walls created with layers of *paint in motion* possess a

lively, vibrant quality that makes a powerful and memorable impression.

Some effects are quite easy for one person to apply and yield excellent results, even to beginners.

Other techniques need time and practice to master; the most complex ones require that two

people work together as a team.

Each technique in this chapter includes a general recipe, complete with a list of tools and

materials, as well as step-by-step instructions. Along with this technical guidance are some

ideas about the best uses for each method and helpful tips to make the process more effective

and successful.

colorwashing

An easy technique, colorwashing hides a multitude of sins; flaws in the base coat will disappear under the almost playful strokes with which the glaze is applied. Because the stroking technique is free, light, and somewhat random, use colorwashing in informal spaces—bedrooms, family rooms, and in homes decorated in a relaxed or rustic style. Aged plaster walls, or walls textured or distressed to achieve this effect, have an even more dramatic appearance when they are lightly colorwashed.

Practice this technique on a piece of board to discover the stroke and resulting effect that you find attractive and satisfying.

HOW TO COLORWASH

TOOLS:

- A wide (4" [10 cm]) brush for large expanses of wall
- A smaller (2" or 3" [5 cm or 8 cm]) brush for smaller spaces
- Small, clean paint can or coffee can

INGREDIENTS:

- A clean base coat in satin (pearl) or shinier
- Glaze for colorwashing (use oil- or water-based products; oil finishes will allow more time before the glaze dries.)

① Tape off and/or mask any areas that will not be painted; apply the base coat with a roller. Allow the paint to dry thoroughly.
② Thoroughly mix the glazing liquid; dip your brush in about a third of the way, knocking off any drips into the can.
③ Starting with an upper corner, work across and down the wall, applying the glaze in a dance-like movement of the brush. Use a crisscross, zigzag, or short, curvy stroke. Continue applying the glaze, redipping the brush as needed, until each wall is complete.

NOTE:

Glaze has a somewhat short working time; each manufacturer's product may be a little different. If the glaze has dried and there is a pronounced *stop point* or line in the colorwash application, you can paint over the mistake with the base color, allow it to dry, and colorwash again with the glaze.

stippling

Stippling glaze on a painted base creates an especially elegant effect; it looks wonderful applied to moldings, window trim, and cabinetry. This technique will subtly enhance either walls or trim in formal rooms full of luxurious fabrics and light-boned furnishings.

Stippling is a subtractive process; the glaze layer is stippled immediately after it is applied, which removes some of the glaze. Working quickly is a must for this technique, so work with a partner for best results. Using an oil-base coat and oil-glazing medium will give you more time to work.

HOW TO STIPPLE

TOOLS:

- A good stippling brush (use the largest brush you can comfortably handle, and invest in a brush of high quality. A large staining brush with lots of bouncy bristles can substitute, if a stippling tool cannot be found.)
- A small roller (4" [10 cm]) for applying glaze (use a roller sleeve with 1/2" [1 cm] nap)
- Rolling tray with disposable tray liner

INGREDIENTS:

- A clean base coat in satin (pearl) or shinier
- A glaze for stippling

You will need two people to complete this effect: one to roll the glaze on; one to stipple it off.

① Tape off and mask all areas adjacent to the surface being painted; apply the base coat with a roller; allow the paint to dry thoroughly.

② Work from top to bottom, and left to right; work quickly. The person applying glaze should load the small roller lightly, then roll it on from top to bottom; then the second person stipples the freshly rolled glaze.

③ To stipple, pounce the brush lightly – in a straight-on movement, not at an angle – against the glazed area, then remove the glaze taken up by the brush. (Either wear pants that you don't care about, or keep copious amounts of paper towels right next to you so that you can wipe off the stipple brush after each pounce.) The more you stipple an area, the more glaze will be removed, and the finer the finished effect will become.

④ Work with even pressure on the brush, at even speed. Complete a whole area (a full run of molding or baseboard, one wall, or an entire window frame) before stopping.

⑤ When doing whole walls, do opposite walls together with the corners of the adjoining walls taped off. After the first pair of walls dries, tape them off and do the second pair.

sponging

Sponging is the simplest of the broken color effects; using a natural sea sponge, the impressions made by its pores when patted on a clean base coat create the effect. Use paint over paint, or glaze over paint, or multiple layers of glazed, sponged effects.

Sponging can be casual and countrified, imitating the look of antique granite—and spongeware. It can be elegantly impressionistic, using several colors of glaze to create an abstract suggestion of a froth of blossoms. In general, large and irregular sponge pores create a more casual appearance; small, uniform pores look light and delicate, suitable for formal spaces.

HOW TO SPONGE

TOOLS:

- One or more natural sea sponges (If a uniform look is desired, examine sponges carefully and pick those with very similar pore size and configuration.)
- Paint tray with disposable tray liner

INGREDIENTS:

- A clean base coat
- Paint or glaze for sponging

1. Tape and mask off areas that will not be painted; apply base coat, and allow to dry thoroughly.
2. Rinse, then wring out the sponge very thoroughly, so it is just moist, not wet.
3. Pour about 1/2" (1 cm) of paint or glaze into paint tray; dip sponge into the paint or glaze lightly, as if you were dipping strawberries into sugar.
4. Blot the sponge lightly on a paper towel or paper plate; then pat it very lightly on the wall. Do not press the sponge to the wall; a light touch gives a more defined impression.
5. Continue sponging in this fashion, remembering to keep the sponge's pores free of paint fragments (examine the sponge frequently and pick off any bits of dried paint.) Continue to keep the sponge lightly moist.
6. Sponging with glaze will produce a translucent pattern; using paint provides an opaque impression. Translucent glaze also combines with the opaque color beneath it; thus the combination of a yellow base with an applied blue glaze sponge pattern will produce green where the two colors overlap. This mixing does not take place when sponging a painted effect with opaque paint.
7. To sponge into corners, try this tip. Instead of using a small version of the sponge used on the walls, use an old paintbrush with splayed bristles. Lightly dip the ends of the bristles into the paint, blot on a paper towel, then touch the brush into the corners with the same light, bouncing motion you use with the sponge.

ragging on/off

Bunched-up rags or plastic bags make wonderful tools for ragging paint or glaze on or off a smooth base coat; the random folds create lively abstract patterns in the paint. Depending upon the material used, the tightness/closeness of the creasing, and the color combination, you can create an infinite number of looks, from soft and casual to restrained and formal.

Ragging on consists of applying paint or glaze to a base coat; ragging off is the process of removing portions of a smooth glaze overcoat by taking up portions of the glaze with crumpled fabric or plastic. Since application techniques are always simpler than subtractive methods, where applied products must be removed, ragging on is easier for the beginner. Like stippling, ragging off is best accomplished with a partner.

HOW TO RAG ON

TOOLS:

- Old, lint free rags, cut up into 20" (51 cm) squares (these can be purchased at paint stores by the box; or, cut up old sheets, or cotton T-shirts.)
- Paint tray and disposable tray liner

INGREDIENTS:

- Good base coat, satin (pearl) or shinier
- Glaze for ragging on

① After taping and masking off areas that will not be painted, apply smooth base coat and allow to dry thoroughly.
② To make the ragging tool, scrunch up the rag to the size and shape of a shower pouf; make sure this ball has ridges that will add interest to the ragged effect.
③ Dip the ragging pouf lightly into the paint; blot it on a paper plate or towel so that it isn't drippy.
④ Pounce the ragging pouf *lightly* on the wall. Continue dipping, blotting, and pouncing. This is a randomly patterned effect, so it's all right to go over an area that has already been pounced.
⑤ Retouching this effect is easy. Simply paint over the area you don't like with the base coat, and reapply glaze with the ragging pouf.

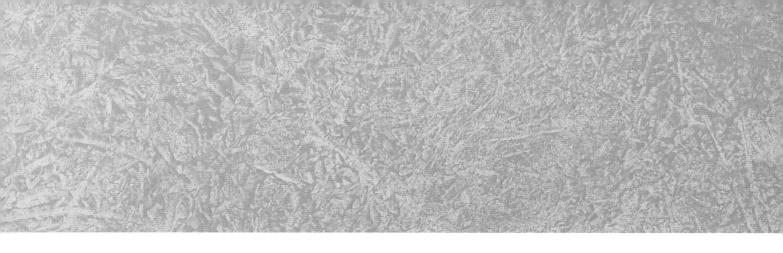

HOW TO RAG OFF

TOOLS:

- A quantity of thin plastic bags (the type used to cover clean clothes at the dry cleaner's is best for fine looks; plastic supermarket or department store bags create a looser appearance.)
- Roller and sleeve with 1/2" (1 cm) nap
- Roller tray and disposable tray liner

INGREDIENTS:

- Good base coat in satin (pearl) or shinier
- Glaze for ragging off (oil-based glaze is best because of its longer working time.)

1. Tape off and mask areas that will not be painted; apply base coat and allow to dry thoroughly.
2. This effect needs to be done quickly, to keep ahead of drying glaze. As with stippling, work with a partner. One person rolls on the glaze evenly with a lightly loaded roller; the other uses the bunched-up plastic bag to remove glaze; as with most broken color effects, a light touch creates the clearest impression, too much pressure creates smears.
3. After removing glaze, blot it up on a paper towel; when the bag begins to have little bits of glaze start to dry on its surface, discard it and take another clean bag.
4. Keep moving, and keep the pattern connected so there are no lines or blank spaces on the wall. Make sure to work all the glaze as you go, so no large blank spots develop on the wall.

PAINT BOX

Rules for Painting Any Broken Color Effect

KENDALL KLINGBEIL, THE ARTIST WHO PAINTED ALL OF THE EFFECTS IN THIS CHAPTER, OFFERS SEVERAL HARD-AND-FAST RULES FOR GETTING THE BEST RESULTS WHEN PAINTING SPECIAL EFFECTS:

- ALWAYS HAVE LOTS OF PAPER TOWELS ON HAND. USE THE SLIGHTLY MORE EXPENSIVE, CLOTHLIKE BRANDS. THEY WORK BETTER.

- BUY A LITTLE BOX OF LATEX GLOVES (UNLESS YOU ARE ALLERGIC TO THIS SUBSTANCE) TO PROTECT YOUR HANDS WHEN PAINTING, ELIMINATING THE NEED FOR FREQUENT WASHING AND VERY DRY SKIN.

- PRACTICE THE CHOSEN EFFECT ON A PIECE OF BOARD BEFORE APPLYING IT TO THE WALL. IN THIS WAY, YOU CAN CHECK THE COLOR AND TECHNIQUE BEFORE COMMITTING TIME AND ENERGY TO A WHOLE-ROOM PROJECT.

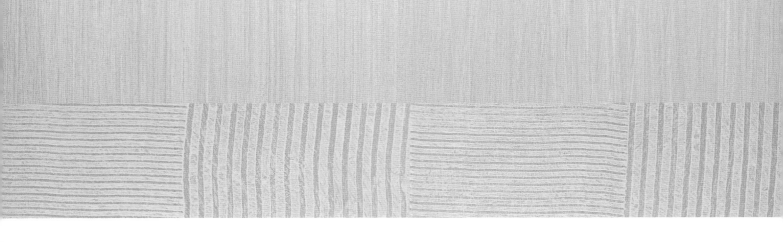

dragging/combing

Similar to a graining effect, a dragging brush or combing tool is pulled through a layer of glaze that has been applied over a smooth base coat.

This action creates a pattern of lines that can be elegant – dragged moldings, cabinets, doors and furniture look very rich – or countrified and casual, depending on the tool used.

Since dragging is done top to bottom or left to right with a stiff-bristled dragging brush, a steady hand is needed to keep the lines going straight.

Dragging and combing are subtractive processes by which glaze is removed with the painting tool, so unless the area being dragged or combed is small and manageable for one person, work with a partner.

HOW TO DRAG/COMB

TOOLS:
- Dragging brush or combing tool
- Roller and sleeve with 1/2" (1 cm) nap
- Paint tray with disposable tray liner

INGREDIENTS:
- Good base coat with satin (pearl) or shinier paint
- Glaze for dragging (oil base has longer working time)

① Tape and mask off areas not being painted; apply smooth base coat and allow to dry thoroughly.

② Working alone or with a partner, roll on glaze, and immediately draw the dragging brush or the combing tool through the glaze in the desired pattern. After drawing the brush or tool through the glaze, wipe off the tool before dragging again; this prevents excess glaze from building up and making fuzzy, unattractive lines in the paint. When painting cabinets, molding, or furniture, paint in the direction of the wood grain.

③ Be careful of your pressure with the tool at the beginning and end of a dragging or combing line; excessive pressure can cause blurry lines. You may want to practice this technique a few times on sample boards before trying it on a wall or piece of furniture.

stenciling

This is another easy effect, achieved by application rather than subtraction.

While there are hundreds of precut stencils available from commercial manufacturers, making your own is very easy and satisfying. Copy a motif from a favorite fabric, an historical border, even elements of one of your child's drawings, and transform it into a stenciled effect that has personal meaning.

Stencils may be applied with brushes or sponges; the sponged look is a good way to get a subtle stencil image. Because glazes are a bit more slippery than paint, they are not an appropriate medium for filling in a stencil. Use latex or acrylic paint.

MAKE YOUR OWN STENCIL

TOOLS:

- A photocopy or freehand outline of an image you want to use for the stencil; enlarge or reduce the image to the desired size.
- A sheet of clear Mylar or Denril (sold in pads at crafts stores)
- Razor blades, a utility knife, or (best) a stencil burner or woodburning tool with a very fine point
- A fine point marking pen

① Placing the photocopy or freehand outline of your stencil design under a sheet of Mylar or Denril, trace the pattern onto the plastic or, if you are confident with the stencil burner or other cutting tool, simply cut the plastic sheeting along the lines of the pattern, then remove the cutouts. Make multiple copies if a large number of repeats will be needed.

② Stencils can be used for the regular stenciling process; cutouts may be used for reverse stenciling. Both Mylar and Denril are fairly thin, so it should be possible to cut more than one stencil at a time.

NOTE:

When using a stencil burner or cutting tool, work on a fireproof cutting board or a piece of tempered glass.

TO STENCIL

① You will need the stencil, paint, and a tool (brush or sponge) to apply the paint. Choose colors that complement the base; a stencil base can be a smooth coating or a broken color effect. Apply the stencil as a ceiling, wainscot or baseboard border, or as an all-over pattern, like wallpaper.

② If the stencil is compact, just hold it in place while painting over the opening for the design; large or complex designs will need to be positioned with light tack masking tape or repositionable spray adhesive.

TO REVERSE STENCIL

Decide on a motif – leaves, flowers, geometric shapes – and make as many cutouts of these as needed to execute the pattern. Then stick the cutouts in place on a dry, base-coated wall with spray removable adhesive. Paint any applied broken color effect – sponging, stippling, color-washing. Apply the paint right over the cutouts.

When the effect has dried, remove the cutouts, and their pattern will stand out from the broken color effect. This technique looks subtle and lovely when base and broken color hues are closely related.

crackling

Crackling duplicates the alligatored appearance of wood that has layers of paint, cracked from years of repeated exposure to heat, light, and moisture. The aged, distressed appearance of this effect makes it a good choice for country, or colonial, style interiors.

Because crackling medium initiates a chemical process that cannot be controlled, it is somewhat different from other broken color effects. Most home painters will not want to use this product on an entire wall, but crackled moldings, window trim, cabinetry, and shelving can give the patina of age to a room.

HOW TO CRACKLE

TOOLS:

- Bristle brush, sponge brush, or roller

INGREDIENTS:

- Base-coated surface
- Crackling medium
- Latex paint for top layer to be crackled

There is no need to repaint a surface being crackled, as long as the color is satisfactory for an undercoat, and the surface is clean and free of serious flaws.

① Tape off and mask any areas that will not be crackled.
② Using a brush, roller, or sponge brush, coat the painted base with crackling medium and allow it to dry; follow manufacturer's instructions. The thicker the application of crackling medium, the more the top layer of paint will crack.
③ Paint the top layer of paint over the crackling medium, and wait.

Cracks will appear as the paint dries, revealing the undercoat and giving the surface a colorful, aged appearance.

marbling

Imitating the look of marble is a great effect wherever marble is logically used in a home – mantels, trim, tabletops. Painting marble on whole walls is not only difficult but looks out of place, except in the most glamorous and luxurious interiors. While it is a somewhat complicated technique, using marbling in a small area makes it easier for one person to complete successfully.

HOW TO MARBLE

Use water-base products for this effect so that there will be less waiting time between layers of paint.

TOOLS:

- Stippling brush
- Rags for ragging on
- Feathers to apply accents (goose or other large bird feathers work well; can be purchased at craft supply stores)

INGREDIENTS:

- A clean, smooth base coat in the appropriate background color (use a piece of real marble as a palette guide, or create your own fantasy marble from favorite colors)
- Three or more shades and tints of latex glazing liquid

① Tape or mask the area the will not be painted; apply base coat and allow to dry thoroughly.

② Apply glaze using a rag on, or rag off over stipple technique to get the cloudy, layered effect that can be seen in marble's surface. Let this layer dry.

③ Apply an additional layer of ragged-on glaze in another color; push it around the surface to imitate the random patterns. Allow this layer to dry.

④ To apply the fine vein lines seen in real marble, dip the edge of a feather in the glaze; it will create a filmy line on the surface. Move the painted feather around and it will create a very natural pattern.

⑤ You may want to experiment with marbling on a practice board before attempting a larger project.

parchment

This is a somewhat advanced applied effect; it is a great technique to use for the look of translucent clouds in the sky. It is an all-paint effect; water-base products will work just fine.

GETTING THE LOOK OF PARCHMENT

TOOLS:

- An old, soft, angled paintbrush works best for this effect

INGREDIENTS:

- Use two closely related tints or shades of latex paint.

1. Use a blend of the two colors to paint the smooth base coat; allow paint to dry thoroughly.
2. Using the first color, dip the brush into the paint, blot, then press the brush onto the wall with small, circular back-and-forth motions. Work from upper left corner of the wall, across and down.
3. With the second color, repeat the motion, using the same stroke as step 2 and working next to and around the previous strokes.
4. Step back frequently to be sure the effect is not spotty.
5. Do one wall at a time, without stopping, so that the look is consistent. This is a physically demanding, energetic painted effect; don't attempt it if you tire easily.

Parchment walls are an extremely elegant look for a foyer, living room, or master bedroom.

lace effects

Use widths of real lace as reverse stencils to create this fabulous look. It is somewhat costly because of the fabric, but it will make a gorgeous treatment for the wall above a chair rail in a dining room. If you want to moderate the cost, use the look of lace as an accent treatment, on door panels, drawer fronts, or tabletops.

Do not attempt to create lace effects on a wall without help, which you will need to attach the lace to the wall (once spray adhesive goes on, it can stick to itself, or you!)

TOOLS:

- Scissors
- Tape
- Measuring tape

INGREDIENTS:

- A clean, dry base coat
- Sufficient yardage of lace to cover the entire wall area to be treated with a lace effect
- Removable spray adhesive
- Spray paint for reverse stenciling
- Protective clothing (hat, gloves, mask, eye gear)

① Remove the selvage of the lace fabric; then lay out the pattern as you want it to appear on the wall. You may want to tack up the lace to test the look before you stick the fabric down for painting.

② Working with a partner, spray the back of the lace with spray adhesive. Stick lace to the wall from top to bottom, working from the top center out, up, and down, smoothing as you go, until the lace is laid out in the desired pattern.

③ Do not neglect this step! Spray paint casts tiny drops a good distance. Make sure that everything in the room is covered, and block off the doorways to adjoining rooms.

④ Before spray painting the lace, don protective gear so that paint doesn't get into eyes or on skin.

⑤ Spray paint the lace thoroughly; read and follow manufacturers instructions for drying time. When paint is dry, remove the lace.

NOTE:

While painting a whole wall is expensive and a rather difficult procedure, use this idea to create some easier effects. For example, using lace doilies cut in half and positioned along a ceiling, then stencil painted, will create a delightful scalloped lace border for a little girl's or a guest bedroom.

CHAPTER FOUR

Tools of the Trade

PAINTING ROOMS REQUIRES MANY DECISIONS, BUT SOME THINGS ARE INDISPENSABLE: TO GET

GREAT-LOOKING RESULTS, YOU MUST HAVE THE RIGHT EQUIPMENT. A good place to find out

what you need is the tool kit that a professional painting contractor brings to the job. Take

a look at what's inside:

painting prep equipment

○ **BASICS**

A DROP CLOTH covers furnishings, rugs, and anything within a room that won't be painted. Use plastic sheets (1 or 2 mils. thick is fine) to cover furnishings; these are available in various sizes, depending on the coverage needed. Invest in a canvas drop cloth for covering floors as you work, particularly if more than one room will be painted; the canvas is sturdier and less slippery than plastic.

AN ALUMINUM-SHADED CLAMP LIGHT with a 100-watt bulb, and a heavy-duty EXTENSION CORD provide the power to illuminate surfaces for smooth wall preparation and thorough paint coverage.

A four- or five-foot (1.2 or 1.5 meter) STEPLADDER will be needed for ceilings eight feet (2.4 meter) or higher. For lower ceilings, a two-foot (0.6 meter) stepladder is easier to move around.

○ **SMALL PREP TOOLS**

Use flathead and Phillips head SCREWDRIVERS to remove switch and outlet plates and loosen overhead and wall light bases and other hardware from the surfaces that will be painted.

One or more PUTTY KNIVES smooth areas repaired with joint compound or other patching material. These tools are also useful for scraping peeling paint; they come in sizes from one inch wide to more than six inches wide. Wider versions are known as tape knives.

A WIRE BRUSH is good for sweeping away peeling paint from moldings, trim, and around windows. These come in a variety of shapes and sizes.

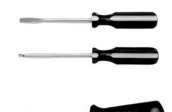

A UTILITY KNIFE or SCISSORS should be on hand for various cutting chores.

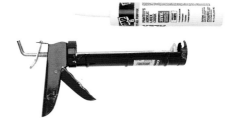

wall prep materials

DRYWALL TAPE is used to join pieces of gypsum wallboard when they are installed. It's also a great product for covering cracks and small holes in the wall surface.

Many painting contractors recommend JOINT COMPOUND for creating a skim coat to smooth over a deteriorated wall, and for patching holes and cracks. They find that premixed joint compound is easier to use than other patching products, such as Spackle, plaster of paris, plaster, or drywall compound.

Buy SANDPAPER in several grit sizes for various smoothing chores. Coarse sandpaper has a grit size of 20-60; medium is 80-150; and fine grit paper is 150 or higher. Sandpaper is available in inexpensive sheets; use lightweight paper for curved surfaces, heavier weight for flat surfaces. For easier handling, spend a bit more and buy sandpaper in sponge or block form.

CAULK is used for filling joints; it can close the gap between sections of molding or baseboard and the wall. Apply it with a CAULKING GUN; follow manufacturer's instructions for using this tool; you may want to practice the technique before using the caulking gun for your paint project.

FOR SAFETY

Clear plastic SAFETY GOGGLES protect eyes from dust and grit, especially when working on overhead areas. A DUST MASK will prevent inhalation of plaster dust and other airborne particles produced during wall preparation.

Other protective gear includes a PAINTER'S HAT, to keep dust, peeled paint, and liquid paint away from hair. Rather than letting paint touch skin, wear DISPOSABLE GLOVES when working with paint prep products and the paints themselves. Wear old clothing when prepping and painting; if you plan to paint a number of rooms, invest in a pair of painter's pants.

painting equipment

Once the walls have been prepared for painting, assemble the tools for applying paint:

☐ **ROLLING TOOLS**

Rolling paint is the fastest way to cover a wall, particularly for a smooth, unbroken finish. To accomplish this, buy a good metal ROLLER TRAY that holds the paint; roller tray liners made of plastic eliminate the necessity for heavy cleanup between paint colors. Just dispose of the used liner and pop in a new one for the new color. To spread the paint, select a good quality, sturdy ROLLER FRAME and the appropriate sleeves for the job. ROLLER SLEEVES (also called roller covers) come in a variety of naps, from short to long. Use the wall surface being covered as the guide to nap length; the smoother the wall surface, the shorter the nap. Synthetic roller sleeves, made of polyester, Dynel, or other manmade fibers, are used with water-based paints. Sleeves made of natural fiber, such as mohair or lamb's wool, are used with oil-based paints. Quality sleeves have thick, dense nap to promote good paint coverage.

For roller-painting ceilings, buy an extension handle for the roller frame; these are available in three- to five-foot (0.9 to 1.5 meter) lengths. The extension handle can also provide additional leverage when running the roller across a surface.

brushes

Rollers are a good choice for large, flat areas, but BRUSHES are desirable for places that are not easily rolled: corners, edges, molding, and carved or detailed woodwork. Use brushes with synthetic bristles (nylon or polyester) for water-based products, and brushes with natural bristles for oil-based paints. For brushing paint on broad, flat surfaces, a brush three or more inches wide is desirable; choose one that fits your hand comfortably. For trim and cutting in paint to corners and edges, brushes one to two inches wide with an angled end are often preferred to make this job easier and neater. Some interior painters prefer to use a round sash brush for window trim and small pieces of molding.

When choosing brushes, go for quality. Though premium brushes can be expensive, they will last a long time if properly cleaned and stored (see Paint Practice for cleanup tips.) Before buying a brush, check to see that bristles are secure within the ferrule, the metal band that wraps around them. Brushes with split-bristled, tapered ends hold paint better and ease smooth application. Ruffle through the bristle end with a thumb, and give bristles a slight tug; bristles falling out of a new brush are a sign of poor quality, and stray bristles can ruin a smooth paint job.

PAINTING PADS can be used for covering hard-to-paint places such as the spaces behind pipes, bathroom fixtures, or radiators. Some pads are equipped with angled handles for reaching into tight crevices with the pad.

○ **FOR ANY PAINT JOB**
Spills happen. Always have on hand a good supply of PAPER TOWELS and CLEAN RAGS. Keep a household sponge and a BUCKET OF CLEAN WATER on the job site during prep and painting; have the appropriate cleaner for oil-based paints (usually mineral spirits or turpentine; check instructions on

the paint label) for cleaning equipment. Since oil-based paints are more difficult to remove from equipment, invest in a brush spinner for the task of keeping the natural bristle brushes used with oils in top condition. Don't forget to pick up a handful of PAINT STIRRING STICKS; retailers usually provide them free of charge.

PAINTER'S TAPE may look like masking tape, but the right product for masking off areas that will not be painted is a light tack product that does not leave its adhesive residue behind. Talk to the paint retailer about the various tapes; one variety of blue tape can be left in place for days and will still be easy to remove. MASKING PAPER, sold in rolls of varying widths, can be used to protect larger areas that will not be painted.

specialized painting tools

Broken color and other special painted effects require specific tools for achieving their distinctive looks. While everything from bunched-up plastic bags to a feather duster can be used to create visual effects in a wet paint medium, these are the tools to create the most popular looks:

SPONGING

For applying this decorative effect, NATURAL SPONGES make the best applicators. There are several types of natural sponge, with different pore configurations; some varieties have regularly spaced, even pores, while other sponge surfaces have an irregular combination of large and small pores. Choose a large sponge for the wall, and a smaller sponge of the same variety and pore type for working into corners and tight spots.

CHAPTER FIVE

Paint Practice

AFTER GATHERING PAINT AND MATERIALS AND SELECTING A COLOR AND TECHNIQUE, THE TIME TO

PAINT HAS ARRIVED. This chapter helps organize an approach to room painting to provide great

results, with ideas culled from many painting contractors and decorative painters who have long

experience in painting practice.

testing color

Nearly every wall needs some preparation before applying paint; repairs and priming are key to the final appearance, and this chapter walks you through the steps for setting up a great base for any paint project. Nonetheless, the time and effort needed for prep work can be trying for do-it-yourselfers who are impatient to see color on the walls. A tiny manufacturer's chip—or even a four by eight (10 cm by 20 cm) sample card—can only provide a hint of how the color will look when painted on the wall. It is a much better strategy to have a little fun and try the color and technique before buying!

COLOR PREVIEW

To serve the very human need for instant gratification, the time before the furniture is moved, drop cloths are draped, and equipment is organized is the perfect occasion to give yourself a preview of the color and technique you have chosen.

TEST SAMPLES

The first step in a great-looking paint job is to create a sample of the smooth or broken color application, and test it in the room you plan to paint. Before purchasing all the paint needed, buy a small sample of the product or products that will be used. The smallest size some manufacturers make for custom color may be a quart, but this experiment may save much more in money and time spent applying several gallons of the wrong custom color!

TEST BOARD

Using a piece of poster board or foam core about eighteen inches by twenty-four inches (46 cm by 61 cm), paint the color directly on the board, using the technique that will be applied to the walls. Once the color is dry, take a day or two to live with the color; see how it looks at different times of day, bathed in the natural and artificial light that normally illuminates the room.

CHECKING THE HUE

Move the board around; place it in a doorway and approach it from another room or area of the house, to see how the new hue works with visible colors in adjacent rooms. With this experiment, using a sample while the furnishings are in place, it becomes much easier to see whether or not the color and application are right for the space.

PAINT BOX

Testing Your Colors

WHEN USING SEVERAL COLORS, PAINT ONE BOARD IN EACH COLOR TO BE USED IN THE ROOM, AND POSITION THE BOARDS WHERE THE COLOR WILL BE PAINTED. **A DESIGNER'S TRICK FOR JUDGING** THE BALANCE BETWEEN COLORS IS TO CREATE THE BOARDS IN PROPORTION TO THE AMOUNT OF SURFACE THEY WILL COVER.

THUS, A SAMPLE BOARD OF **TRIM COLOR** THAT REPRESENTS ABOUT TWENTY-FIVE PERCENT OF THE SPACE IN THE ROOM SHOULD BE ONLY ONE-QUARTER OF THE TOTAL SIZE OF THE SAMPLE BOARDS— WHEN THE TWO BOARDS ARE PLACED SIDE BY SIDE, IT BECOMES EASIER TO SEE HOW THEY WILL ULTIMATELY WORK TOGETHER.

prepping the room

Once color and technique are decided, take these steps to get ready to prime and paint.

◻ **WALLS**

- Before moving any furniture, appraise the walls in bright light; use sticky notes or pencil marks to indicate wall flaws that will need special prepping with sanding or joint compound. A clamp light with an aluminum shade provides strong illumination to make this task simpler. This step is particularly important when the final finish needs to be smooth and glossy; once the paint is on the walls, the flaws will ruin an otherwise great paint job.

◻ **SET-UP**

- Remove all fragile knick-knacks, place remaining furniture in the center of the room, and roll up area rugs. Cover furniture with a plastic drop cloth; if you have one, use a canvas drop cloth for the floor. Otherwise use a thick plastic one or large sheets of brown paper.

◻ **SWITCH PLATES**

- Remove the decorative plates that cover switches and wall outlets; loosen light fixtures and protect them with masking paper (or cover with plastic or paper bags).

◻ **TOOLS**

- Gather all prep tools and put them on a table (protect the table first with a drop cloth or a piece of flattened corrugated box); the table can be the central base of operations, so tools don't get lost. Or put everything together in one central spot on the floor. Don't forget to watch your step!

preparing surfaces

If walls are new or fairly smooth, the prepping should go quickly. Loose paint or plaster can be removed with a putty or tape knife. Screw holes or taped seams should be filled with joint compound or other repair medium. Once the filler dries (follow directions for drying time carefully),

the surface can be sanded smooth. Unless rough, distressed walls are desirable for the final finish, remember that a smooth base is a must for achieving a polished paint job.

◻ **COMMON REPAIRS**

Attend to nicks, dents, cracks, and spaces between walls and molding; these problems constitute the major repairs before painting walls.

◻ **FILL GAPS**

After scraping loose paint or removing flakes of plaster, the next step is to fill in any gaps and indentations with the chosen compound — plaster, joint compound, and drywall compound, plaster of paris, or Spackle. Apply the selected product with a putty or tape knife; wipe the knife clean between each pass on the wall surface, and the work will progress more quickly.

◻ **CAULK CRACKS**

For spaces between walls and trim or baseboards, caulk may be preferable to other repair media, as it can be applied with a caulking gun to fill in these narrow spaces, and the excess wiped away with a sponge.

◻ **SAND SURFACES**

Always follow manufacturer's instructions for drying time of any repair compounds. Once all repaired surfaces are thoroughly dried, they may be sanded smooth. Give plenty of attention to smoothing window trim and moldings; since these surfaces are often painted in flaw-revealing, glossy paints, extra care will ensure the best result.

PAINT BOX

Lighten Your Load

FULL PAINT CANS ARE HEAVY! USE EMPTY PAINT BUCKETS OR CLEAN COFFEE CANS FOR HOLDING PAINT WHEN WORKING ON THE CEILING, TRIM, OR MOLDINGS; POUR A SMALL QUANTITY FROM THE LARGE CAN INTO THE BUCKET OR COFFEE CAN.

○ **CLEANING UP**

Prep work can leave behind a residue of dust over the wall surface; before applying primer or paint, do not neglect to clean all the prepared surfaces. Vacuum the walls, clean them with a tack cloth, or wash them so that no residue remains. Be sure all surfaces are thoroughly dry before priming or painting.

applying color

Now comes the fun part: applying the colors and techniques you have chosen to enliven your rooms. Though it may be difficult to contain your excitement, remember that you have given this decorating process much time and thought; it will be worth your time if you execute your plan carefully.

○ **PRIMING**

With the exception of raw wood to which milk paint is being applied, most surfaces will need a priming coat to help the smooth base coat of color adhere to the surface and dry to perfection. Nearly every manufacturer makes primers that pair with their paints for good adhesion and successful results.

PAINT BOX

Cleaning Sleeves and "Cutting In"

BEFORE PAINTING AND PRIMING, CLEAN THE ROLLER SLEEVES, WHICH MAY CONTAIN LOOSE FUZZ THAT CAN STICK TO THE PAINTED SURFACE AND WREAK HAVOC WITH THE PAINT JOB. **CLEAN SLEEVES FOR WATER-BASED PAINT WITH WATER**; SLEEVES **FOR OIL-BASED PAINTS** CAN BE CLEANED WITH THE APPROPRIATE **SOLVENT** (USUALLY MINERAL SPIRITS).

BEFORE ROLLING THE MAJOR PORTION OF CEILINGS, **DO THE BRUSHWORK FIRST.** PROFESSIONALS CALL THIS "CUTTING IN," WHICH MEANS TACKLING THE AREAS THAT THE ROLLER SLEEVE CANNOT COMFORTABLY REACH—**THE CEILING EDGE**, AND THE AREA AROUND DETAILS SUCH AS **LIGHT FIXTURES** OR **CEILING MOLDINGS** AND **DECORATIONS** IN RELIEF. IF THE ROOM HAS BEEN PREPARED, THE LIGHT FIXTURE BASE SHOULD BE REMOVED FROM THE CEILING, OR MASKED SO THAT PAINT WILL NOT SPLATTER.

Using a Paintbrush

MANY PROS RECOMMEND GRASPING THE BRUSH BY THE METAL FERRULE, FOR BETTER CONTROL. **DIP THE BRUSH** ABOUT ONE-THIRD TO HALFWAY UP THE LENGTH OF THE BRISTLES, **TAPPING THE BRUSH** AGAINST THE CONTAINER TO ALLOW THE DRIPS TO FALL BACK INSIDE, FOR CLEANER APPLICATION.

BRUSH A THREE- TO FOUR-INCH (8 OR 10 CM) BAND AROUND THE **CEILING EDGE** AND AROUND **FIXTURES.** THEN YOU WILL BE READY TO ROLL THE CEILING.

- **OIL-BASED VS. WATER-BASED PRIMERS**
  In general, oil primers should be used with oil-based paints, and water-based primers applied as the undercoat for latex and acrylic paint products.

- **PRIMER AND SURFACE**
  Different primers prepare different surfaces; special priming products exist for every kind. For your painting project, consult the paint manufacturer's instructions, and the paint dealer, to get the right priming product for the job. As with all paints, adhere carefully to the specified drying times for primers; coating a still-damp, primed wall with paint can cause all kinds of problems.

- **PAINTING CEILINGS**
  Because ceiling drips can do damage to the rest of the room, be sure that all areas below the ceiling are covered with drop cloths or masked. Don't forget the tops of doors, interior shutters, or wall-mounted fixtures.

- **ROLLER WORK**
  Roller work should proceed in roughly three-foot by three-foot (0.9 by 0.9 meter) areas for the best coverage. Starting from one corner, mentally divide your ceiling space into segments of this size, working back and forth across the room. After thoroughly stirring the paint, and using a liner in the roller tray, pour paint from the can into the tray, to a depth of about an inch (3 cm) in the deep section of the tray. Fill the roller sleeve with paint and roll it back and forth in the tray so it is fully coated but not drippy.

HOW TO ROLL

First, roll the paint in a rough "W" across the first area. Then, without adding more paint, roll out the painted "W" over the three-foot (0.9 meter) section. Continue this process until the whole ceiling is painted. Be sure that the area is well lighted, and examine the work in progress.

MISSED SPOTS

Do not add paint when a spot is missed; smoothing over can be done with a dry roller sleeve so fresh paint is not added to a spot that is already drying.

COVERAGE

While flat finish, white ceiling paint usually provides good coverage in a single coat, allow the paint to dry before deciding on a second coat. If a special effect will be used on the ceiling, complete it before beginning to paint the walls.

PAINTING WALLS

Once the neck-cramping work of ceiling painting is finished, the walls come next.

MASKING

If the ceiling is white, and the wall will be painted in a different color, mask the edge of the ceiling before doing the wall brushwork. Mask trim, window, and door edges, and the tops of base-boards, unless these will be done in the same shades and gloss as the walls.

EDGES AND FIXTURES

Use the same techniques as with the ceiling, cutting in with a brush at edges and around fixtures and outlets. Then roll in three-foot by three-foot sections, working top to bottom, left to right, one wall at a time.

PAINTING DETAILS

Decorative trim around ceiling edges, as well as windows, doors, and baseboards often gets special treatment with a higher-gloss finish than walls and ceiling, because they are most vulnerable to dirt, finger marks, and other blemishes that will need regular cleaning.

CONTRASTING COLORS

Painting these details in contrasting or complementary colors can also be an effective strategy for giving a room definition and refinement. In either case, the work should be carefully done.

DETAIL MASKING

Mask the line between trim, moldings, baseboards or windows, and the adjoining walls. Burnish the tape with a blunt instrument (a putty knife or similar tool) so that paint will not seep underneath the tape. Be sure that the floor beneath the painting area is protected by newspaper or drop cloth from drips, spills, and spatters.

PAINTING DOORS

When painting doors, many pros just remove hardware, rather than masking it, as many metallic knobs and locks are now coated with finishes that can be ruined by cleaning with anything stronger than water. This eliminates the need to cut in paint around knobs and latches, making the job go more quickly.

PAINTING WINDOWS

Anyone who has ever painted a room will acknowledge that painting windows, especially those with many small panes of glass, is a particular challenge.

Here are some recommendations from the pros:

When painting double hung windows, paint the outer sash first. Keep both sashes open, and apply paint in a thin layer. Move the window up and down as painting proceeds, so that neither sash gets painted shut. When painting the thin wood bars around the panes (called muntins), some professionals recommend that these parts be painted without masking the glass.

SCRAPING VS. MASKING

Paint that gets onto glass can be easily removed by scraping with a razor blade, provided paint removal is done soon after the paint dries. Pros note that masking, and then removing tape from these small spaces, can be more time-consuming than just scraping away the drips from the glass. Tape that stays on too long (except for blue painter's tape) can leave a gummy residue more difficult to remove than dripped paint!

Hue Variations from Can to Can

WHEN WORKING WITH COLOR, BEAR IN MIND THAT, EVEN WITH CUSTOM-MIXED CANS OF PAINT, THERE MAY BE **SLIGHT VARIATIONS** IN THE HUE FROM CAN TO CAN. TO AVOID INCONSISTENT COLOR, "BOX" THE PAINT BEFORE APPLYING IT TO THE WALLS. POUR AND **MIX ALL GALLON CONTAINERS** IN ONE, LARGE FIVE-GALLON BUCKET. THIS WILL ASSURE UNIFORMITY OF COLOR THROUGHOUT. THESE LARGE RECEPTACLES, WITH TIGHT-FITTING LIDS, CAN BE PURCHASED AT ANY PAINT STORE.

Painting Window Muntins

AFTER PAINTING WINDOW MUNTINS, **SCORE THE DRIPPED PAINT** ALONG THE EDGE OF THE GLASS WHERE IT MEETS THE MUNTIN. USE THE SCORE MARK AS A GUIDELINE FOR SCRAPING, SO THAT ONLY THE WINDOW GLASS, NOT THE NEW PAINT JOB, GETS SCRAPED.

Storing Leftover Paint

LEFTOVER PAINT CAN BE **SAVED FOR TOUCH-UPS** IF PROPERLY STORED. CAREFULLY CLEAN THE LID OF THE PAINT CAN SO THAT NO PAINT REMAINS ON THE LIP OF THE CAN OR THE EDGE OF THE LID; CLOSE TIGHTLY. STORE CANS IN A COOL, DARK PLACE, AWAY FROM ANY HEAT SOURCE. DO NOT STORE PAINT WHERE IT WILL BE EXPOSED TO FREEZING TEMPERATURES, AS FREEZING WILL RUIN IT.

finishing the job

After painting, examine the whole job in good, bright light before putting away equipment and cleaning up. Look for any areas the paintbrush missed, and fill them in. When the paint has dried thoroughly, scrape off any drips and spatters with a razor blade, sand them smooth, clean the dust, and retouch.

DISPOSAL

Remove all masking tape and clean equipment (soap and water for latex, mineral spirits or manufacturer-specified cleaner for alkyd). Empty latex paint cans can be allowed to dry, then tossed out (Do not throw liquid paint in the trash.) Dispose of alkyds, their containers and tools according to local hazardous waste disposal rules (There are usually special collection days or disposal centers.)

HOW TO GET THE PERFECT COLOR

Decorating rooms with paint requires a synergy of skills: buying the right products, in the right colors, and using them artfully to achieve a desired effect. In the following chapters, readers can see beautiful effects with paint-finished rooms and decorative vignettes that reveal harmonious relationships of color, architecture, and furnishings; they succeed aesthetically. But more importantly, *Painting Rooms* takes the extra step to tell the reader why they work so well.

Successful palettes encompass the relationships of colors to each other, to the furnishings they surround, to light streaming from windows and from interior sources, to the needs and tastes of the people who dwell within the spaces. Some understanding of all these relationships will enable any do-it-yourselfer to choose color more confidently.

The text for this section offers guidance for painting with each major color of the spectrum, and includes the use of neutrals. It provides pointers for observing and selecting the shades, tints, and special effects that capture inspirations culled from nature and daily living – the sources for most decorating ideas. This section offers recommendations for combining a favorite color with other hues that will enhance and complement that color. It divulges tips from professional designers and painters, whose years of experience can add to the reader's repertoire of skills. So, whether your favorite vase or the color in a summer sunset inspires you to paint, this section contains ample instruction for putting a chosen hue to work to create a beautiful interior.

CHAPTER ONE

Painting with Blue

SO EASY ON THE EYE, THE WINNER OF EVERY COLOR POPULARITY CONTEST, BLUE IS A VERSATILE PERFORMER IN THE HOME PAINT PALETTE. THE SERENE, THOUGHT-PROVOKING QUALITY OF THIS HUE SETS A TRANQUIL TONE FOR WORK, STUDY, AND REST, MAKING BLUE AN APPEALING CHOICE FOR KITCHENS, HOME OFFICES, BEDROOMS, AND BATHS. As useful in the home's public spaces as it is in private ones, blue can easily serve as a key decorating color for an entire home.

Blue has many positive associations; blue chips are the best stocks, blue ribbons the top awards. This prized connotation has a long history; before the invention of synthetic pigment, blue was made by grinding precious stones to powder. Ultramarine blue was made in this fashion and used sparingly by artists to depict the heavens and other lofty subjects. Today, modern manufacturers provides us with an enormous range of blues to match every decorating inspiration, in products accessible to all.

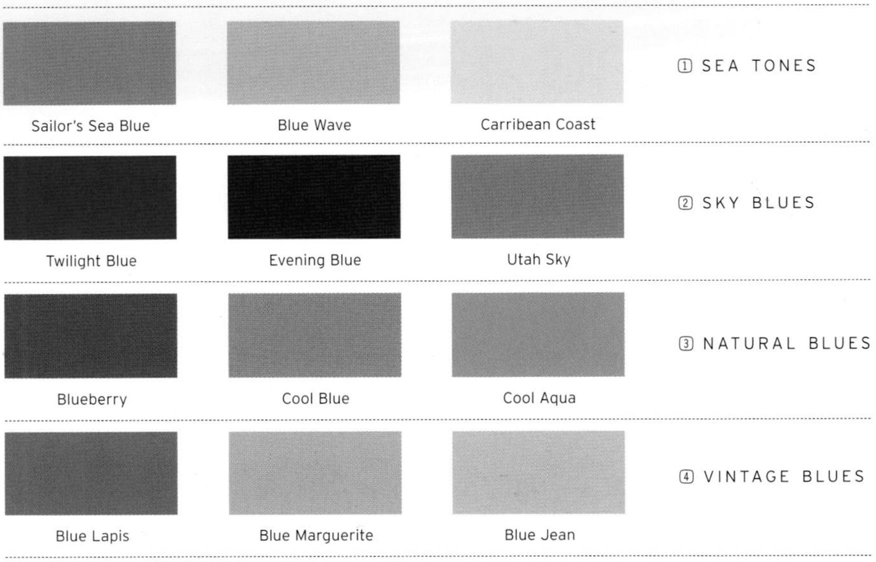

Pale blue walls make a good backdrop for natural wood furniture; the pale orange tone of the wood is a natural complement in the spectrum to light blue. Old washboards painted in the other primary hues show how a muted primary scheme works well in this country setting.

① SEA TONES

Sailor's Sea Blue Blue Wave Carribean Coast

② SKY BLUES

Twilight Blue Evening Blue Utah Sky

③ NATURAL BLUES

Blueberry Cool Blue Cool Aqua

④ VINTAGE BLUES

Blue Lapis Blue Marguerite Blue Jean

Even without the harbor view, pale blue-gray walls enhance the contemplative feeling of this room under the eaves. White trim amplifies the color's depth and complexity. White furnishings and pale floors mirror the room's subdued tone, and dark wood accessories, such as the graphically strong, thumb-back Windsor chair, have been added to stand out in the soft surroundings. Touches of primary bright color make good accents in this room; note how the red journal pops out among all the receding tones.

According to formalized color theory, the natural complement of blue on the spectrum is orange. Paint a room using these two colors together to create an appealing harmony; note the pleasing effect when polished, reddish-orange colored wood furniture such as maple or mahogany is paired with blue walls.

Putting aside the theoretical, look for good partners for blue by observing it in nature. Many blue flowers have white or yellow centers; look for blue/white or blue/yellow combinations on the following pages and see how well they work.

Another surprisingly effective complement for blue is green. Observing blue flowers surrounded by their green leaves and stems proves the point; a green couch or chair in front of a blue painted wall makes the same, harmonious statement. Many shades of blue work well together in a monochromatic scheme. Should this decorative pattern prove a bit chilly, it can quickly be warmed with a few accents, such as decorative pillows or tabletop objects in the primary colors of red and yellow.

sea and sky effects

Few things are as soothing to the soul as an afternoon at the beach spent gazing at the ever-changing sea, where the colors constantly shift in response to weather, wind, and the angle of the sun. To capture the colors of the water and sky in your home, observe the play of light in the rooms to be painted. The quality of the light at the time of day a space is used determines whether a sparkling, light-struck blue, a pale gray-blue, or a deep, saturated tone is most appropriate. In general, paint morning-lit spaces with clear blues. For rooms usually illuminated by incandescent lights, use different shades of blue.

PAINTING WITH SEA TONES

Rooms for contemplation and rest, such as a bedroom, home office, sun porch or spa bathroom, benefit from colors blended in warm sea tones. Light colorwashes or sponged patterns of blue green over a lighter ground provide a subtle and soothing backdrop for quiet or solitary activity. Look at marine paintings, and notice that the artist will usually employ many colors to create the play of light on water. Replicate this dynamic effect with multiple layers of color that are applied by colorwashing, stippling, or sponging; use a pale gray/light blue, and finish with a slightly darker blue or blue-green. Such an effect will provide depth and complexity to walls in hallways, powder rooms, or other spaces that have simple, or few, furnishings. Single layers of color also evoke the sea's many moods. The ocean in late afternoon, when the low angle of the sun or rolling fog dims the sparkly surface, often pales to a soft gray-blue, a tranquil tone appropriate for a quiet sitting room, office, or meditation space.

PAINT BOX

Painting Multiple Layers

WHEN APPLYING COLOR IN MULTIPLE
LAYERS, START WITH THE LIGHTEST COLOR
PAINT AND FINISH WITH THE DARKEST,
TO AVOID THE SOMETIMES CHALKY
APPEARANCE OF LIGHT-OVER-DARK.

*Recreate the tranquil tones of a
landscape by the sea with walls
colorwashed in a coastal blue
over raw, rough plaster. The
blue-white palette carried
throughout the room creates a
serene, cooling effect in a space
designed for summer dreaming.*

Painting a light-struck stairway in the colors of sky and clouds creates a dramatic, celestial effect for those who climb the steps.

APPLYING SKY BLUES

Consider painting a ceiling in a refreshing alternative to plain white—blue hues that suggest a clear daytime sky. Puffy, cloudlike patterns applied by rag-rolling, stippling, sponging, or even stenciling, on a sky-blue ceiling create a floating sensation for the child or adult gazing upward at this effect. While clouds typically decorate a bedroom or nursery ceiling, they might also comfortably grace the upper reaches of sitting rooms, libraries, and other spaces where people relax. On walls, apply sky tints to create a feeling of vertical movement in a home. Picture a stairway with steps in natural wood complemented by sky-blue risers; they move upward to a landing with the walls painted in the same blue. This produces an almost celestial effect, especially if there is sun streaming in through a window or skylight.

NIGHT-SKY EFFECTS

Walls or ceilings that capture the look of a night sky provide an intimate enclosure for a bedroom, study, or other cozy space. Dark, deep blues such as navy, midnight, lapis lazuli, or indigo can be dramatic and luxurious. In a hallway or den, use a glossy or glazed dark blue finish that reflects lamplight to make the space seem rich and elegant, particularly if the walls are hung with pictures in gilded frames. Another dramatic look is a deep blue ceiling, stenciled with small white or gilded stars, lit from below by wall sconces or lamps. Since dark paint will make a ceiling seem lower, painting one in deep blue is an effective remedy for high or vaulted ceilings.

using natural blues

Look to the natural world for an infinite selection of inspirations. The iridescent glow of a dragonfly, the cheerful hue of a bluebird, the delicate tint of a blue crab's shell as it skitters along the rocks at water's edge — all these creatures brighten their surroundings, just as their colors would enliven a room. The garden is also a source for brilliant blues to paint in a decorating scheme. Use the spectacularly bright hue of a delphinium or bachelor's button to paint cabinets, architectural details, or trim in kitchens or baths equipped with lots of white. Although white connotes cleanliness and good hygiene, too much white in an already bright space promotes glare; eye-soothing blue makes an excellent complement.

The frosty rime on a blueberry or juniper berry gives the fruit a powdery appearance that belies its juiciness. This muted blue makes a great wall color that enhances the look of natural wood. Think of it for a dining area or any seating space filled with natural-toned furniture.

Vivid blues practically sparkle with intensity, especially in semi- or high-gloss sheen. Such eye-catching brights are a particularly good foil for expanses of white space, such as the dining nook beyond this blue doorway.

*Glittering blue-green prisms in
a vintage chandelier inspired
the satiny walls of this long cor-
ridor, hung with framed prints,
photographs, and mirrors that
capture and reflect the light.*

painting
with vintage blue

Few ceramic patterns are as recognizable as the
blue-gray dishes and cups, decorated with classical
designs in white relief, first made by potter Josiah
Wedgwood in the eighteenth century. This distinctive blue jasperware has been an inspiration for
many blue-decorated rooms ever since.

Many vintage blues are distinguished by their
shading; important rooms at Colonial Williamsburg,
as well as the country blue of many historic
Scandinavian interiors, have a touch of gray. Such
subtle, light-enhancing color provides a delicate
aspect to rooms that are furnished with elegant,
fine-boned furniture, or bleached or natural-toned
floors, for an overall pastel feeling.

Vivid primary blue walls and stairs stained an equally bright yellow combine for a striking palette in this vintage farmhouse room. While milk paints in more muted shades are a standard treatment in antique homes, using intense hues adds contemporary flavor to classic styles.

CHAPTER TWO

Painting with Red

RED GETS NOTICED. JUST AS THE DAMSEL IN THE SCARLET DRESS ATTRACTS EVERY EYE IN THE

ROOM, ROOMS PAINTED RED HAVE A NATURAL MAGNETISM, MAKING THIS A LOGICAL COLOR CHOICE

FOR ANY SPACE WHERE PEOPLE GATHER — ENTRYWAYS, LIVING AND DINING ROOMS. Red makes such

a memorable statement that one of its many tints and shades finds its way into almost every

home palette. Use red's dramatic flair by painting it on a single wall in an otherwise neutral-

colored space. This strategy works to highlight any objects or furnishings placed on or in front

of the red wall, creating an instant focal point. Painting a single surface to stand out is a

contemporary treatment, particularly effective when interior architecture consists of smooth

planes without trim and molding details.

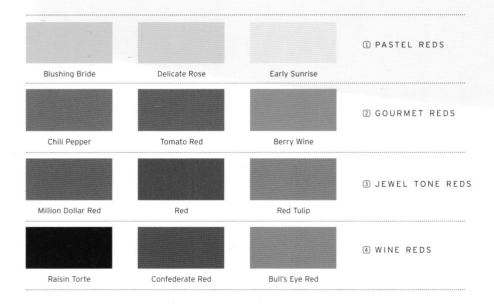

① PASTEL REDS

Blushing Bride   Delicate Rose   Early Sunrise

② GOURMET REDS

Chili Pepper   Tomato Red   Berry Wine

③ JEWEL TONE REDS

Million Dollar Red   Red   Red Tulip

④ WINE REDS

Raisin Torte   Confederate Red   Bull's Eye Red

Strong patterns, textures, and decorative objects blend in a rich harmony when surrounded by walls in the shade of fine red wine. The deep claret tone mutes a disparate collection of exotic furnishings for an effect that is inviting and supremely comfortable.

When considering which colors work best with red, picture a bouquet of long-stemmed red roses or a vase of red Emperor tulips. Their green foliage creates harmonious surroundings for the brilliant red flowers. Similarly, green – red's complement – can work as a trim or carpet color in rooms with red walls; think green with a bit of yellow for deep-toned reds, and green with a dash of blue for more orangey reds. Observe other red flowers and their foliage for additional, appealing red-and-green combinations.

Red also creates a related color scheme in rooms with natural wood detailing – molding, doors, and cabinetry, which, in their unpainted state have a somewhat orange hue. Walls can be painted in an unbroken, matte finish for a cozy appearance, or colorwashed for a lighter, country feeling. Complete this scheme with accents close to red on the spectrum – red-violet, or yellows with a touch of red in them.

Language scholars note that red is the first color to receive a name in nearly every culture, and child development specialists have determined that red is the hue that a baby's eyes will target in his early glimpses of the world. This primitive connection to red makes it a natural choice for the décor in children's rooms, though it need not be confined to a scheme of primary colors. Use red as a key color in a painted wall mural, or as a stenciled border of silhouettes just below the ceiling. Sponge on red over a light background for a bright but subdued wall treatment, reminiscent of the sponge-decorated pottery that brightens many country-style homes.

Not just for frilly bedrooms, pink walls enliven formal spaces as well. Complemented by quantities of greenery and light-catching crystal chandeliers, this pastel sitting room creates a harmony of softly elegant texture and light.

pastel red: painting with pink

Young women often have their first experience with pastel red in the hospital nursery, where girls are swaddled in pink blankets. Thus this pale tint has a common association with little girls' bedrooms and all things frilly and feminine. Yet pink performs well beyond this narrow decorating pigeonhole. Pink walls create softly illuminated social and workspaces, such as living rooms, libraries, or offices, where furnishings bask in its flattering light.

Pastel pink can range from cool – touched with a bit of blue – to a warmer hue with a slightly yellowed tone that moves the resulting color toward coral and other seashell tints. The intensity and source of light that shines on pink walls and other pale-painted surfaces will make a significant difference in how the color is perceived. Intense sunlight can overheat warm pink, and conversely, dim light can make cool pink look drab. Although people fret more about the final appearance of very dark or bright colors, their pallor disguises the trickiness of pastels. Since pale tints contain a significant percentage of white in their mix, the resulting color will have the light-reflecting quality of white paint. To gauge a pastel's appropriateness for a particular room, always take the intermediate step of testing the chosen hue with a large sample board, paying particular attention to the color as it appears when exposed to all the room's light sources.

Windowless kitchens, and those
with wide expanses of white,
sometimes have a hard, high-
tech quality that needs some
colorful relief for the eye. Here,
raspberry walls contrast with
bright white equipment, while
enhancing the soft sheen of
stainless steel fixtures and
kitchen tools.

PAINT BOX

Disguising Less-than-Perfect Walls

RED ROOMS LOOK RICH AND ELEGANT
WHEN THE WALLS ARE GLAZED IN A
MODERATE TO HIGH SHEEN, YET A SHINY,
SMOOTH COATING ALSO DRAWS ATTENTION
TO FLAWS IN THE SURFACE. TO DISGUISE
LESS-THAN-PERFECT WALLS, USE A BROKEN
PAINT TECHNIQUE SUCH AS SPONGING OR
RAG ROLLING, WHICH GIVES THE PAINTED
SURFACE DIMENSION AND DEPTH WHILE
CONCEALING MINOR DEFECTS.

The stimulating warmth of appetizing shades of red make them popular hues for painting walls in restaurants and home dining rooms as well. Rag-rolled shades of spicy red contribute to the glowing coziness of this formal dining room, masking minor wall defects and complementing the rich red-browns of antique furnishings. Note how the red background sharpens details of framed vintage needlework.

applying gourmet reds to rooms

So many red foods exist in the natural world that manufacturers have taken this cue and lined the grocery shelves with thousands of packages that feature red graphics and images. Its mouth-watering quality makes red an excellent color choice in rooms designated for eating and socializing. Such a colorful stimulant will make dining rooms, kitchens, and entertaining spaces as lively as the guests within.

Not everyone thinks of red for the kitchen, as its assertiveness might be just too much excitement at breakfast. Yet one of the cooler reds—shades with a bit of blue in them—creates a wonderful contrast with the large expanses of white cabinets and appliances so popular in contemporary kitchens. This juxtaposition seems to relax the sharpness of raspberry red or cerise, while softening the austere brightness of white fixtures and furnishings. Any workspace—kitchen, laundry, even the home office—with a monotone scheme, whether white, beige, gray or tan, feels more comfortable when these fruity reds are added to the palette.

Shades of spicy red work extremely well in rooms occupied in the evening hours; candles and other indirect lighting patterns serve to increase their friendly glow. Many decorators like to specify one of the rich shades of red for dining rooms, as this color not only whets the appetite for food, but also provides a rosy background that makes a room's occupants look their best.

USING RED DETAILS

A luscious sundae bedecked with whipped cream and a single, glossy maraschino cherry makes a great analogy for the way in which bright red works as an accent color in rooms. Use high-gloss red—the color of toy wagons and shiny fire engines—to bring forward architectural details in rooms painted white, cream, or other neutral colors. For a crisp, finished look, pick out elements such as trim, cabinet knobs, and the outline molding of raised paneling. Such a treatment enhances the happy, lively look of children's rooms, where red trim completes a polished, primary scheme in a white-walled space with blue and yellow furnishings.

applying jewel-tone reds

The red of precious and semiprecious stones is a clear, sparkling shade that radiates warmth. Use it for a glowing sitting room that no one will want to leave, or as a welcoming embrace in a front hallway. White trim, or white upholstered furniture, tone down the brightness of jewel reds while maintaining an overall look of sophisticated comfort. A bright red room can be the exclamation point in an otherwise subdued home palette; chances are, it will also be the space that guests will remember best.

using the shades of red wine

In the glass, a fine red wine sometimes looks brown, or almost black; held up to the light, the depth of its crimson glow becomes apparent. This corresponds to the transformation of deep, dark red walls when they are illuminated. Deep reds have long been used on walls to mimic the effect of fine wood paneling, a painted treatment that is enhanced by architectural features such as applied molding and raised panels. Dragging a coat of darker red over a lighter red can provide more of the appearance of wood grain; finished with a coat of clear glaze, walls look lustrous and rich by lamp or candlelight.

Because iron oxide is a pigment accessible to almost every culture, dark reds have not been reserved for faux-wood treatments in elegant dining rooms. Palettes for farmhouses around the world contain some version of the dark reds drawn from local clays and sediments. For country houses, red-brown paint can color moldings, doors and other wood trim, cabinets in a farmhouse kitchen, or stencils across a raw plaster wall. This color combines with all types of wood for a soft, warm monochromatic scheme, and creates a lovely backdrop for rustic painted furniture and folk art accessories. Use milk paint for its soft and authentic country look, or acrylic paint in a flat finish, to duplicate the vintage, matte appearance.

Walls colorwashed in a deep farmhouse red conform to the rustic flavor of a dining room furnished with treasured finds from country auctions and flea markets. Using the rich, dark tones provided by old-fashioned, natural earth pigments is an authentic and historically accurate wall treatment for antique houses in rural settings.

Ruby red walls demonstrate the power of a bright color to illuminate a small space. The homeowners have made this formal room the centerpiece of their apartment, which is painted in a palette of primary hues. The tricolor scheme is successful for several reasons. While the red is an intense shade, yellow and blue walls have lighter values, so the resulting scheme is harmonious and eye-pleasing. Notice also how white is used as a unifying trim color, to separate the hues and enhance their clarity.

PAINT BOX

Enliven with Red

USE CRIMSON DETAILS TO ENLIVEN
THE TYPICAL PINK-AND-WHITE
BEDROOM, ADDING BREADTH TO A
MONOCHROMATIC PALETTE.

CHAPTER THREE

Painting with Yellow

IF COLOR IS LIGHT MADE VISIBLE, THEN YELLOW IS THE BRIGHTEST LIGHT IN THE SPECTRUM. THINK OF A PROCESSION OF YELLOW RAINCOATS STREAMING OUT OF THE LOCAL ELEMENTARY SCHOOL ON A RAINY MARCH MONDAY—HOW THEY CHEER THE LANDSCAPE AND THE HEARTS OF EVERYONE WHO SEES THEM. Such is the uplifting effect of yellow, and a perfect reason to paint with it somewhere in a home's interior. Yellow paint brightens a windowless hallway or a dimly lit room under the eaves; it is sunshine in a can. Apply intense, golden yellow as a trim color in a dark-paneled, rustic den; glossy details pop out from the subdued background. Then pick up the yellow accent in decorative details: a woven throw, pillows, or a bowl of golden delicious apples.

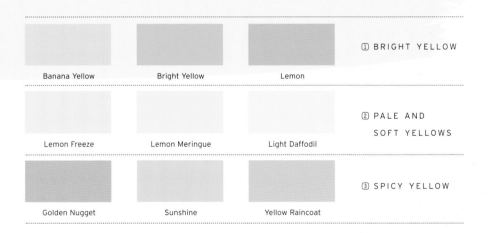

			① BRIGHT YELLOW
Banana Yellow	Bright Yellow	Lemon	
			② PALE AND SOFT YELLOWS
Lemon Freeze	Lemon Meringue	Light Daffodil	
			③ SPICY YELLOW
Golden Nugget	Sunshine	Yellow Raincoat	

Two shades of golden yellow—a lighter base with a darker layer of glaze ragged off—create a glowing setting for casual and memorable meals. This treatment gives ordinary sheetrock walls the textured appearance of stucco, and creates a rustic background for contemporary decorative objects and art.

Lemon yellow walls enhance this kitchen's spacious dimensions. Use expanses of white, plus wood floors and furnishings, to temper the impact of this strong hue. Decorate with bright accents, such as the flowers and abstract prints, as they seem to glow more brightly against the sunny background.

High-gloss yellow paint, a staple for kitchens and baths where brightness is a plus, reflects light like no other hue in the spectrum. Apply shiny treatments in yellow wherever more light and good washability are important: home offices, play rooms, family rooms, hallways leading to private sections of the home. Use bulbs labeled "warm" in fluorescent fixtures to avoid any possible greenish glare.

Yellow provides a pleasing background in rooms with plentiful live greenery and good natural light: enclosed sun porches, breakfast rooms, or any space constructed around a greenhouse window. Colorwash yellow over a lighter ground such as white or ivory, to create an air of soft informality in such indoor/outdoor spaces.

A natural choice for morning-lit bedrooms and kitchens, yellow walls make great surroundings for waking up, or the first cup of coffee. Striping or sponging yellow on white walls in a bedroom will immediately energize the surroundings. Yellow combines harmoniously with so many other colors that few changes in decorative accessories will be needed.

Because of its inherent brightness, yellow may be applied in rooms of all sizes, from cavernous to compact. A monochromatic scheme, using two or three tints or shades of yellow, creates a cheerful, sociable space. Monet's dining room at Giverny is such a two-toned testimonial to the power of yellow, and no one who sees it forgets its brilliant beauty.

painting with bright yellow

Tropical yellows—the colors of ripe bananas, lemons, or a toucan's beak—look lively paired with white trim, or accompanied by other hues from southern latitudes, such as hot pink, mango, or turquoise. While these combinations are most at home in climates where palm trees thrive, high-voltage colors can also work under cooler northern light, particularly when their intensity is tempered by expanses of white or light neutral colors. In a kitchen, this means lemon yellow walls with white cabinets—or the reverse. In a bright yellow bedroom, aqua accents and off-white trim and linens can tone down this energizing hue.

Painting Kitchen Cabinets

NO MATTER WHAT COLOR YOU CHOOSE, PAINTING OLD CABINETS CAN EFFECT AN INSTANT AND DRAMATIC FACELIFT IN THE KITCHEN. SOME POINTERS TO REMEMBER:

• IF CABINETS HAVE WOOD (NOT GLASS-PANED) DOORS, IT'S NOT NECESSARY TO PAINT CABINET INTERIORS, WHICH ARE NOT VISIBLE UNLESS THE DOORS ARE OPEN. THIS WILL SAVE MANY HOURS OF EMPTYING AND THEN REFILLING THE CABINETS. A GOOD COMPROMISE IS TO PAINT THE INTERIOR EDGES AROUND THE DOORS AND DRAWERS. CLEAN ALL THE SURFACES THAT WILL BE PAINTED; MANY PROS USE TSP (TRISODIUM PHOSPHATE). THE CLEANING WILL REMOVE GREASE AND DIRT THAT ADHERE TO OLD WOOD FINISHES.

• SAND THE GLOSSY SURFACES TO PROMOTE GOOD ADHESION OF THE PRIMER COAT. USE THE BEST QUALITY PRIMER AND PAINT. BECAUSE KITCHEN CABINETS GET A LOT OF HANDLING, PROS LIKE TO USE OIL-BASED PAINTS, IN SEMI- TO HIGH-GLOSS SHEENS. ONE COAT OF PRIMER AND TWO COATS OF FINISH PAINT SHOULD PROVIDE THE NECESSARY COVERAGE. BECAUSE ALKYDS CREATE NOXIOUS FUMES, THE KITCHEN MUST BE VERY WELL VENTILATED, AND EACH COAT OF PAINT MUST DRY THOROUGHLY TO INSURE GOOD ADHESION. WHILE PAINTING CABINETS WITH A LONG-LASTING PAINT FINISH MAY BE SOMEWHAT TIME-CONSUMING, THE COST OF PAINTING (EVEN IF YOU HIRE A PRO) WILL STILL BE MUCH LESS EXPENSIVE AND DISRUPTIVE THAN INSTALLING NEW CABINETRY.

Primary yellow walls create a happy setting for a child's bedroom or playroom; complement this sun-bright look with a pale blue ceiling sponged with clouds. Or, if the ceiling is high and the child is a budding astronomer, create a night sky above the yellow walls, accented with tiny, glow-in-the-dark stars. Using the sky image on ceilings will mitigate yellow's energizing property at bedtime, creating a peaceful feeling when young ones gaze upward from their pillows.

The bright yellow of egg yolks or sunflowers can also renew and revive a dated kitchen, when applied in a discernible sheen, from satin to high-gloss, on kitchen cabinets. Add new hardware and window treatments to complete a very cheery and cost-effective rehab of older stained-wood cabinets.

Revive a dated kitchen by painting old wood cabinets and adding new hardware. Here, butter yellow cabinets in a glossy finish are paired with lavender-blue walls, providing a cheerful country setting for cooking and dining.

using pale yellow

A pastel tinted yellow glaze over a white, ivory or beige base achieves subtle effects that gently illuminate rooms. Walls that are sponged, rag-rolled or stippled in this fashion provide the illusion of sunlight through sheer curtains on walls. While the combination of white and yellow is a traditional pairing, increase the color value by using other pastels as complements. Pale violet upholstery looks luscious against yellow walls; pale pink or robin's egg blue can also make refined partners for this hue. A pastel scheme brightens dim interior rooms, and looks especially refreshing with pale wood furnishings.

painting with soft shades of yellow

The most gently sparkling jewel in the spectrum of gems, topaz has a subdued yellow tone that adds a dignified glow to walls when used as a paint color. Yellow toned down with a dab of gray and warmed with a touch of red has an elegant appearance that pairs well with formal furnishings. It creates a subdued undertone when used in broken color treatments – as the undercoat for a blue-green crackle finish, or the base coat for red glaze dragged over moldings, doors and window trim. Topaz is the color of late afternoon light, as the sun slips toward the horizon; it makes a warm and appetizing shade for an elegant dining room.

Pale, buttery yellow walls in a living or dining space make a wonderful backdrop for colorful painted furnishings and accessories; cobalt blue or turkey red in particular stand out against this setting. A grouping of celadon green pitchers or vases will also catch the eye when surrounded by light yellow.

Soft-toned yellow walls—the color of topaz—create an elegant backdrop for formal furnishings and rooms with generous proportions. Subdued yellows balance with the gleam of dark, polished wood, and enhance other mid-toned colors. Notice how blue-green trim elements in the dining room beyond this foyer take on added richness in the company of this gentle shade of yellow.

PAINT BOX

Using White with Pastels

WHEN CREATING A SOFT, PASTEL ROOM, TAKE CARE NOT TO OVERWHELM ITS COLORFUL ATTRIBUTES WITH TOO MUCH BRIGHT WHITE. USE MORE SUBTLE TONES OF WHITE IN THE COMPANY OF PALE TINTS, SO THAT THE PASTEL SURROUNDINGS LOOK DELICATE, RATHER THAN WATERED-DOWN.

SUBTLE TINTS OF YELLOW, SUCH AS PRIMROSE OR VANILLA CREAM, CREATE GENTLE SURROUNDINGS IN A BATH OR POWDER ROOM, WHERE A RESTFUL FEELING AND FLATTERING COLORS ARE IMPORTANT. WHITE FIXTURES WITH A VINTAGE LOOK, AND WHITE TILES WITH DECORATIVE PATTERNS CREATED WITH TINY BLACK OR COBALT BLUE TILES, COMPLETE A SOPHISTICATED AND COMFORTABLE SCHEME PAIRED WITH PALE YELLOW WALLS.

Pale yellow walls with vintage fixtures give this bath a refined, soft look. Mosaic detailing along the edges of the white tile and porcelain and brass accessories enhance the polished, period atmosphere.

Achieving the spicy look of curry requires two or more layers of toned-down yellow, with a darker, yellow-ocher glaze ragged over a smooth coat in a lighter hue. This luxurious room looks warm and mysterious using a complementary palette of yellows and deep violets. The ceiling border is an intricate relief pattern of vines and leaves, picked out in the lighter yellow to create an elegant and subtle harmony with the walls.

Few combinations match the glamour and sophistication of black and gold. The effect of gold-veined marble has been replicated by a broken color treatment on the wall facing the entry to this elegant, high-ceilinged foyer. The glowing focal point is enhanced by the adjacent satiny black walls, and by a collection of opulent objects on a carved and gilded table.

applying spicy shades
of yellow

Mustard, saffron, and curry lend a snap to many ethnic dishes, and the deeper shades of yellow to which these spices give their names set a country mood when used on walls or trim. Mustard details for doors, windows, and perhaps a simple stenciled border along a wall's ceiling edge, define a room's dimensions when walls are painted in deep green, blue or red. Pick up this trim color with decorative pillows, lampshades, or nubby woven rugs for a warm, informal look.

Spicy yellow on the wall works like many deep-toned shades. It is enclosing and comforting, and a great foil for brilliant colors and sparkling accents. Chinese red or black lacquer furniture and deep, soft-cushioned seating in dark-bright hues – sapphire or emerald – create an indulgent, opulent ambience for a den or sitting room, when paired with walls rag-rolled in the lush yellow of saffron.

using yellow
with metallic accents

Yellow has an illuminating effect in formal rooms, and marries well with elegant gilding and luxurious appointments. Ironically, decorating dictums in earlier centuries cautioned against using yellow in the company of gilt or gold metal, and many historic rooms show yellow walls with silver gilt framed art. Achieve a modern take on this archival scheme, and pair yellow walls with silver metallic furniture and fixtures for a sharp, contemporary blending of light and shine.

Yellow glazes can be mixed with metallic gold powders to create a shimmering effect over a lighter base coat. A sponged layer of this mixture is dazzling in a small dressing room or powder room, giving the space an air of regal elegance.

Gilded frames glamorize art and prints, and gilded details will do the same in formally furnished rooms. Moldings and trim can easily be detailed by brushing on gold metallic paint. If a room lacks such architectural ornament, it can be applied by stenciling a simple gold motif, such as a Greek key or egg-and-dart pattern around the ceiling edge. Similar decorative details can enhance a simply painted mantel; mask a narrow stripe around its perimeter and brush in a gold edge.

Use gold accents to enliven rooms painted in dark colors. Forest green, deep plum, rich brown, navy blue – these and most saturated colors are enriched with light-reflecting touches of gold. Create a stenciled border using gold and a contrasting accent color at ceiling or wainscot height. If paneling or doors have been painted in a dark color, pick out the details – the molding around wainscoting, the edges of door panels – in gold paint. In a vintage room from the gilded ages of the past – Georgian, Empire, or Victorian – applied architectural ornaments in rooms can be highlighted in gold for an authentic period look. Apply gold in proportion to a room's degree of luxury; embellished and tasseled swags, velvets, and taffetas can balance quantities of gilt more successfully than more modest fabrics, or highly patterned room furnishings. To get the right balance when painting trim, paint one detail at a time: one linear strip of molding, or one band of plaster trim around a ceiling fixture. It is always easier to add gilded details than it is to remove them.

CHAPTER FOUR

Painting with Green

GREEN IS THE MAGICAL CHANNEL BETWEEN THE SUN AND THE EARTH AND ALL OF LIFE THAT IS

NOURISHED BY THESE ELEMENTS. Rare indeed are the flowers and fruit that do not bloom or

ripen against the backdrop of the many shades and tints of this life-sustaining hue. It is nature's

neutral, and those who love green discover that it has the same wonderful, mystical power

in the home.

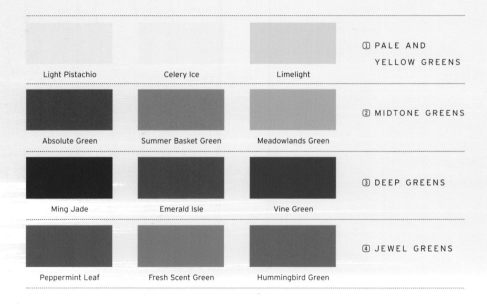

Light Pistachio	Celery Ice	Limelight	① PALE AND YELLOW GREENS
Absolute Green	Summer Basket Green	Meadowlands Green	② MIDTONE GREENS
Ming Jade	Emerald Isle	Vine Green	③ DEEP GREENS
Peppermint Leaf	Fresh Scent Green	Hummingbird Green	④ JEWEL GREENS

The pleasing, airy atmosphere created by large windows and expansive views is enhanced by a kitchen design that brings outdoors in. Soft green walls and pale wood cabinetry, floors, and furnishings have a comfortable, natural feel, making this room a most relaxing space for cooking and gathering.

The complementary relationship
of red and green extends to
all the tints and shades of each
hue. Here, coral-red walls are
subdued using two tones of blue-
green trim and decorative accents;
the palette is softened by the
balancing act performed by colors
at opposite ends of the spectrum.

Almost any selection of colors can assert themselves in green surroundings. Positioned in the center of the spectrum, green can harmonize or complement any one of the other colors with ease. Think of a summer field, full of yellow, violet, blue, pink and red flowers; each can show off its vivid hue against the background of green leaves and stems. In this same fashion, green becomes a harmonizing base coat for other color combinations used in broken color treatments. And just as the many hues of green in forest and meadow can comfortably coexist and please the eye, so too can layers of different tints or shades of green create a monochromatic and appealing finish on walls. Versatile and comfortable, green creates harmony, unity, and vitality in room settings.

Just as other complementary schemes contain the element of surprising harmony – blue and orange, yellow and violet – the potential of a red and green pairing goes well beyond its use as a traditional Christmas palette. While pure red and intense green may make a team too energetic for most spaces, using these two colors in light- or dark-toned combinations creates palettes suitable for a variety of décors. Light green trim paired with coral red walls makes an elegant surround for light framed, painted furnishings. Rough walls colorwashed in red and trimmed with green have a warm, country feel. The reverse palette – green walls with red trim – looks rich and formal with such furnishings as a red-based Oriental rug, and deep-cushioned upholstery that uses either red or green as a major fabric color. This setting can also set off and enhance shining lacquered tables and chairs, with green assuming its role as an enhancer and harmonizer of color and texture.

painting with pale green

Pastel green – think of pistachios, celery stalks, or the tiniest hint of new growth emerging from the ground – has enjoyed a resurgence in the home palette not seen since the Art Deco era of the 1930s. This fresh hue creates a feeling of serenity and a clean, healthy appearance in rooms where it is applied. Not surprisingly, pale green finds its way to bedrooms, baths, and other spaces where tranquility rules. Artfully colorwashed or sponged on walls, or painted in a satiny smooth coat, pale green brings a springlike quality to interiors that delights the eye and calms the beholder.

A collection of objects in pure, primary hues blends harmoniously before a background of soft green, revealing this color's amazing capacity to unify and enhance the clarity of objects it surrounds. Green is a spectral color that can easily function as a neutral in rooms.

applying yellow green

An interesting adjunct to soft pastel green is its
more yellow neighbor on the color wheel: chartreuse. While this intense green hue has enjoyed
popularity as a fashion color — albeit briefly —
in several recent decades, its ability to combine
cheerfully with expanses of white, with natural
wood, and with touches of strong colors such as
turquoise make it worth consideration for painting
rooms. The bit of yellow in this hue can bring a
lovely touch of light to rooms that could use more
sunshine; mitigating its acidity with white and
bright blue creates a pleasing and lively palette
that will withstand the fickle whims of fashion.

using midtone greens

Pure bright green, toned down with gray and
touches of blue or yellow, creates a variety of soft
shades that effect a tranquil atmosphere in rooms.
Use these hues to stencil leaves or vines in an
appealing pattern along wall perimeters. To apply
a Monet-like impression of flowers blooming in
fields, sponge a layer of soft green glaze on walls,
in the company of other sponged hues that imitate
blue crocus or yellow narcissus. To step into a bedroom with this abstract, but mural-like decoration
feels like being enfolded in a painting.

Apply a midtone green, touched with a bit of gray,
to moldings around windows and doors, especially
those apertures that frame a view to woods, garden, or fields. The soft green trim seems to dissolve the distance between indoors and out, making a natural vista part of the interior decoration.

*Walls colorwashed to achieve
the tang of lime juice provide
lively counterpoint to the white
fittings in this bath. Yellow-
greens can be especially effective
in small spaces; mitigate their
sharpness with accents of pure
bright hues for balance. In this
room, turquoise window trim
is a bright detail in the right
proportion to harmonize the
expanses of white and chartreuse.*

Gray-green provides handsome surroundings when applied in a smooth coating to walls; its gentle tone creates a muted backdrop for wall-hung collections, and is particularly suited for walls displaying detailed, patterned objects. The beauty of decorated plates and platters, which would be hidden in a china cabinet, comes to life when arranged on a soft green wall.

Gray-green, along with many subdued shades of blue-green, enhance many vintage interiors. Not only does this color range harmonize with furnishings and accessories of the Arts and Crafts period at the turn of the twentieth century, gray-green is also a classical choice, one of the hues in the Wedgwood spectrum of the eighteenth century. Smooth gray-green walls make a flattering environment for a grouping of Mission-style furniture, and at the same time, this wall color will harmonize with the delicate carvings and curves of Federal and Georgian furnishings.

painting with deep green

The lush, dark colors of an evergreen forest or the leaves of holly and ivy make dramatic statements in the home. Sitting rooms and hallways hung with paintings in gilt frames look elegant and dramatic with shiny, deep green walls outlined with glossy white trim. Fill this setting with luxurious appointments—burgundy red velvets, shining dark wood furniture, and sparkling crystal—and feel enveloped in comfort and ease.

A vintage treatment pairs dark green walls in a flat finish with ivory or taupe trim, a somewhat muted combination that combines gently with country antiques—painted furniture, folk art, old patchwork quilts in many calico colors. Reverse the combination—taupe walls with spruce green trim—as a background for a neutral scheme accented with touches of blue or red in chair cushions, pillows, or window valances.

Using a soft gray-green for dining room walls helps reveal the intricate details of a display of vintage Staffordshire dinnerware. The same shade, applied to the frames and moldings of patio doors, creates a seamless passageway, permitting garden greenery to visually enhance the interior as well as the patio.

Dark green walls in the bathroom, with white or natural wood trim and fittings, create a feeling of warm repose—a perfect environment for a soak in the tub. Since this is a setting for letting the imagination roam free, give the bath a rustic feeling. Wash raw umber over tan for the look of rough plaster walls, then stencil or hand-paint trailing dark green vines around door and window moldings. The bath becomes a lovely private grotto, and a relaxing retreat.

working with jewel-tone green

Emerald and turquoise are gems prized for their brilliance, and they illuminate rooms with an inner light. A translucent emerald glaze ragged over a lighter green smooth coating can make a sitting room or inner hallway glow; add another layer of clear glaze combined with metallic powder for a lustrous, sparkling treatment that needs no further adornment.

Turquoise—sometimes seen as a shade of green-blue, at others as a blue-green—can add accents of intense color to rooms with a neutral palette. It balances sharp yellows, oranges, and reds, giving rooms a Southwestern feel when used with this color range. Using turquoise full strength on a wall makes a powerful color statement, an intense glow that can be softened with furnishings of rustic light wood, or bright white trim and moldings. Like walls in other strong hues, turquoise harmonizes with large pieces of wood furniture with a distressed or hand-hewn look, primitive objects, and the strong sunlight of southern latitudes.

Dark green walls can be lively and warm, and provide a strong but gentle field for objects placed before them. Details of sculpture and gilding are sharpened; this hallway scene shows how green can ease the eye like a soft neutral shade. Also note how pleasing the pairing dark green makes with the blue walls and ceiling in the dining room beyond.

PAINT BOX

Protecting Broken Color Finishes

PROTECT BROKEN COLOR FINISHES IN THE BATH, AND IN OTHER ROOMS WHERE HANDS MAY TOUCH WALLS OR MOISTURE CAUSE DAMAGE. APPLY A CLEAR SEALER SUCH AS POLYURETHANE, WHICH IS AVAILABLE IN ALL GLOSS LEVELS. CHECK WITH THE PAINT DEALER TO MAKE SURE THE SEALER WILL ADHERE TO THE CHOSEN PAINT SURFACE.

As a member of the green family, even high-intensity turquoise can function as background to collections of objects. A grouping of botanicals, suspended by visible lines, creates a high-impact impression when mounted over the turquoise ground. In this room, the rustic wood mantel and white trim balance turquoise's color power.

CHAPTER FIVE

Painting with Violet

VIOLET SPEAKS OF MYSTERY AND POWER AND HAS BEEN APPROPRIATED THROUGH THE AGES BY SORCERERS AND ROYALTY ALIKE. A SECONDARY HUE MIXED FROM PRIMARY RED AND BLUE, THIS NEAT BALANCE BETWEEN WARM AND COOL HAS RECENTLY BEGUN TO EARN A MORE IMPORTANT PLACE IN THE MODERN HOME PALETTE. Victorians loved violet and used it everywhere, from the exteriors of their "painted lady" villas to dining rooms and parlors. While it has often been chosen for feminine bedrooms and pampering baths, this color can create dramatic and harmonious schemes throughout the home in living rooms, dining rooms, and even kitchens.

Everyone knows the traditional connection between lavender and lace, but violet functions equally well as a pleasing backdrop for modern, sculptural furnishings. Mid-tone violet has the intensity of warm gray, so that it creates a feeling of comfort and ease amid the sharp geometric planes and shiny finishes of contemporary spaces.

A pastel scheme lends elegance to this contemporary guest room; the gentlest touch of violet enhances this room's contemplative quality. Pale violet, teamed with white trim and spare black-lacquered accessories, plays the role of a meditative neutral, softening the room's angles and contributing to an atmosphere of restful quiet.

Lavender Mist	Misty Lilac	Whisper Violet	① SOFT VIOLET
Purple Hyacinth	Crocus Petal Purple	California Lilac	② NATURAL VIOLET
Twilight Magenta	Amethyst Cream	Enchanted	③ CONTEMPORARY VIOLET
Gentle Violet	Dark Lilac	Grape Gum	④ DEEP PURPLE

Soft violet effects a warming environment for this dining room, bringing out the rich glow of sculptural wood table and chairs, and dramatically framing the contemporary painting.

using soft violet

A few moments after the sun sets, the sky streaks with pastels in a rainbow of colors. Among these hues are clouds tinted an elegant lavender. This inspiring combination sets the tone for a lovely broken color wall finish, using a smooth background of pale blue or pink, and sunset clouds of pale lavender pounced over the base with a sponge or a rolled rag. Consider such a finish for a sitting room or bedroom, a soft effect for a cozy space that inspires reflection. Or use a pale violet for a smooth painted wall, and one other pastel — pale pink, peach, and a whitened sky blue — as a trim color.

In a monochromatic scheme, a mixture of tints and shades of violet can be as lovely and fresh as a spring garden full of pansies, violets, lilacs, and tulips. This combination, applied in a broken color effect, lends a soft, contemplative quality to a spa bathroom or powder room, and creates a comfortable setting in a guest room.

A fine-arts approach pairs violet with its complement — yellow — a pleasing combination one can observe in nature in nearly every season: violet and daffodil, morning glory and primrose, aster and goldenrod, deep purple ash leaves and golden maples. Use this team in a dining room or a living room furnished with lots of light-stained wood. Use violet as the wall color with pale buttery trim, or reverse the combination, painting walls yellow with glossy violet trim. The most comfortable duets use the two colors at similar values.

Because yellow and violet have this symbiotic relationship, consider violet walls for a collection of paintings, prints, or photographs in gilded frames, which will glow in this juxtaposition.

Since violet's place in the spectrum falls between red and blue, either of these hues will work with it in a related scheme, used as trim or accent colors, as secondary colors for adjacent walls, floors or ceilings, or as partners in a broken color wall finish. On a wall, sponging clear glazing liquid colored with red or blue over a violet-sponged layer can create the luminous effect of a summer bouquet seen through sheer curtains.

painting with natural violet hues

Violet works in amiable partnership with a variety of colors, and one of the most natural combinations blends it with green. A colorwash of violet over a white or pale gray base, trimmed with stenciled leaves or painted green moldings or wainscoting, brings a spring or summer palette indoors. For an effect that is soft, yet sophisticated, combine such a scheme with white painted furniture in a dining room or white upholstery in a living room.

Violet walls and a lush outdoor landscape soften the formality of gleaming dark wood furnishings in a bedroom lit by foliage-filtered natural light. The lilac paint treatment and bed covers are not overly sweet; using a rug and upholstery in white, and adding judicious touches of a related color — in this case a berry red — give the room an elegant balance.

Using an undercoat of white and a reverse stenciling technique— applying star shapes and a scalloped template along the ceiling— the dusky violet colorwash creates a nursery with a delightfully dreamy wall pattern. The effect creates a serene environment for the newest member of the family.

Accentuate the positives of long, narrow corridors with warm colors and quantities of art. This hallway has adjacent walls painted in the complementary hues of lavender and yellow. Clusters of silver framed prints and a burnished chrome commode table enhance and reflect the limited light, adding sparkle and brightness to the space.

The tiny, pale purple florets of the lilac flower seem to shimmer amid its silvery-green foliage and the tan bark of its branches. Think of this combination in a room setting—pale or pickled wood furniture, with upholstery in one of the gray-greens. Walls might be a smooth, single pale purple tint or a sponged combination of several violet tints and shades; sponge randomly over the violet background with silvery green for an abstract, impressionist representation of these lovely, fragrant blooms.

Bedrooms, often placed in the floor plan at the rear of the house, frequently offer the most natural views: toward a backyard garden, fields or woods, or distant hills. Windows surrounded by walls painted violet help bring the outdoors in, as greenery is more noticeable in violet's company. The effect is soft and serene, just the right note for rooms set aside for dreams and rest.

using purple accents

Violet is a favorite children's color, as the popularity of certain purple dinosaurs will attest. With its regal connotations, violet can certainly please a resident young princess, and also takes its place in the playroom, used in its brightest tints along with the primary hues. Think about bright, shiny violet as a trim color in a child's room, for closet doors, window shutters, and wood furniture. While such an accent scheme works well with white walls, consider using it as trim when walls are a related color, sponged either in red or in blue. Or apply yellow—violet's complement—in a pale tint on the walls, using purple as a trim color and white for furniture and curtains to softly subdue the bright contrast.

Shades of plum have long been used in country schemes, and add to the coziness and warmth of spaces used for eating and gathering. Restore an old kitchen by painting wood cabinetry in a rich plum; detail moldings and pulls with a brighter violet hue to add contemporary flair.

Violet also works well in the company of soft gray, used as a trim color, or painted on a single wall to create a focal point. Broken color effects using violet as the top color have a pleasant warmth and softness when applied over a gray ground.

using violet in contemporary settings

The word purple sometimes conjures a vision of antiques, lacy antimacassars, maiden aunts, and bone china teacups. Yet this hue has begun to find its way into many modern and even minimalist interiors. A cool interior of flat, unadorned planes gathers warmth and definition with color, and lavender is sufficiently understated to work with modernist patterns of studied simplicity.

To create an effect of shadow play in an otherwise sun-struck space, use lavender on the vertical planes of a room in a single direction—all walls facing east, for example—while other walls are painted white or beige. Such a scheme provides contrast and spatial definition in a room without moldings or other architectural details.

Another common feature of contemporary homes, a high-ceilinged hallway, has a vertical volume that can make it feel cavernous. Painting walls in soft violet can humanize and soften such large-scale spaces.

PAINT BOX

OBTAIN THE EFFECT OF SOFTLY TINTED CLOUDS ON WALLS OR CEILING BY USING THE PARCHMENT BROKEN COLOR EFFECT DETAILED IN CHAPTER THREE OF THE FIRST SECTION OF THIS BOOK. THIS TREATMENT LOOKS FILMY AND ALMOST ETHEREAL, AS CONTRASTED WITH THE PUFFY CLOUDS THAT CAN BE ACHIEVED BY SPONGING ON A SKY-COLORED BASE.

Many contemporary kitchens have been outfitted with the latest sleek appliances, cloaked in brushed stainless steel for a clean, state-of-the-art appearance. And, just as violet makes a surprisingly good background for metallic finishes in other areas of the home, walls painted in a spring-fresh shade of hyacinth bring a space-age kitchen back to homey reality. Decidedly a fresh take on color in the kitchen, violet blends beautifully with the chrome, stainless, and nickel accoutrements that are now so popular in culinary design.

painting with deep purple

Lustrous eggplants, regal purple velvet, an amethyst brooch — all of these objects glow in the deepest shades of violet. Used on the walls of a cozy sitting room or library, these colors lend an air of intimacy and luxury. While flat-painted, deep purple walls duplicate the look of velvet or suede, using a shiny overcoat of glaze will give the same walls a glowing quality that reflects evening candlelight.

A room painted in deep purple is the perfect setting to use complementary yellow in its most luxurious form. Touches of gilt can be applied to moldings, and brass lamps, paintings with gold-leaf frames, and fabrics woven with golden thread sparkle in the company of violet walls. Think of jewel colors as possible accents for this extravagant scheme; fabrics, rugs, or accessories with hints of ruby, sapphire, or emerald complete the look.

Chrome and stainless steel fixtures, shelves, and equipment seem to glow more brightly in this violet-painted kitchen. The lovely, hyacinth background makes colored glass and fresh produce stand out in sharp relief. Violet seems to recede and blend with silvery objects, so while it is vibrant and fresh in a kitchen setting, it functions almost like a neutral hue in these surroundings.

PAINT BOX

ADD A BIT OF ARCHITECTURAL INTEREST TO PLAIN PAINTED CABINETS BY USING AN ACCENT COLOR NOT ONLY FOR CABINET PULLS, BUT ALSO TO CREATE THE ILLUSION OF A MOLDING WITH A PAINTED STRIPE NEAR THE EDGE OF CABINET DOOR PERIMETERS.

DO THIS WITH TWO LINES OF MASKING TAPE, LEAVING THE DESIRED STRIPE WIDTH AS A GAP BETWEEN THE TWO. TAKE CARE THAT THE LINES ARE STRAIGHT (MEASURE AND CHECK WITH A SPIRIT LEVEL) AND THE CORNERS ARE CRISP. BURNISH THE TAPE TO INSURE THAT EDGES ARE SMOOTH AND PAINT DOES NOT BLEED UNDERNEATH. WHEN PAINT IS DRY, REMOVE THE TAPE TO REVEAL THE STRIPE.

Deep purple, in the saturated shade of an eggplant's skin, creates a delightfully rich harmony with white in this vintage living room. The dark walls cast all the room's beautiful details— the sheen of fabrics, the glow of metallic frames and accessories, the crispness of architectural forms—in sharp relief.

CHAPTER SIX

Painting with Orange

ORANGE IS A SPARK, A BURST OF ENERGY. IT EMBODIES A LIVELY FRESHNESS, WHICH, LIKE THE TANGY FRUIT THAT BEARS ITS NAME, ADDS ZEST TO ANY ROOM IT DECORATES. As an advancing color in the spectrum, orange may seem intimidating to use in any quantity in the home.

Applied in the right proportion and tone, however, its bright warmth provides excitement in the decorative palette.

Incorporate orange in a related color scheme, using yellow and red, its neighbors on the spectrum, to create a comfortable range for the eye. The total effect of all these advancing colors can be softened by using white or beige for trim, fabric, or floor covering; the resulting scheme is bright, but soft.

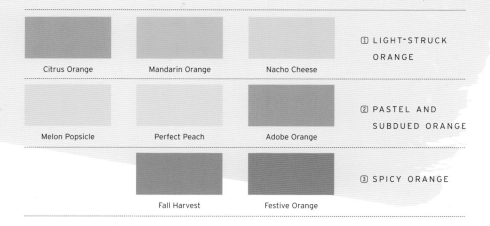

Citrus Orange   Mandarin Orange   Nacho Cheese   ① LIGHT-STRUCK ORANGE

Melon Popsicle   Perfect Peach   Adobe Orange   ② PASTEL AND SUBDUED ORANGE

Fall Harvest   Festive Orange   ③ SPICY ORANGE

Bright orange can override almost any other color, but when it is colorwashed over a creamy base, it becomes translucent and soft, as if seen through a veil, or sheer curtains. This sitting room, rendered with an orange glaze over an ivory base, has the light, shimmering look of sorbet.

Walls painted in the warm shade evocative of ripe persimmons create a welcoming space in an entry foyer or home office. This cheerful color is a soft complement to painted wood; the blue desk looks rich and vibrant in this setting. See how the landscape in the gilded frame seems to acquire greater depth with the backdrop of midtoned orange.

Restrain the vivacious brightness of orange using any one of the broken color techniques. Rag rolling, sponging, or dragging orange over a pale ground adds the spark without too much flame. Consider using orange mixed with a clear glaze to further increase its transparency. Walls given this treatment will surely brighten a dark, windowless nook or hallway.

Apply bright orange paint, full-strength, to effectively focus the eye anywhere it is used. Covering one wall, a door, a window shutter, or a fireplace surround, orange will draw attention to any architectural detail. To make such a statement easier on the eye, use furnishings or accessories in shades of complementary blue or a rich, very dark green.

using light-struck orange

Just as a glass of orange juice becomes the sparkling centerpiece of a breakfast tray, walls washed with orange color illuminate a room that is bathed in morning light. Orange in its lighter tints is a refreshing color to wake up to, particularly if a gentle touch is used with furnishings. Pair orange-painted walls with light woods and floor coverings, pale textiles, and wall and window trim in white touched slightly with yellow, and the result is a sunny, harmonious atmosphere even when the day dawns cloudy. To further soften the attention-getting aspect of this hue, paint walls using orange tinted up with white or toned down with gray (or with its complement, blue) to make a room softer, easier on the eye.

painting with pastel orange

The pale orange pulp of a cantaloupe suggests a soft, pastel palette good for sunny climates, or for warming up rooms in cooler places. The addition of light tints of orange to a palette that contains such colors as icy blue or pale honeydew green provides a temperature adjustment equal to the sun's rays; an equivalent light tint of yellow might fade out in a brightly lit room, but pastel orange holds its own. In a houseful of rooms washed with pastels, pale melon trim throughout provides a unifying stroke of warm color to insure that the overall effect is lively, rather than faded.

Peach-painted rooms flatter many skin tones; peach is a glowing tint of orange that has a bit of red in it. Use it in bedrooms, powder rooms, even dining rooms, as orange – the color of so many fruits – is logically considered an appetite stimulant.

SOFT ORANGE EFFECTS

Late season orange fruits have a toned-down hue associated with the harvest, and a sense of warmth and coziness. Rich but subdued, these shades of festive gourds and mouth-puckering fruit enliven a space without overwhelming it with brightness. Use one of these darker oranges in a foyer to make it inviting and comfortable. The orange midtones also make a particularly good backdrop for painted furnishings.

Peach walls flatter this room's assets; polished wood floors and furniture shimmer as part of a scheme that includes coordinating fabric in related colors on the chairs. A mirrored wall reflects the overall glowing effect, heightening the soft, complexion-enhancing tone of the walls and the rich formality of the furnishings. Creamy white trim is the finishing touch for this elegant space.

Multiple layers of orange glaze, going from pale to midtone, with a final coat mixed with copper pigment, effect a luscious, glowing treatment for dining room walls. Glossy red-orange painted trim and upholstery, and shining accents, including sculptural copper light sconces, complete a glamorous, stimulating environment.

PAINT BOX

Conceal Flaws with Terra-Cotta

TERRA-COTTA IS A GREAT COLOR FOR WALLS THAT ARE LESS-THAN-PERFECT. USE IT AS A WALL COLOR IN A MATTE FINISH, LIKE THE COLOR OF COUNTRY TILE AND CLAY FLOWERPOTS, TO CONCEAL MANY SMALL FLAWS IN AN EXPANSE OF WALL.

painting with subdued shades of orange

Paint a wall with a single coat of light yellow or pale tan; then wash it with one or more coats of orange-tinted glaze for an effect to simulate the broad, glowing evening sky of the American south-west. The bright sun of this hot desert climate invites strong color that will not fade out under its rays. Colorwashed walls, of true rough plaster or a treatment that simulates this look, are an ideal background for rustic furnishings, Native American pottery, desert landscapes, wrought iron sculptures and candlesticks.

The orange of flowerpots and floor tile is a soft color that harmonizes with many decorating styles. Terra-cotta, the Italian words for "baked earth," possesses a homey warmth that makes it a wonderful wall color for public rooms where people gather, such as kitchens, family rooms, and living rooms. Because it is such a subtle shade of orange, it can easily work with bright, contrasting colors, as well as many different shades of blue and green, and not overpower other decorating elements. Rather than a strong statement, terra-cotta makes a wonderful background to the room's décor and activity.

Amber – a jewel-like substance, which catches light and seems to glow from within, inspires a shimmering wall color. Paint a base coat of slightly orange-beige, washed or rag-rolled with an amber-shaded glaze, to provide a luminous treatment. This color blends particularly well with the earthy tones of furnishings and decorations of the early twentieth century Arts and Crafts movement. Copper, verdigris, and hammered bronze – metals used for lamps and hardware in this era – look rich and warm in amber surroundings.

PAINT BOX

Keeping Light Patterns in Mind

KEEP IN MIND THAT LOCAL NATURAL LIGHT PATTERNS ALTER THE WAY COLOR APPEARS IN A DESIGN SCHEME. THOSE WHO LOVE SOUTHWESTERN COLORS AND STYLE, BUT LIVE IN NORTHERN LATITUDES, SHOULD CONSIDER USING COLORS IN A SLIGHTLY MORE TONED-DOWN PALETTE. ADVANCING HUES THAT HAVE A "HOT" APPEARANCE – RED, ORANGE, BRIGHT YELLOW – SHOULD BE TESTED IN THE HOME ENVIRONMENT USING A LARGE SAMPLE OF THE FINISHED EFFECT.

Terra-cotta walls function as a soft backdrop for many styles of furnishings. While it is often associated with rustic environments and country pottery, here the color works to warm effect with an eclectic grouping of furniture and accessories. Bright red – the small model cars on the lower shelf of the side table, and the background of the period print – works well with terra-cotta, as do other intense primary hues and bright orange. This subdued orange background enhances blue-green furnishings, such as the wicker chair and pottery pitcher.

Walls that glow are the effect of multiple layers of related colors that imitate light shining through amber beads. Wash a darker orange over a creamy base coat with a slight tint of yellow-orange to produce this luminous quality, which enhances many earth-toned objects and furnishings. Here, the walls make an appropriate vintage statement; amber was popular in the Arts and Crafts period, when such objects as the green art pottery and angular oak furniture heralded a break with highly-decorated Victorian formality.

spicy orange effects

Cinnamon, nutmeg, allspice, and cumin are pungent spices in subtle shades of orangey brown; their colors warm up the surroundings in any home, but blend especially well with country-style furnishings and natural materials. Subtle color variations among these spices create a pleasing palette for adjoining rooms, or a whole house.

The deepest tones of orange have a quiet, but intense warmth. These spicy, seemingly brown, colors work well in country interiors because of their earthy quality. Like all dark shades, spicy hues will glow more brightly when juxtaposed with white or cream-colored trim; this contrast will also make the space more formal, just as white collar and cuffs dress up the sports jacket.

using the metallic sheen of orange

Consider how a rack of hanging copper pots, or a wall covered with a display of copper molds can enhance a kitchen. Then consider the effect of a coppery orange wall: a yellow-orange base, sponged or washed with a coppery metallic tinted glaze. This shimmering wall could be the ideal place for a collection of kitchen wares; a grouping of colorful plates, a collection of water pitchers lined up on a plate rail, or an assortment of trivets would all stand out on such a glowing backdrop.

*Cinnamon walls and pale
orange-brown clay floor tiles
make a monochromatic background for an array of country
furnishings; crisp white trim
gives this sitting room a touch
of formality. Seen through the
doorway, walls painted with a
lighter tint suggest a different
spice, blending well with the
front room and creating a sense
of visual harmony.*

CHAPTER SEVEN

Painting with Neutrals

TO UNDERSTAND THE ROLE OF NEUTRAL COLORS, CONSIDER A TRADITIONAL WINTER LANDSCAPE

IN A TEMPERATE CLIMATE: SNOW, BARE TREES, FRAGMENTS OF DRIED GRASS, GRAY BOULDERS,

AND LEAFLESS SHRUBS STICKING OUT FROM THE ICY TERRAIN ON AN OVERCAST DAY.

Without an impression of strong color, other visual qualities become apparent; details of form

and texture seem more pronounced. This is the power of a neutral palette, and the reason it

remains an ever-popular strategy for painting rooms.

Black and white and all tones of gray in between, plus the lighter side of the brown family,

constitute those hues that are considered neutral. Yet this label does not mean that using

neutral paints in rooms will result in drab or unexciting spaces. Every paint color makes a

statement, and these shades are no exception. Anyone who has seen one knows the vitality

of a successful black-and-white room, or the enveloping comfort of an all-beige room full of

interesting shapes and textures.

Soft, subtle colors, such as the pale gray-beige used on bedroom walls, act as harmonizing backgrounds for many different neutral tones. The patina of old wood, subtly gilded objects, and fabrics in muted beiges and whites combine in a haven for tranquility and rest.

① SOFT NEUTRALS

Frosted Café	Kahlua And Cream	Butter Pecan

② NEUTRALS THAT MIMIC NATURAL MATERALS

November Skies	Wolf Gray	Wisp Of Mauve

③ BEIGE, BROWN, AND TAN

Big Bend Beige	Sandlot Gray	Santa Fe Tan

One of the most exciting aspects of a neutral palette is its broad flexibility: myriad combinations of whites, grays, beiges, and blacks work together harmoniously. Thus, pairs, triads, or quartets of neutral shades can be ideal for painting walls in broken color effects. A creamy ivory wall with a dragged or combed overcoat in a subtly darker shade of beige or gray creates a hint of pattern and texture in a room with many soft and smooth fabrics and surfaces. Walls with a pale undercoat can also be taped off in a large grid, the squares softly delineated by hand-rubbing beige or tan paint next to the taped areas with a soft rag. When the tape is removed, the painted effect creates an illusion of stone blocks—a lovely backdrop for classical, light-colored furnishings.

When a smooth coat of neutral color paint is used for walls and trim, a successful monochromatic scheme can be built by applying similar values of the same color for upholstery, floors, and most other furnishings. Then, punch up the drama of the scheme with fully saturated details. Use deep brown details—pillows, picture frames, candlesticks—with beiges and tans. Accessorize all-gray schemes with black-lacquered side tables and black-painted baskets. Craft an all-over white scheme, then add one other color, using a neutral such as straw or taupe, or a single bright hue from the color wheel, for accessories such as lamps, throws, and pillows.

applying white paints

Every manufacturer's fan deck of colors contains a large section of whites—sometimes more than one hundred different shades and tints of this supposed non-color. Bright whites make a crisp contrast to almost any other color; often used as a standard treatment for ceilings, they make an adjacent color look more lively and true.

Creamy whites, with a touch of yellow, orange, or brown, have a softer appearance. They mimic warm afternoon light, creating a serene setting for reading and relaxing—a great palette for a library, bedroom, or office.

Using creamy whites in discernibly different sheens on the walls of a room is one way to achieve an interesting, yet subtle, patterned effect. For example, stripe a room with an ivory hue, using eggshell and satin sheens of the same shade. This creates a light, formal look of striped damask. For another elegant hint of pattern, apply subtle stenciled borders in classical motifs along the perimeters of a room using this same serene juxtaposition of gloss levels.

Picking out trim, molding, doors and windows in glossy, creamy white creates a somewhat aged appearance in rooms, especially when these details are paired with walls finished in vintage colors. Off-whites, pearl-whites, and putty tans have this historical connotation for many decorators and designers.

*Walls painted white and
complemented with matching
slipcovered pieces create an
atmosphere of peace and serenity.
Against this soft backdrop,
details of form and texture catch
the eye, which can easily take
in subtle features of the room's
accessories: the patterns of the
plates on the wall, the rustic
surface of the sideboard, the
elegant curved legs of the small
tables near the couch.*

Paint effects that resemble stone evoke a feeling of classical antiquity in a hallway, living room, or any formal space. Here, walls are painted to resemble large blocks of limestone, rendered with a simple technique of taping and ragging off several layers of glaze over a cream base. While this marble mantel is the genuine article, refer to Chapter Three of Section One for painting similar marble effects.

Shades of gray glaze applied to a pearl-gray undercoat create a soft yet lively background for distinctive furnishings in a neutral palette. An artfully distressed black-and-gold bureau seems to glow in this setting.

painting with soft, neutral tones

The gentle qualities of pale neutral colors lend themselves to painting linear or subtle geometric patterns. When used together, soft beiges, tans, whites, and grays will never clash. By vertically taping a white base coat, stripes of any pale neutral tint will energize a room and also provide an illusion of greater ceiling height.

Taping off sections of wall and painting them in a different soft, neutral shade artfully define a room's important features. Surround a large abstract canvas or a hall table with a painted rectangle or square of a neutral shade slightly darker than the base wall color. This subtle "framing" effect draws the eye to such focal points.

using neutral paints to mimic natural materials

Slate, marble, granite, and limestone are durable and beautiful natural materials that have become highly desirable for surfacing walls, floors, and countertops. Yet their distinctive—and expensive—good looks can be duplicated with a bit of practice. A wooden mantel or fireplace surround, artfully painted to suggest stone, creates an elegant focal point for a living or dining room.

Distinguish an entry hall by painting walls to resemble blocks of stone. Using a pale smooth base, tape off walls in squares that suggest quarried sections of limestone or sandstone. Then apply glazes in one or more soft shades that duplicate the chosen stone, rubbing along the taped borders to suggest the subtly shaded edges of cut stone.

Multiple textures increase the comforting appeal of this study, decorated in shades of brown from golden tan to milk chocolate. Rich caramel walls, velvet and leather furnishings, and crisp, white trim combine for a look that is both warm and elegant.

getting the look of granite

Imitate the rich, speckled surface of cut granite on bathroom walls or kitchen backsplashes with a simple sponging technique. Copy the colors of a favorite sample, which may have three or four different neutral shades: tan, white, gray, and black is one combination for a number of varieties from different quarries around the world. Use the lightest color in the granite sample for the base, then sponge in succession with glazes in the other colors, finishing with the darkest shade, allowing glazes to dry between colors. Depending upon the granite look desired, choose sponges in the pore size that will best replicate the sample.

using beige, brown, and tan

The colors of sand, bark, and wood provide a natural and relaxed harmony in rooms. Choosing one shade of the brown family for walls, and furnishing a space so enclosed with other tints and tones of this hue, creates an immediate sense of warmth and security. Because of their comforting, earthy quality, such palettes are often chosen for restful spaces: dens, family rooms, and spa bathrooms. The associations of libraries and spaces for work and reading with materials such as leather and tweed also make a case for painting walls in brown or tan.

Shiny glazed walls in deep chocolate, or warm textured or flat-finished walls in a soft fawn shade, make an elegant background for richly tactile furnishings in nubby fabrics, leathers, or velvets. Add a touch of formality with crisp, white trim. Or, soften and make the effect of brown or tan more rustic and countrified by colorwashing the chosen shade.

Matte black walls provide a
sophisticated backdrop for art
and antiquities, sharpening
the details of each object and
enhancing the impact of their
forms. The strategy of using
light-reflecting metal objects and
white trim lightens the atmosphere of the space so that the
broad black field looks bold,
but not somber.

CHAPTER EIGHT

Change Color to Change the Mood

WHEN TRYING TO DECIDE WHICH COLOR TO PAINT A ROOM, LOOK WITHIN BEFORE LOOKING AT PAINT CHIPS. ASK YOURSELF, WHAT ARE YOU GOING TO USE THE ROOM FOR? HOW DO YOU WANT TO FEEL WHEN YOU'RE THERE? How do you want your guests to feel? Do you want something elegant and reserved or something casual and relaxed? Do you want the room to make you think or to help you relax? In other words, pick the mood to help you pick the color. If you want the space to feel sophisticated, list your thoughts and find colors in magazines or on paint chips that elicit that sophisticated effect. Then, let these tones become your basic palette.

To conclude the color section of *Painting Rooms*, we offer the experience of designer Gregor Cann, who artfully refreshed one room of his house three times, with three different colors, in a single year. The opportunity to present such actual proof of the power of paint was simply irresistible, and we thank Gregor, photographer Eric Roth, and the publishers of the *Boston Globe*, for allowing us to share it on these pages.

orange-yellow paint
for a burst of energy

To create a tropical break inside a wintry climate, paint a room with a brilliant and vigorous orange-yellow, such as safflower. This warm and alive color vibrates with energy, and people seem to noticeably perk up when they walk in the room.

To decorate with such a vibrant wall color, meet its boldness with similar bright accents. Use pillows in bold, bright colors to compete with the walls; paler shades would wimp out. Let the room be about fun and abandon—no need to be reserved. Consider larger and fewer pieces of furniture. Arrange furniture and accessories so that the lines are straightforward, gridlike, and clean.

blue for calm and tranquility

If you want a space to feel cool and kicked back, paint with blue – it lowers the energy and calms the pace. Blue lets your room or home exude a more come-as-you-are attitude, encouraging people to laugh and let go. Accent the room with a lot of whites to give it a crispness, an edge. Use a contrasting white for the furniture and artwork to let individual pieces stand out and take on greater importance. The lesson here: If you want to play up something, contrast it. The floor space is more defined in white. Conversely, the eye blends colors that are more alike, so each piece in the room has less definition. If you want to downplay that couch that needs to be recovered, paint the walls in a shade similar to the sofa fabric.

One blue note: The paler the shade of blue, the more tranquil and cooler, the effect. Blues can make a space seem chilly if you're not careful. Paint, with brighter blues – they are more vibrant and less cold.

PAINT BOX

REMEMBER THAT COLOR AFFECTS ITS NEIGHBORS. CONSIDER THE GOLD LEAF ON THE PICTURE FRAMES AND THE GOLD CHEST: THE GOLD LOSES ITS IMPORTANCE ON THE ORANGE WALLS, COMES FORWARD ON THE YELLOW-CREAM WALLS, AND IS IN YOUR FACE ON THE BLUE WALLS. SIMILARLY, THE SOFA STANDS OUT MORE IN THE BLUE ROOM THAN IT DOES IN THE OTHER TWO.

sophistication with yellow-beige

Create a room that feels poised and sophisticated by using a warm, yellowy beige. To accent and enhance this air of decorum, polish and display your fancy collections: cut glass, polished silver, orchids. Anything that says luxury and elegance. Be aware of the fine line between tasteful presentation and ostentatious display. If you want your home to be inviting but not pretentious, keep the elegance a little offhanded. Contrast glitz with some fundamental stuff—things that don't take machines and money to create, like fruit heaped in a crude clay bowl, firewood stacked on the floor, or roses crowded into a glazed pot.

BOX OF PAINT COLORS

Color inspiration comes from many sources. Some people love to leaf through magazines and books to find rooms they like, and take the pictures to the paint store to compare them with the paint cards. Others take cues from the natural world, looking at landscapes or flower gardens to help construct their interior palette. Many people just like to play with pure color, looking at chips and imagining the various hues on their walls. While Section Two of *Painting Rooms* supplies many vignettes to study, and the text offers many suggestions of colors from nature, this book would not be truly finished without a supply of color samples to contemplate. Thanks to the generosity of Benjamin Moore & Co., the following pages present a sample of the vast spectrum of colors available from this respected company.

Of course, you may also want to visit your local dealer to inspect the hundreds of colors that could not be duplicated on these pages. Enjoy your search for the perfect color!

The colors used in this section refer to the Benjamin Moore® Color Preview System. These colors are printed and may vary from the actual paint colors. Please consult your Benjamin Moore & Co. dealer for the Benjamin Moore & Co corresponding color chips for accurate color. See the Resources (page 138) for contact information. If you would like to use paints from another range, the paint retailer of your choice will be able to advise you on the closest available match.

RAISIN TORTE 2083-10	RED 2000-10	SPRINGTIME BLOOM 2079-40
CRANBERRY COCKTAIL 2083-20	BULL'S EYE RED 2002-20	PARADISE PINK 2078-40
CONFEDERATE RED 2080-20	TOMATO RED 2010-10	STRAWBERRY SHORTCAKE 2000-40
CHILI PEPPER 2004-20	BERRY WINE 2003-30	AUTUMN RED 2087-40
MILLION DOLLAR RED 2003-10	RED TULIP 2000-30	FLAMINGO'S DREAM 2002-40
ROYAL FUCHSIA 2078-30	PEONY 2079-30	FULL BLOOM 2001-50

HYDRANGEA FLOWERS 2008-40	CANDY STRIPE 2079-70	MELON POPSICLE 2016-50
BLUSHING BRIDE 2086-50	MARMALADE 2016-40	PEACH CLOUD 2169-60
TICKLED PINK 2002-50	PEACHY KEEN 2014-40	ORANGE 2011-10
DELICATE ROSE 2008-50	PEACH SORBET 2015-40	FESTIVE ORANGE 2014-10
EARLY SUNRISE 2084-60	SPRINGTIME PEACH 2014-50	RUMBA ORANGE 2014-20
AZTEC LILY 2080-70	PERFECT PEACH 2167-50	ORANGE BURST 2015-20

TANGY ORANGE 2014-30	ORIOLE 2169-30	BUMBLE BEE YELLOW 2020-10
CALYPSO ORANGE 2015-30	ORANGE BLOSSOM 2168-30	NACHO CHEESE 2018-40
ADOBE ORANGE 2171-30	STARTLING ORANGE 2016-10	CITRUS BLAST 2018-30
FALL HARVEST 2168-10	CITRUS ORANGE 2016-20	LEMON SHINE 2020-20
ORANGE PARROT 2169-20	CARROT STICK 2016-30	SUNFLOWER 2019-30
PUMPKIN PIE 2167-20	MANDARIN ORANGE 2018-20	GOLDEN NUGGET 2019-20

YELLOW RAIN COAT 2020-40	BANANA YELLOW 2022-40	LEMON DROPS 2019-50
AMERICAN CHEESE 2019-40	LEMON FREEZE 2025-50	MORNING SUNSHINE 2018-50
LEMON 2021-20	YELLOW HIGHLIGHTER 2021-40	HAWTHORNE YELLOW HC-4
BABY CHICK 2023-20	BRIGHT YELLOW 2022-30	JASPER YELLOW 2024-50
SUN PORCH 2023-30	YOLK 2023-10	YELLOW LOTUS 2021-50
SUN KISSED YELLOW 2022-20	YELLOW FINCH 2024-40	LEMON MERINGUE 2023-60

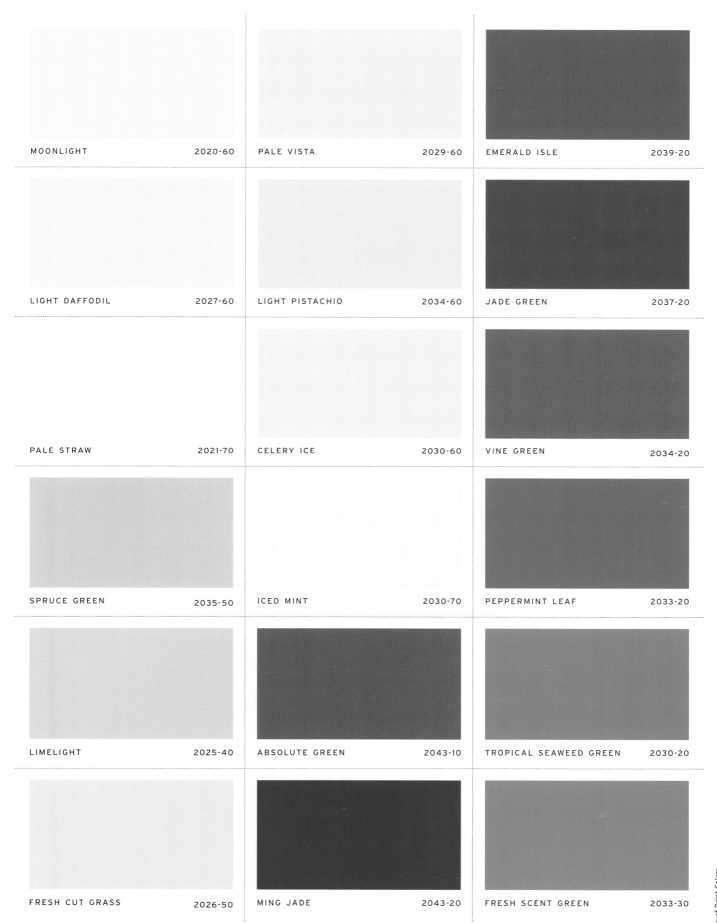

MOONLIGHT 2020-60	PALE VISTA 2029-60	EMERALD ISLE 2039-20
LIGHT DAFFODIL 2027-60	LIGHT PISTACHIO 2034-60	JADE GREEN 2037-20
PALE STRAW 2021-70	CELERY ICE 2030-60	VINE GREEN 2034-20
SPRUCE GREEN 2035-50	ICED MINT 2030-70	PEPPERMINT LEAF 2033-20
LIMELIGHT 2025-40	ABSOLUTE GREEN 2043-10	TROPICAL SEAWEED GREEN 2030-20
FRESH CUT GRASS 2026-50	MING JADE 2043-20	FRESH SCENT GREEN 2033-30

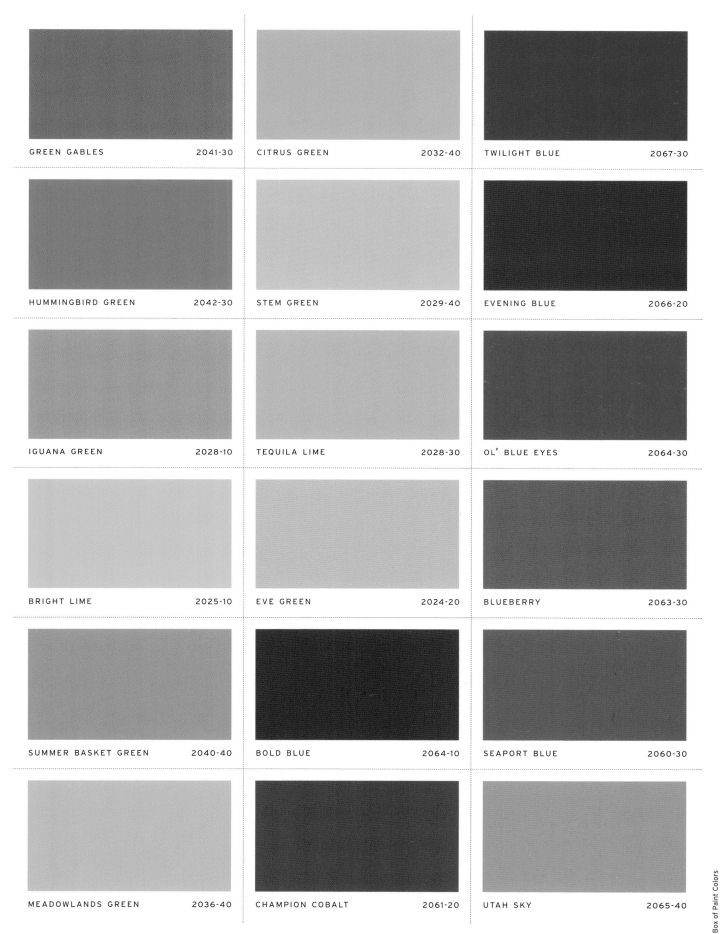

GREEN GABLES 2041-30	CITRUS GREEN 2032-40	TWILIGHT BLUE 2067-30
HUMMINGBIRD GREEN 2042-30	STEM GREEN 2029-40	EVENING BLUE 2066-20
IGUANA GREEN 2028-10	TEQUILA LIME 2028-30	OL' BLUE EYES 2064-30
BRIGHT LIME 2025-10	EVE GREEN 2024-20	BLUEBERRY 2063-30
SUMMER BASKET GREEN 2040-40	BOLD BLUE 2064-10	SEAPORT BLUE 2060-30
MEADOWLANDS GREEN 2036-40	CHAMPION COBALT 2061-20	UTAH SKY 2065-40

SAILOR'S SEA BLUE 2063-40	BLUE LAKE 2053-40	BLUEBELLE 2064-60
CLEAREST OCEAN BLUE 2064-40	BLUE MARGUERITE 2063-50	WHITE SATIN 2067-70
BLUE LAPIS 2067-40	BLUE JEAN 2062-50	BLUE HYDRANGEA 2062-60
BLUE WAVE 2065-50	CARIBBEAN COAST 2065-60	BASHFUL BLUE 2065-70
COOL BLUE 2058-40	COSTA RICA BLUE 2064-50	HARBOR FOG 2062-70
COOL AQUA 2056-40	TURQUOISE POWDER 2057-50	PURPLE LACE 2068-60

LAVENDER MIST 2070-60	GRAPE GUM 2068-20	PASSION PLUM 2073-30
PALE IRIS 2073-60	DARK LILAC 2070-30	TWILIGHT MAGENTA 2074-30
LILY LAVENDER 2071-60	GENTLE VIOLET 2071-20	LILAC PINK 2074-40
PURPLE CREAM 2073-70	AUTUMN PURPLE 2073-20	PURPLE HYACINTH 2073-40
MISTY LILAC 2071-70	MYSTICAL GRAPE 2071-30	PURPLE EASTER EGG 2073-50
WHISPER VIOLET 2070-70	SCANDINAVIAN BLUE 2068-30	CROCUS PETAL PURPLE 2071-40

CALIFORNIA LILAC · 2068-40	BLACK IRON · 2120-20	MELLOWED IVORY · 2149-50
SPRING PURPLE · 2070-40	JET BLACK · 2120-10	WHITE MARIGOLD · 2149-60
VICTORIAN TRIM · 2068-50	BABY SEAL BLACK · 2119-30	ALPINE WHITE · 2147-70
EXOTIC FUCHSIA · 2074-50	BLACK BERRY · 2119-20	EASTER LILY · 2150-70
AMETHYST CREAM · 2071-50	TOUCAN BLACK · 2118-20	ADOBE WHITE · 2166-70
ENCHANTED · 2070-50	UNIVERSAL BLACK · 2118-10	CANDLE WHITE · 2164-70

PATRIOTIC WHITE 2135-70	SANDY WHITE 2148-50	EVENING DOVE 2128-30
ICE MIST 2123-70	YELLOW FREEZE 2020-70	WOLF GRAY 2127-40
ASPEN WHITE 2027-70	LION YELLOW 2158-60	EXCALIBUR GRAY 2118-50
MOONLIGHT WHITE 2143-60	IVORY TOWER 2157-70	NOVEMBER SKIES 2128-50
WOODLAND SNOW 2161-70	FINE CHINA 2156-70	BEACON GRAY 2128-60
SUGAR COOKIE 2160-70	TIMID WHITE 2148-60	SILVER CLOUD 2129-70

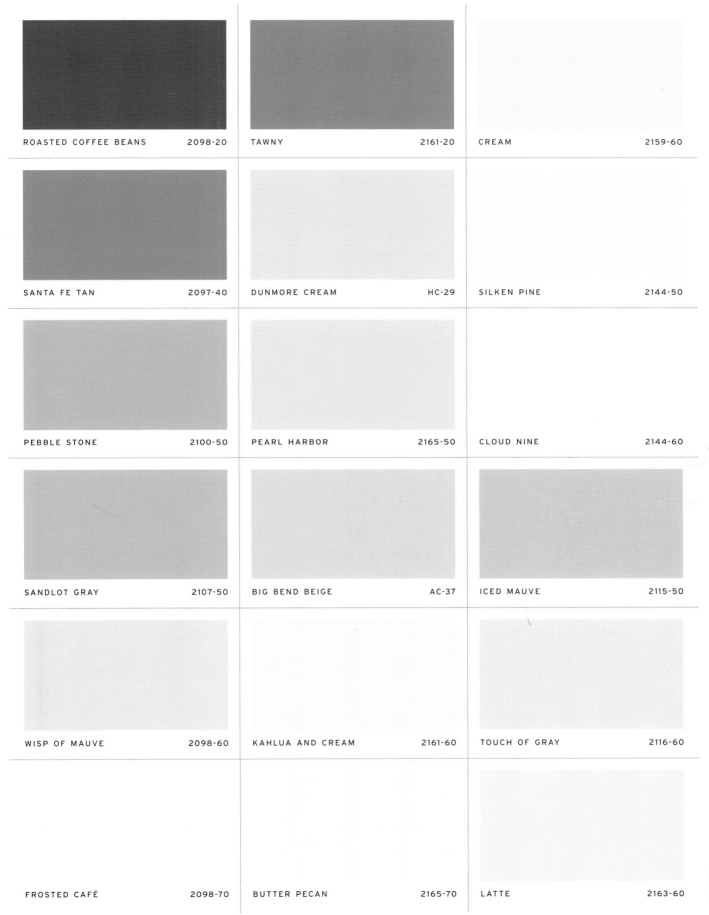

ROASTED COFFEE BEANS 2098-20	TAWNY 2161-20	CREAM 2159-60
SANTA FE TAN 2097-40	DUNMORE CREAM HC-29	SILKEN PINE 2144-50
PEBBLE STONE 2100-50	PEARL HARBOR 2165-50	CLOUD NINE 2144-60
SANDLOT GRAY 2107-50	BIG BEND BEIGE AC-37	ICED MAUVE 2115-50
WISP OF MAUVE 2098-60	KAHLUA AND CREAM 2161-60	TOUCH OF GRAY 2116-60
FROSTED CAFÉ 2098-70	BUTTER PECAN 2165-70	LATTE 2163-60

Resources

paint manufacturers

Use these phone numbers and/or Web sites to locate dealers in your area, and find answers to specific questions about manufacturers' products. Unless otherwise noted, companies listed offer multiple product lines of oil- and water-based paints; most also manufacture glazes, primers, and other products for interior painting.

ACE
www.acehardware.com/paintbrand/paintbrand.asp

BEHR
3400 W. Segerstrom Avenue
Santa Ana, CA 92704
1-800-854-0133 (extension 3 for store locations; extension 2 for technical questions)
www.behrpaint.com

BENJAMIN MOORE
51 Chestnut Ridge Road
Montvale, NJ 07645
1-888-BENMOORE
For your closest Benjamin Moore dealer please call 1-800-6PAINT6 (1-800-672-4686) or visit their Web site at www.benjaminmoore.com. Benjamin Moore is a registered trademark and Color Preview is a trademark of Benjamin Moore & Co.

CALIFORNIA PAINTS
1-617-547-5300 ext.1

CRAYOLA® PAINTS
This is a line of paints manufactured by Benjamin Moore. In addition to a range of Crayola® colors, such specialty products as glitter paint, chalkboard paint, and glow-in-the-dark paint are available for special painted effects. For more information, call the Benjamin Moore customer service number (1-888-BEN-MOORE) or access the company's Web site and search by the brand name.

DEVOE
1-800-654-2616
www.devoepaint.com

DUTCH BOY
1-800-828-5669
www.dutchboy.com

FINNAREN & HALEY PAINT COMPANY
This is a regional company with retail outlets in Pennsylvania, New Jersey, and Delaware.
Conshohocken, PA
1-800-843-9800
www.fhpaint.com

GLIDDEN
1-800-221-4100
www.gliddenpaint.com

PITTSBURGH PAINTS
1-800-441-9695
www.pittsburghpaints.com

PRATT & LAMBERT
1-800-289-7728
www.prattandlambert.com

SHERWIN-WILLIAMS
1-800-4-SHERWIN
www.sherwin-williams.com

super premium paint brands

The following group of paint companies is distinguished by their high-quality, premium priced products. The approach to color of these brands is quite complex; each paint color is composed of multiple pigments (up to a dozen, sometimes more); pigment is the most expensive component in paint, and thus these paints have a retail cost of more than double that of other high-quality paints. However, in addition to the complexity of their color system, these paints also provide a wall finish that is distinctive for its depth and luminosity of color.

FARROW & BALL
British Manufacturer. Mail or online order paints (oil enamels cannot be shipped to Arizona or California.) Sample pots available; manufacturer recommends customers send for product literature and/or samples before making a quantity order.
Phone (in Toronto, Canada) 1-845-369-4912 (limited distribution at select U.S. outlets)
www.farrow-ball.com

FINE PAINTS OF EUROPE
Exclusive importer of Holland-made Schreuder Paints. Fine Paints offers many high-quality products for preparation, plus best-quality paintbrushes and other equipment. In addition to its line of 940 fan deck colors and Classic European colors, Fine Paints also offers Martha's Fine Paints, a collection of nearly 100 colors developed in collaboration with Martha Stewart Living Omnimedia, Inc.

Sample .25 liter pots are available for 99 colors of the company's Obolux ä matte acrylic paints. Distributed nationwide through select local dealers, and by mail order.
P.O. Box 419
Route 4 West,
Woodstock, VT 05091
1-800-332-1556
www.finepaints.com

DONALD KAUFMAN COLOR COLLECTION

Another producer of premium, full-spectrum color paints; these are available through two retail outlets, one in New Jersey and the other in Santa Monica, California. For information, call 1-800-977-9198

ecofriendly paint products

Many of the paint manufacturers listed above have low- or no-VOC paint lines; the following companies make only low- or no-VOC products. Many are produced with alternative ingredients with low or very little toxicity. For specific information about the products, contact the manufacturers at the phone numbers and/or Web sites listed.

AMERICAN FORMULATING & MANUFACTURING (AFM)

350 W. Ash Street #700
San Diego, CA 92101
1-800-239-0321 (leave name to receive product brochure)
1-619-239-0321 (for technical information)
Safecoat products: primers, paints, clear finishes, sealants
www.afmsafecoat.com

BIOSHIELD PAINT CO.

1365 Rufina Circle
Santa Fe, NM 87505
1-800-621-2591 (orders; catalog)
1-505-438-3448 (questions; comments)
Casein (milk) paint, colorwashes, organic color pigments, gloss and satin enamel paint, plus a wide assortment of paintbrushes, specialty finish brushes, and painting combs.
www.Bioshieldpaint.com

CHEM-SAFE PRODUCTS COMPANY

P.O. Box 33023
San Antonio, TX 78265
1-210-657-5321
Enviro-Safe Paints (available in flat, satin, and semigloss)

INNOVATIVE FORMULATIONS CORPORATION

1810 S. 6th Avenue
Tucson, AZ 85713
1-800-346-7265
Ecological and Canary lines of paint have no known carcinogens or neurotoxins. (available in flat, eggshell, semigloss, gloss)

MILLER PAINT CO., INC.

317 S.E. Grand Ave.
Portland, OR 97214
1-503-233-4491
Miller Low Biocide Paint (available in flat, satin, and semigloss)
Solvent-free, low-biocide, low-fungicide paints.

MURCO WALL PRODUCTS

300 N.E. 21st Street
Fort Worth, TX 76106
1-800-446-7124

SINAN CO.

(makes fungicide-free latex paint, in high gloss enamel and flat finish)
P.O. Box 857
Davis, CA 95617-0857
1-530-753-3104
www.dcn.davis.ca.us/go/sinan

AURO NATURAL PAINTS

Made in Germany and packaged as a powder, made exclusively from natural sources.

THE OLD FASHIONED MILK PAINT COMPANY

For over 25 years, this company has manufactured and distributed genuine milk paints. The product is sold at retail around the U.S. (call or check Web site for dealers), or by direct mail order.
436 Main Street
P.O. Box 222
Groton, MA 01450
1-978-448-2754
www.milkpaint.com

more information about paint

Questions about the ingredients of a high-quality paint? The PAINT QUALITY INSTITUTE provides the facts, plus loads of professional pointers on getting the best result for your painting labors. The Institute's Web site has lots of answers. Visit at www.paintquality.com

The NATIONAL PAINT AND COATINGS ASSOCIATION (NPCA) offers a Web site providing extensive information about paints, painting, and choosing paint colors. The site also provides easy links to many commercial how-to Web pages. Visit at www.paintinfo.org

Want to do the research, then hire a pro? The PAINT AND DECORATING CONTRACTORS OF AMERICA (PDCA) is a 115-year-old professional organization to which 3100 painting companies belong. Their Web site provides helpful hints about hiring a pro, plus a convenient 800 number to find local, trained, and licensed painting contractors in your area. Visit the PDCA Web site at www.pdca.org and click on "consumer information."

LEARN ABOUT LEAD

Homes built before 1978 may have existing paint that contains lead as its hiding agent. Before disturbing a surface that may possibly contain this toxin, learn the facts. The U.S. ENVIRONMENTAL PROTECTION AGENCY staffs a lead hotline and offers information on its Web site about detecting, abating, and/or eliminating a lead paint problem in the home. Hotline staffers will send on request a comprehensive packet of informational brochures (which are also downloadable from the Web site). Contact them before painting. The NPCA consumer Web site described above (www.paintinfo.org) also offers links to comprehensive information about lead paint.

NATIONAL LEAD INFORMATION CENTER
1-800-424-5323
EPA Web site: www.epa.gov/lead

MORE COLOR ADVICE

Which colors are hot this year? And which colors are emerging as the trendsetters in home furnishings? The COLOR MARKETING GROUP'S membership is composed of 1700 Color Designers whose task is to "interpret, create, forecast, and select" colors for all kinds of commercial goods and businesses. Check out their Web site at www.color-marketing.org; click on "site-at-a-glance" and then "news releases" to get the latest word on fashionable colors.

The color wheel is a very logical way to approach color selection; a well-constructed wheel can provide instant information on harmonious combinations of the primary, secondary, and tertiary hues. The COLOR WHEEL COMPANY produces a series of color wheels for artists, designers, and consumers to help them construct pleasing palettes based on the relationships of spectral colors on the wheel. Their 9 1/4" color wheel and Interior Design wheel provide lots of information about color, and are reasonably priced. For product listings and prices, contact:

THE COLOR WHEEL COMPANY
P.O. Box 130
Philomath, OR 97370-0130
1-541-929-7526
www.colorwheelco.com

While most large home stores and specialty paint stores offer good selections of painting tools and equipment, the following offer helpful information or specialty supplies on their Web sites.

GREGOR CANN
Cann Design
1-760-318-7925 (West Coast)
1-617-293-6078 (East Coast)
canndesign@aol.com

tools

THE WOOSTER BRUSH COMPANY
Wooster, OH 44691
1-800-392-7246 (customer service)
www.woosterbrush.com
Manufacturers of more than 2000
different painting products, including
brushes, rollers, and other tools. The
Web site has painting tips and offers a
good overview of innovative products
for painting.

special-effects supplies

MCCLOSKEY SPECIAL EFFECTS
(a division of the Valspar Corporation)
Wheeling, IL 60090
1-800-345-4530 (product information)
McCloskey makes a variety of glazing
products for broken color effects, and
the company offers a number of helpful
brochures along with their products
that supply tips and hints for successful
finishes.

FAUX LIKE A PRO
P.O. Box 1420
Brookline, MA 02446
1-617-713-4320
www.fauxlikeapro.com
This company's comprehensive Web site
offers technique advice, a live chat
room, and an online store for ordering
paints, tools, and books. Designed for
professional faux-finishers, the Web site
is also a great learning tool and source
for interested amateur painters. The
company has its own line of special
effects paints.

AMERICAN HOME STENCILS
10007 S. 76th Street
Franklin, WI 53132
1-800-742-4520 (M-F, 8-4 CST)
www.americanhomestencils.com
Order stencils and supplies on line or
request catalog. This company offers
Robert Simmons stencil brushes, reasonably priced products recommended
by the decorative painters who designed
the samples used in Chapter Three of
Painting Rooms.

ADELE BISHOP STENCILS
P.O. Box 477
Campbellville, Ontario,
LOP 1 BO, CANADA
www.adelebishop.com
Fax: 1-905-854-1243
Large selection of stencils and stenciling
supplies. Catalog $4 U.S. Place orders by
mail. No credit cards.

L.A. STENCILWORKS
16115 Vanowen St.
Van Nuys, CA 91406
Toll free: 1-877-989-0262
www.lastencil.com
Large selection of stencils, including
many contemporary designs. Multiple
designs can be used together to create
interesting decorative murals.

decorative painters

Find these through designers and home
decorators near you.

BONNIE'S PLACE
27 Westchester Avenue
Pound Ridge, NY 10576
1-914-764-8699

Index

Photo Credits

Abode, 68; 74 (top); 80; 88 (right); 105; 107

Sandy Agrafiotis, 71

Fernando Bengoechea/Franca Speranza srl, 58; 74 (bottom); 78

Antoine Bootz, 3 (middle); 62; 70; 72; 73; 83; 95

All studio photography by Bobbie Bush

Grey Crawford/Beateworks, 67; 81

Report Bilder-Dienst/Freundin/Dietrich, 79

Courtesy of Glidden Paints, 37 (top left); 38 (bottom right) 39; 40 (top); 41 (bottom left)

Steve Gross & Susan Daley, 55

John Hall, 104

Brian Harrison/Elizabeth Whiting Associates, 3 (top), 65, 99

Keller & Keller, 56

Tom Leighton/Elizabeth Whiting Associates, 90

Peter Paige/Antine Shin LLC, 61

Spike Powell/ Elizabeth Whiting Associates, 64; 97

Greg Premru, 52

Eric Roth, 2; 59; 66; 82; 84; 86; 91; 100

Eric Roth/Cann Design, 94; 98; 108-113

Eric Roth/Astrid Vigeland Design, 103

Keith Scott Morton, 77; 87

Brian Vanden Brink/Stephen Foote, Architect 3; 54

Steve Vierra/Ida Goldstein Design, 96

Steve Vierra/Gayle Reynolds Design, ASID, 96

Andreas von Einsiedel/Red Cover, 57

Henry Wilson/The Interior Archive, 88 (left); 93

All studio photography by Bobbie Bush

About the Author

JUDY OSTROW is an independent journalist who specializes in writing about the home, its architecture, interior design, and renovation. Her articles have appeared in many national magazines, including *Home*, *Natural Home*, *This Old House*, and special publications of *House Beautiful* and *Woman's Day*. She has painted many rooms of the home she shares with her husband and two children in Westchester County, New York, and is currently planning the painted interior of the family's vacation house in Maine.

acknowledgments

Many hearts, hands, and minds collaborate in the making of books, and this project is no exception. I sincerely thank you all:

Martha Wetherill, acquisitions editor at Rockport, who guided this project with composure and insight wherever these qualities were needed; photo editor Betsy Gammons, who persevered to find just the right images; art director Susan Raymond, who created the book's beautiful graphic framework; and project manager Barbara Rummler, whose encouraging e-mails and calls kept me writing through the many twists and turns from our original outline.

This book would not be as beautiful, nor the guidance as expert, without the knowledge and artistic inspiration of Kendall Klingbeil, who created all of the painted effects in Chapter Three.

I also thank John Lahey of Fine Paints of Europe for his thoughtful insights about paint quality, Leslie Harrington of Benjamin Moore for allowing us to share with readers a selection of colors from the company's enormous fan deck, and Rudolf Reitz of BioShield Paints for some ecofriendly paint samples. I am also grateful to the many helpful paint dealers and contractors who willingly shared their experience and knowledge of paint, tools, and tips.

Finally, I thank my family: my husband, Sam, daughter Rachel and son Adam, for their cooperation during the hectic months of writing; and my parents, for their continual encouragement throughout the years of my writing life.

Artist KENDALL KLINGBEIL has been painting home interiors for more than twenty years. Her work has been featured in *The New York Times*, and she currently works as a decorative painter for Bonnie's Place in Pound Ridge, New York; her fine-arts paintings are exhibited at the Lionheart Gallery, also in Pound Ridge.